Politics, Finance and the Role of Economics

POLITICS, FINANCE AND THE ROLE OF ECONOMICS

An Essay on
the Control of Public Enterprise

C. D. Foster

London School of Economics and Political Science

London: George Allen & Unwin Ltd
Ruskin House   Museum Street

First published in 1971

© George Allen & Unwin Ltd, 1971

ISBN 0 04 338051 4

To Kay who preferred Oxford

Printed in Great Britain
in 10pt Times New Roman type
by Unwin Brothers Limited
Woking and London

Preface

Some will say 'What difference could the Common Market make to the relations between Government and Public Enterprise which is the main topic of this book?' The answer must surely be that there would be changes in detail–in pricing rules and taxation–which would bulk large in legislation and in managerial pre-occupations for several years; but that the fundamental questions I consider are unlikely to be affected. The relations between Parliament, Government and Public Enterprise should stay as they are, until some enterprises merge with their European counterparts. If I am right that the extent and scope of public enterprise will, in any case, increase, and that the problems of its control will become still more important and complicated, such trends will not be altered by entry. It will remain a problem for Britain to solve for its own public enterprises. Sovereignty is not lost quickly; and in these areas it may never be lost.

To write this book is to invite criticism that one has gone beyond one's competence. I believe it a book which would not have been written as it is except by an economist. It does not question the logic of the usual economic apparatus developed to analyse the nationalized industries, but does wonder if this has been as relevant a development of economic techniques to match their problems as was possible. For the most part of it is not an economics book but an analysis of what it was like to work as an economist in government at a particularly interesting and eventful time; and an exploration of the institutional framework which constrains the economist. If I were a professional political scientist or expert in public administration this book could be more scholarly. If it had been the habit of government to employ political scientists and experts in public administration on a short term basis as it did economists, one of them might have written a better institutional book. Across the Atlantic many more have had the experience I was privileged to enjoy. Historians, political scientists and economists there have tried to explain and understand the workings of the political system from within. In Britain, as in America, formal descriptions of political machinery and the memoirs of those who have retired tend to give misleading impressions of the political system which are in important respects strikingly different from the reality as I experienced it. This is beginning to be widely realized; and because the Schlesingers, the Sorensens, the Neustadts and the Galbraiths, as well as many others, have described the actual workings of American Government from within, while there are almost no comparable books about British Government, there is a tendency for those standing outside the British machine to use American models to intuite the way the British system works. What else–beyond

5

hearsay – can they do? But while there may be similarities between the inner workings of different political systems, one argument of this book is that there are also profound differences–largely unrealized by those without and infrequently analysed by those within. To generalize, it seems to me that if as a nation we can maintain and develop the traditions of our political and administrative system, protecting it against increasing pressures to change its nature, we will have cherished something of the highest value; because our system is potentially more rational and less necessarily at the mercy of pressure groups than some others. It will be clear from what follows that I am far from thinking our political system incapable of improvement. The foundations however, seem to me to be excellent.

I must not exaggerate what I have attempted in this book. The most I can claim for it is that it is a clear and possibly penetrating light on a small area which may reflect light onto other areas by analogy. During my four years as a senior official at the Ministry of Transport my experience of what was going on in the more central Departments of Government was necessarily limited, though one had enough contacts to get some impression of the rest. Neither is it a history of the preparation and passing of the 1968 Transport Act. I do not know whether I could have attempted such; but if I could, its realization would have been prevented by the Official Secrets Act which necessarily constrains what an ex-civil servant may write. It seemed to me, however, that it was possible for me to write a book about one area where I had experience – public enterprise. While neither memoirs nor contemporary history nor contravening the Official Secrets Act, it might illuminate usefully some of the processes of Government.

I would like to express my gratitude to all those from whom I have learnt and who have in many and various ways made this book possible. The opinions are, of course, mine whether they relate to events that occurred while I was in Government service or to those before or later. I have had no access to unpublished official papers since I left the Ministry of Transport in the Autumn of 1969. Among those I can acknowledge as having helped me by reading and commenting on drafts or through discussion are the Rt Hon. C. A. R. Crosland, the Rt Hon. R. H. S. Crossman, Sir Ronald Edwards, Sir Henry Johnson (Chairman, British Railways Board), Professor A. J. Merrett, Mr Harold Osborn (National Freight Corporation), Mr D. E. A. Pettit (Chairman, National Freight Corporation), the Rt Hon. Lord Robens of Woldingham, PC, DCL, LLD., Professor W. Robson, Mr Michael Shanks, Professor W. G. Shepherd of University of Michigan (who challenged me to be bold enough to begin this book), Mr W. G. Thorpe (Deputy Chairman, British Railways Board), Sir Arnold Weinstock, and Professor Aaron Wildavsky of the University of California, Berkeley (who made me consider the place of rationality in politics more deeply than I otherwise would have done). I am grateful to my father for the index.

To some of these I owe a more specific debt. I must thank Professor

Robson especially for the time he gave generously from the abundance of his knowledge of the subject and from his wisdom to improving the historical accuracy of my draft. The remaining inaccuracies are mine.

I wish to acknowledge my debt to Sir Arnold Weinstock for the encouragement and opportunities he has given me to observe how incisively and dexterously he exercises financial control and compare this with the practices of the public sector. What I observed reinforced some of the conclusions I had come to, and modified others.

Above all I am most grateful to the Ministers I have served and for the opportunities, experience and leadership they gave me: the Rt Hon. Barbara Castle, the Rt Hon. Richard Marsh, the late Stephen Swingler, John Morris, Neil Carmichael and Robert Brown. Because Stephen Swingler died so sadly at the height of his powers, and without as yet an opportunity of showing what he could have achieved as a Minister with responsibility for a department, I would like to remember him as idealistic, intelligent, enthusiastic, an excellent debater dedicated to making up his mind on what he believed to be right and then doing all he could to help accomplish it.

My greatest advantage was in serving Barbara Castle, with her rare combination of qualities: imagination, constructive power, resilience and an ability to put a clear mind to each new subject and master it. She was a perfectionist who had extraordinary powers of leadership which galvanized a department from a state of normal routine efficiency into a powerful machine working as one to a common end. While I do not refer to her often by name in this book, her influence pervades it.

C. D. FOSTER

London School of Economics

Contents

Part I

THE POWERS OF BOARDS
AND MINISTERS

Chapter 1

A DIVIDING LINE

It would be a facile view of nationalization which saw it only as a process by which what was private was expropriated and absorbed into the state. Statutorily, nationalized industries are the creations, the creatures, of Parliament and they are responsible ultimately to it. But for most part Parliament does not exercise this responsibility directly. It delegates a number of powers and duties to Ministers who therefore undertake the responsibility for it. However, the powers of Ministers are far from absolute. The Boards of the nationalized industries have always been meant to have a considerable independence. Thus the relationship is triangular. The Boards have received powers and duties from Parliament and these constitute a (qualified) independence. The relevant Ministers have also been given powers and duties in relation to the Boards which are what qualify the Boards' independence. The most important day-to-day relation becomes that between a Minister and a Board. The old and difficult question is to determine where the authority of the Minister ends and the independence of the Boards begins. The statutes are not clear on this.

The question has a wider relevance. There are other semi-independent public corporations and agencies, whose number seems to grow whatever Government is in power. This trend looks as if it will continue as social life, and therefore Government becomes more complicated. As a result of the Heath Government's declared intentions, they will grow in number as similar bodies are moulded within Government and pushed out, yet not so far as to become wholly private. Generally these other bodies are less commercially directed than the nationalized industries, but the same difficulty of deciding the dividing line between a Minister's powers and the autonomy of these statutory bodies will often occur.[1] Perhaps an

[1] There is no definitive list of public enterprises, partly because there is no single legal form but an almost infinite gradation, and partly because the bodies vary from the almost completely commercial to bodies administering grants voted by Parliament. But to give some notion of the number and scope of bodies

even wider relevance can be claimed for the discussion of this difficulty. Essentially the same problem may arise within Government departments. We usually think of the divisions of a department and the many other agencies which are formally part of it, as being under the *orders* of its Permanent Secretary and Minister. Yet this is a slippery concept. Juniors have their pride and, necessarily, some independence. Even if they wished to be authoritarian, it is less easy for senior officials to control closely what is going on below them as departments get larger. More independence has to be delegated, and, if the increasing complexity of social life and Government makes it true that a Permanent Secretary and his senior officials cannot run a department as if it were a coterie, this is still more true for Ministers. The time they have to know what is going on in detail is severely limited. They have to take more on trust. It is not surprising that recently the Civil Service and, still more recently, the Conservative Government have got interested in the possibility of adapting more formal methods of control that have been developed by business. Despite their differences, these management systems work on the principle that managers should be set objectives; that their accountability should be set in relation to these. They will not have a free hand in how they will reach their

---

which are semi-autonomous and which present the same problem of finding a dividing line between autonomy and public accountability, here is a list of relevant public enterprises drawn from two of the most knowledgeable authorities, W. A. Robson, *Nationalized Industry and Public Ownership* (Allen and Unwin, 1962) and W. Thornhill, *The Nationalized Industries; An Introduction* (Nelson, 1968). In chronological order they are: Trinity House (1514), the General Post Office (1656), the Public Record Office (1838), the Charity Commissioners (1853), the Mersey Docks and Harbour Board (1857), the Prison Commissioners (1877), the Public Trustee (1906), the Port of London Authority (1909), the Forestry Commission (1919), the State Management District for Liquor Control in Carlisle (1921), the Central Electricity Board and the British Broadcasting Corporation (1926), the Commissioners for Crown Lands (1927), the Medical Research Council and the Racecourse Betting Control Board (1928), the London Passenger Transport Board (1933), the Air Registration Board and the Title Redemption Board (1936), BOAC (1939), the British Council (1940), the Arts Council, the Bank of England and BEA (1946), as well as the new Towns Act enabling the setting up of new town development corporations, the National Coal Board and the British Transport Corporation (1947), the Colonial Development Corporation and the Overseas Food Corporation (1948), the Gas Boards and the Iron and Steel Corporation (1949), the White Fish Authority (1951), the Atomic Energy Authority and the Independent Television Authority (1954), the Air Transport Licensing Board (1960), as well as many municipal public enterprises, the regional hospital boards and many mixed enterprises. Many of those listed above have, of course, been reorganized subsequently, but relatively few have disappeared from the public sector.

objectives. There are means to their ends which they will not be allowed to use. Even so it is a purpose of these systems to define, more closely than is traditional, the area within which a person has freedom of decision. Of course, there is a strong difference between internal management documents which define powers and duties and something laid down in statute. The first can be both more flexible and, as we shall see, more precise. But there is the similarity too.

It seems to me that the question of how there can be effective political control over what matters – indeed the decision as to what does matter – combined with effective delimited freedom for the subordinate bodies, remains one of the most important in public life. It could be discussed in any or all of the three contexts mentioned: the nationalized industries, other public corporations and statutory agencies, or as it operates within the formal of structure of Government itself. But there are great advantages in arguing the issues as they affect the first. There has been more public understanding of these issues as they affect nationalized industries and also a long history of discussion. Both in legislation and elsewhere there have been more rigorous attempts to define the relationships. That the purposes of nationalized industries have been regarded as *mainly* commercial has made it easier to think clearly. (I am far from thinking that, in either statute or practice, the dividing line has been sharp, only that it has been easier to see how a clear distinction between the authority of Ministers – and Parliament – and the freedom of nationalized industries could have been described.) The techniques – cost-benefit analysis and its derivatives like programme budgeting – which make it possible to sharpen the functions of less commercially motivated bodies, have only recently been developed. They make it possible to talk of social purposes with a rigour which was rarely possible in the past for the non-commercially directed bodies, both those which are statutorily separate and those which are within Government. Without these techniques one could not begin to talk about their functions rigorously. Yet, even though the reliance of these last on the new techniques would have to be greater, if one were to wish to clarify the limits of their autonomy and the powers of Ministers over them, the problem is essentially the same. Though they have hardly begun to be used except for the isolated project, these new approaches ought to be important for the nationalized industries in relation to their social policies and obligations. If we can say anything useful about this problem, for them the problems of adapting a solution to the rest would not be so formidable.

But there is another reason for the focus of this essay. In their

13

report on Ministerial Control, the Select Committee of the House of Commons on Nationalized Industries[1] attempt a frontal assault on the whole question. In coming to an opinion they interviewed Ministers and their civil servants, Chairmen of the Boards of several nationalized industries and some of their officials, as well as independent experts. Since nationalized industries are the creations of Parliament, how the Select Committee believes the triangular relationships should be interpreted is of the first importance. Moreover, it is of high quality in detail. It is thoughtful and reasoned. It is unlikely that the subject will get as thorough a working out for many years; and yet it seems to me that the resolution of the old difficulty they have come up with – which is the expression of an attitude they have been developing in a series of reports over more than fifteen years – is logically fallacious and practically dangerous. Because it blurs the argument at crucial points its tendency should be opposed, not only in relation to the nationalized industries, but elsewhere, wherever in Government there is a need to define a relation between a higher and a lower body.

[1] Select Committee on the Nationalized Industries, First Report, Session 1967/8, *Ministerial Control of the Nationalized Industries*, 3 vols, HMSO, 1968. We will want to refer to this often. References to paragraphs in the *Report* (vol. 1) will be shown by bracketed numbers in the text. References to the numbered questions in the *Minutes of Evidence* (vol. 2) are shown as bracketed numbers preceded by 'Q'.

Chapter 2

THE SELECT COMMITTEE ON THE NATIONALIZED INDUSTRIES

In their report on Ministerial Control, the Select Committee plainly saw the issue as we have described it in the last chapter: how to fix the limits of ministerial control and of Board freedom. Their interest was not academic. Board Chairmen told them that over the years Ministers and civil servants had increasingly interfered in nationalized industry affairs to a point that one Chairman, Sir Ronald Edwards, said 'has not gone beyond the degree which I would regard as tolerable' (Q. 248), while falling no great distance short of it. Another, Lord Robens, spoke more strongly: Government intervention was already 'intolerable' (Q. 503). The Committee's disposition was to agree with the Chairmen. Ministerial intervention ought to be reduced. Thus they looked for principles which would confine the Minister's function to what they frequently called 'strategic' control, relinquishing to the nationalized industries the 'tactical command' (75–8, 147–9).

There is an old canard people often fall into of saying that something is true in theory but false in practice. In a logical moment no one would say such a thing, for if the facts do not support a theory something is wrong with the theory. The Select Committee fell into a similar trap. They were not the first, and it would have been merely pedantic to object if it had not been the cornerstone of their argument. In trying to resolve the limits of ministerial (and parliamentary) control they rested largely on a distinction between *policy-making* and *implementing policy*: '. . . in the opinion of the Committee . . . it was the intention of Parliament that Ministers should be primarily concerned with laying down policies . . . which would guide the operations of the individual industries and should not intervene in the management of the industries in implementing those policies' (876). This was to determine the difference between strategic and tactical command.

Now it can easily be shown that this distinction is a chasm. Take one of the most definite and well understood policies a body

15

could be required to follow: profit maximization. One could attempt (as a Minister) to lay down a policy of profit maximization and to leave it to a Board to implement that policy. The difficulty is that the Minister or anyone else is not in a position to have an opinion on whether the policy the Board took did maximize profits unless he knows the alternatives the Board rejected; in short, unless he has the facts on which the Board took its decision. The same is true of far, far simpler policies. Suppose that the policy laid down for an Immigration Office is that it is to allow in all except undesirable aliens. Then, logically, a Minister does not know whether the policy is observed unless he too is in possession of the relevant facts, that is, the passports and whatever are the files which say if a particular alien is undesirable. Of course what is lurking here is the question of *trust*. If Ministers – and Parliament – either did not care how well the policies they laid down were executed, or if they had such perfect trust in the Boards that they did not question their policies would be followed, a dividing line between policy-making and implementation could be made to work. (The first would be rather like formulating a theory but not minding how well it fitted the facts; the second like theorizing, and assuming that the truth and meaning of whatever one had thought up was agreed by everyone.)

But Ministers and Parliament are not as *laissez-faire* as either dividing line would imply. A common reason for relying on the distinction is a wish to shed responsibility and delegate choice. Take the situation where an administrator believes that too much of his time is being taken up trying to settle a class of issues. He may look first for a formula to help him out by generalizing the principles on which the cases are to be decided. But if he cannot find one, he may decide it simply is not worth his time going on trying to decide these cases, each on its own merits; so he delegates the decision to a lower level, making some general statement of 'policy' but not such as to affect the practical freedom of the lower level in coming to a decision. (If he could, then it would mean he had found a workable formula.) But the Select Committee is not saying that on all important issues Boards may be left to interpret policy as they please because the content of what they do is not important enough to be put before Ministers given the other claims on ministerial time. Neither is it saying that one should trust the Boards to the extent of assuming they will interpret Parliament's and the Minister's wishes without any control. The Select Committee itself recognizes that there are two major concerns of a Minister on behalf of Parliament: the first is that a Board should pursue certain social and national ends; the second is that a Minister should have 'oversight' over the efficiency with which Boards pursue the policies laid down for them. Thus the simple distinction between the Minister's job of laying down policies and the Board's of implementing them, collapses. The question then becomes one of trying to settle how far a Minister may go to see that his own and Parliament's policies are being carried out efficiently.

The Select Committee recognizes that circumstances may need something more than laying down policies, in their sense: 'Where necessary (Ministers) must have in reserve the means of seeking to improve the efficiency of management. But they must not do managers' jobs for them. Control should be exercised in five ways. . . . First, Ministers should select, appoint and, if necessary, not reappoint members of Boards. Secondly, Ministers must have the ultimate right to information . . . that touches on their efficiency, revenue or expenditure. But . . . information should not be sought simply because of its inherent interest, or to discover whether everything is being done properly. . . . Thirdly, Ministers and their officials must have opportunities for discussing with their industries, on the basis of the information given them, questions of efficiency which cause them concern. Fourthly, Ministers should oversee the execution of pricing and investment policies, as far as possible by agreeing proper techniques and appraisal criteria and not by detailed and specific intervention. Lastly, Ministers should have the power to carry out occasional special efficiency studies so as to judge the efficiency with which policies have been, or are being executed.'(142)

The point about this is that it goes far indeed in countenancing intervention by Ministers. If the Minister thinks the situation warrants it – and he is the judge of this, not the industry – he can intervene much more than any Minister does now. From past experience the Boards would regard the exercise of powers in this form as intolerable. Short of actually taking over the management itself, no merchant bank could wish for more power if it felt it had to analyse the situation of an unsatisfactory client to whom it had lent money. Later I will argue that, practically, the right of appointment to the Boards is less potent than it may at first seem. But the right to all information relevant to any revenue or expenditure (investment) decision, if the Minister has reason to think that a wrong decision has been made, is strong medicine.[1] (In the terms

[1] Lord Robens told the Committee he had refused his Ministry some information because he felt it time-consuming and pointless (QQ. 524, 525); and his is not the only Board which has felt its Ministry has no absolute right to information. One can see the point: while it costs nothing to ask for information, it does to give it.

of the argument of the last chapter it makes it possible for him to take an opinion on whether his policies have in fact been implemented. If it were relevant he could see every last passport.) So is the right to put the consultants in.

If this was all there were to the Select Committee's views there would have been no point in writing this book, certainly none in focusing on the opinions of the Select Committee. They had made a distinction without a difference. As is so often the case with a report which is the product of many minds, what is said in one place is contradicted in another. An interventionist Minister could use the Select Committee to justify more intervention than is now normal. (He could attempt to insist on getting more information. He could ask to see the 'books'. He could put in the consultants in cases of doubt which at present would be bitterly resented as unprecedented intrusion.) A non-interventionist Minister could also congratulate himself on how well he was following the precepts of the Select Committee.

There is more texture to the Select Committee's views than this. The Committee does not, I believe, face up to the difficulty of when a Minister may use these reserve powers. But they do have a suggestion which in various forms they hope will avoid the need. This brings them back to their central notion: the distinction between policy-making and implementation. In the past many attempts have been made to define the autonomy of nationalized industries by reference to concepts which the Committee recognizes, as most observers have done, to have been fatally unclear: distinctions, for example, between responsibility for policy and 'day-to-day' management; between questions of public interest and commercial judgement; and indeed the distinction between policy and implementation itself. The Committee did not see itself rejecting these unclear notions, but as building on the ideas latent in them. They argued that a cause of repeated and increasing friction was that ministerial policies had not been stated clearly enough (114–21). This was true of policies in general but also of more limited financial and economic objectives: 'The use of certain unambiguous pricing and investment criteria should be standard for the economic control of the nationalized industries' (35). Of social policies also: 'once the social obligation' of a Board 'has been selected, it is most important that it should be precisely defined' (712). Not only should policies be defined more rigorously but 'there should be a clear demarcation of responsibilities' between Minister and Board (145). Thus it is not surprising to find the Committee saying that in the past 'the very lack of clarity about objectives and policies acted as a constraint on the industries' management freedom' (199) or that it created a 'no-man's land' between the Minister and Board 'too often filled with warring forces disputing for its possession' (123).[1]

I would wholeheartedly agree with the Select Committee that lack of clarity about objectives has been a prime cause of muddle, friction and deficit in the past. Indeed, an important part of the 1968 Transport Act with which I was associated was based on that premise. The railways had been given an impossible and sapping task in being required to keep a more or less commercial profit-and-loss account and balance-sheet, at the same time as being required to operate social (which also happened to be in many many cases, loss-making) services. The deficit that resulted, given the strains, was not a deficit in the sense it indicated logically a deficiency in Board achievement.[2] Neither was it a deliberate payment by the Government to support services which it believed socially and politically desirable. While the strains were probably greater on the railways than on any other nationalized industry, a serious element of muddle and obfuscation exists for all nationalized industries until their objectives have been similarly sorted out, as was attempted for several transport industries by the 1968 Act. In general, I think it fair to say that there are rather too few clear policy statements by either Ministers or by Boards.

However it seems to me that the Select Committee have been oversold on the possibility of clarification and the benefits of clarity. They are almost eighteenth-century in their belief in the power of reason and the possibility of persuasion. They are of the enlightenment, too, in believing that there are certain economic (and other) policies which can be set out as criteria at a high level of abstraction without involving detail, and yet can be tight enough for the purposes of public accountability. We will return to this later and to the arguments of those who believe clarification a waste of time.

But first, most oddly, they seem to have accepted that Ministers are able to lay down binding statements of policy. There are many constraints on their ability to do this, some even statutory.[3] To these let us turn first.

[1] The nationalized industries also complained of the lack of clarity, especially on fuel policy (QQ. 192–204, 215, 218, 230–5, 508–10, 529).

[2] But even when due allowance was made for the cost of running 'social' services, there was almost certainly a very heavy deficit. See pp. 58, 142 below.

[3] It seems curious that the Select Committee never called a lawyer to give evidence. It might have helped them, for instance, if they had called the late Mr Richard Hankey, CB, Deputy Treasurer Solicitor then senior lawyer at the Ministry of Transport, whose knowledge and understanding of the legal aspect of the nationalization statutes was extraordinary.

Chapter 3

WHOSE IS THE POLICY?

The first place to look for statements of nationalized industry is in the statutes governing them. There will be sections setting out, or amending, a corporation's powers and duties. The National Freight Corporation, for example, as created by the 1968 Transport Act had these duties:

(a) so to exercise their powers, under, or by virtue of this Act, as, in conjunction with the Railways Board:

  (i) to provide, or secure or promote the provision of, properly integrated services for the carriage of goods within Great Britain by road and rail; and

  (ii) to secure that, in provision of those services, goods are carried by rail whenever such carriage is efficient and economic;
  and in discharging their duty under sub-paragraph (ii) to have due regard to any indication of the needs of the person for whom the goods in question are to be carried and to the nature of the goods;

(b) in connection with those services, to provide such other services and facilities as appear to the Corporation to be expedient and;

(c) to have due regard, as respects all those transport and other facilities, to efficiency, economy and safety of operations.'[1]

These are the broad duties of a Board which has taken over nationalized roads goods transport and railway freight marketing as its principal activities. As with other Boards, sections follow laying further duties on the Board and on the Minister in relation to the Board, besides stating what powers they are to have to exercise these duties. (Powers are also given to the Treasury and possibly to other Ministers, e.g. the Secretary of State for Scotland in some cases, but not in this.)[2]

[1] Transport Act 1968, *Public General Acts*, part 2, ch. 73, pp. 2097–8.

[2] In the Select Committee's *Minutes of Evidence* (pp. 336–41, 428–30, vol. 3, pp. 134–5) there are succinct descriptions of Ministers' powers. There are 73 exercized by the then Ministry of Power, now the Department of Trade and Industry, in relation to the fuel industries, not all relating to any one industry. Of these, 10 are exercised subject to Treasury approval or consultation, 2 are

It is tempting to skim over all this rapidly as incantation. But in relation to *policy*, harder, more definite injunctions are scarcely to be found. (The more definite duties and powers relate to matters once removed from policy: the power to make Board appointments, to prescribe the form of accounts, to approve borrowing, etc.). Even the financial policy powers and duties are just about as imprecise. As many have pointed out,[1] the injunction, commonly found in some form, to 'break even, taking one year with another' is strictly meaningless until the period is defined over which the Board is to break even – and in a statute it never is. Similarly, the Minister's role in relation to the approval of capital expenditure, though always present, is also always vague. Ministers are commonly given the power to approve a 'general programme' of capital expenditure, or to 'approve the lines' of such a programme (45). This is vague because, while seeming to indicate a rather generalized form of approval it does not rule out a Minister's satisfying himself in detail before feeling able to approve.

Implicit in the Select Committee's report is that all, or perhaps almost all, policies are capable of expression as economic criteria. Also running through the Committee report and questioning of witnesses may be a view that it could have been because of lack of the relevant (economic) expertise that policies failed to be expressed clearly. I would not feel able to pass an opinion on the preparation of earlier legislation, or on similar legislation by other departments, but during the preparation of the 1967 Transport Bill,[2] economic criteria were worked out in some detail. Some of this was part of the railway and London Transport inquiries.[3] The working group

---

powers shared with the Secretary of State for Scotland and 1 with the Minister of Transport. The then Ministry of Transport listed 29 powers in relation to the principal nationalized transport undertakings, 6 involving Treasury approval. The then Board of Trade listed 29 powers in relation to the Air Corporations – 13 shared with the Treasury. While the sheer number of powers especially concerning the fuel industries does seem extraordinary – and one wonders how necessary many must be – not more than a handful are important for the discussion of the question of ministerial control. Many of the rest relate to contingencies which have hardly ever arisen, many to purely procedural matters, the appointment of auditors, determination of the form of accounts, etc.

[1] C.f. D. N. Chester, 'Note on the Price Policy Indicated by the Nationalization Acts', *Oxford Economic Papers*, N.S., vol. 1, no. 1950.

[2] It became the 1968 Transport Act (after passing through and being amended by Parliament).

[3] Reported in the *Railway Policy* (Cmnd. 3439) and *Transport in London* (Cmnd. 3686) White Papers respectively. The staff for these inquiries into the two Boards were partly Ministry experts, partly outside consultants. The chairmen were Mr John Morris, MP for the Railway Inquiry and the late Mr Stephen Swingler, MP for the London Transport one.

which spent a long summer discussing and preparing the basis of the National Freight Corporation spent some time also on the economic criteria which would enable it to decide (i) when 'it would be efficient and economic' to carry goods by rail; and (ii) how one could devise a criterion and a profits-sharing system which would mean that the economic solution (nationally) was also one which would maximize the profits in this respect of both the railways and the NFC. A sub-committee of accountants and economists[1] was set up to study the matter; with help from the operators it came up with criteria capable of very precise formulation. In general there was an attempt to consider what every party – for example, not only the Boards, but also the private operators and their customers – might be expected to maximize.[2] And in cases relevant to legislation several detailed expressions of these commercial and economic criteria were worked up. They did affect the determination of policy and the drafting of legislation, but they were not put into the Bill in words which would be (a) familiar to economists or (b) otherwise precise by the Select Committee's standards.

There were powerful reasons for adopting no more than variations on the usual somewhat vague forms of words:

(1) Precise words are usually avoided in legislation because of the danger that they will be amended in the House or in the Committee, slightly, but in a way which alters their economic content significantly. What may seem pernickety forms of words are an almost irresistible temptation to one kind of MP to tinker. When such an amendment is raised by him, many of his colleagues and even Ministers defending the Bill may be too bored with this kind of issue and too impatient to defend the original form of words.

(2) The briefing of Ministers for the Committee stage of a Bill is a most elaborate and impressive procedure. Literally volumes of notes are provided to cover each subsection of each clause and each amendment, whether Government or Opposition. While the note on each is terse and to the point, a long Bill means much paper. This is a formidable problem of digestion for Ministers who have to defend the Bill and repel Opposition amendments. More than a small number of tricky clauses requiring rather detailed notes will, quite reasonably, not be popular.

(3) Precise words are also avoided in drafting because of the risk that another Minister, or even the same one, will later wish to think differently, because policies or circumstances change. If criteria are

---

1 Chaired by Mr A. C. Burney, CA., now Sir Alec Burney.
2 See the speech by Mr Carmichael reported below, p. 24.

worded in the usual way, there is a chance that the change of mind can take place within the framework of the Act. But the more precise the original words, the greater the probability that new or amending legislation will be needed. This might be impossible, or imply considerable delay, because of the normal pressure on parliamentary time.[1]

(4) Like most professions, economists spend a lot of time talking to each other and so develop a vocabulary of terms which they understand and which they sometimes make the mistake of thinking have an equally obvious meaning to the world outside. A parliamentary draftsman, faced by what he regards as quaint economic speech of no particular significance to anyone except economists, will redraft in words which make sense to him. In particular he will have difficulties with the concept of 'maximization', so essential to economists (and given the actual difficulty of defining maximization precisely in economics, one can see why).[2]

Thus one can see why precise expressions of policy tend not to appear in statutes even though Parliament undoubtedly has the power to be more precise if it wished. (It is perhaps noteworthy that the Select Committee did not demand greater clarity in legislation, only from Ministers and Boards.)[3] This is perhaps one reason why it is usual to precede, or accompany, major Bills with one or more White Papers. A reasoned, well argued White Paper indicates a thoughtful Bill. In them a Minister can discuss his ideas more conversationally and with less worry about the exact meaning of what is said. He can also give the reasons why he rejected other methods of achieving a solution. Again, he could express his policies with the precision the Select Committee would seem to want. But

[1] Where precise wording is required, in practice it is common to give the Minister, or some other body, power to do this by regulation. But to give Ministers the power to fill in the details of economic criteria by regulation would almost certainly not get through the House. It would give Ministers too much power.

[2] There is a lengthy literature in economics on the problems of trying to define and test the proposition that firms maximize their profits. G. C. Archibald explains the difficulties in a particular context more rigorously than most, in 'Testing Marginal Productivity Theory', *Review of Economic Studies*, June 1960.

[3] It is interesting to contrast British and American practice here. In Britain, what seems at times an almost infinite care is given to the meaning of words in legislation, to cross-referencing to other legislation and to making sure that all is consistent. In America, one gathers that much less attention is given to this. Quite contradictory statutes can lie on the statute-book as a result. It is then the duty of the courts to reconcile them. It is not clear that the filling out of economic criteria by judicial interpretation makes the economist feel that his meaning is getting across any more than in the British system.

23

he does not do this. By and large, the same, more or less exact statements of economic criteria were available when the 1967 Transport White Papers were written as influenced the legislative drafting. (The drafting of the Bill and the White Papers was roughly simultaneous.) But once again the same reasons militated against precision, as well as some others:

(1) What may seem extreme precision in a White Paper, especially if the Government does not give it as much importance as the economist does, might alienate some support which ambiguity could retain.

(2) A Minister may reasonably wish to have some freedom to change his mind before the deadline of enactment. (If there are points where a Minister has not yet fully persuaded his colleagues, on these obscurity may be mandatory.)

(3) A White Paper is meant for MPs and secondly for interested laymen (all of whom will probably read it fast). Thus the civil servants who draft the White Papers are no keener than the lawyers to make stretches of their prose arid and tortuous with what they see as the verbosity and idiosyncracies of the economist.

But far more important than these is a certain pointlessness in striving after too much exactness in a White Paper. It has no statutory force and, by the time its Bill is law, there are bound to have been amendments which make parts of it irrelevant or misleading. The changes, as with the Transport Bill, can be substantial.[1]

Thus one might expect the precise expression of ministerial policy to come after legislation, possibly as another White Paper, or as regulations, or perhaps as a considered ministerial statement in

[1] The fullest expression of the management and economic philosophy of the Bill was not in a White Paper, for which it was thought to be too detailed, but in a speech by Mr Neil Carmichael, MP (then Joint Parliamentary Secretary) to the Management of Transport Workers Conference, June 25, 1968. In it great stress was laid on clarity and consistency of objectives, as indeed was common in all speeches made by Ministers. It went on to state . . . 'the selection of commercialism or profitability [was] the overriding management objective . . . Some may be astonished that the Government is asking all its transport undertakings to adopt profitability as their management objective. You may wonder how this is to be squared with the unprofitable services to be provided by the railways. The answer is, of course, that in future the railways will be paid to run such services and that the financial arrangements will be such that in no case will it be unprofitable for them to do so. As you will know, the Transport Bill provides that the Government and the new passenger authorities can pay grants for unprofitable passenger services. The basic idea here is a contractual one by which Government and local bodies meet any shortfall in the services they demand.'

Parliament, or as directions to the Board. But this does not happen. The Chairman of a nationalized industry who was to ask for a White Paper or equivalent ministerial statement, or even for a letter from the Minister setting out his thoughts on what the policy of the Board should be, would be told that this was *ultra vires*. If the Chairman were to set down his own interpretation of what was implied for him by the new legislation, it would be improper for a responsible Minister to say that he agreed (or disagreed). To understand this one has to draw a dividing line between the powers and duties Parliament lays on Boards and Ministers. A Minister can make policy statements about the second but not the first. This is quite simply because Parliament lays on the Board, not on the Minister, the general duties and powers of conducting the affairs of the industry. To return to the National Freight Corporation, it is the duty of the Board 'so as to exercise their powers, under, or by virtue of this Act, as, in conjunction with the Railways Board (i) to provide, or secure or promote, the provision of properly integrated services for the carriage of goods within Great Britain by road and rail', etc.[1] When introducing a Bill a Minister is putting proposals to Parliament, but when it has become an Act, he would be attempting to interpret the will of Parliament if he were to place an interpretation on any duties except those laid on himself.

That the interpretation of its duties is the responsibility of the Boards does not seem to have been faced by the Select Committee, but that this was so was recognized in an extreme form by the Chairman of the Electricity Council (though some other Chairmen did not seem to have seized the point). The statutes give Ministers powers to make general directions in the 'national interest'. The power has only been used some three times, but it is an undoubted ministerial power. (It has not been used more often because it is held that 'national interest' has to be defined very narrowly. It should not be a blanket permission for the Minister to have his will by calling it the national interest.) Sir Ronald Edwards considered the possibility of conflict between such a direction and his statutes: 'I have personally taken the view that I would never question the Minister's power to give a general direction . . . I would not really want to go into the constitutional issues . . . However I can see circumstances where we might be pressed – and this is purely theoretical . . . – to do something substantially inconsistent with our statute. The overriding guide in our statute, after all, is that we have to run an efficient and an economical industry. If I thought that what we were being asked to do was inconsistent with that,

[1] See p. 20 above.

25

then I think one would have to consider one's position in a very serious way indeed' (Q. 209). Asked 'if considering one's position usually means refusing to obey the order, or going', he replied: 'Yes, it does – does it not?' (Q. 210).

All this affects the possibility of Ministers' adopting a repeated suggestion of the Committee that there might be annual ministerial policy statements *settling the broad lines of Board objectives*, 'an annual general-cum-special directive after which the industry is allowed to get on pretty well on its own' (Q. 1379). Ultimately they did not recommend such an annual statement, but for different reasons. They were after two things: both the idea of a general policy statement and the idea that Boards should be protected from rapid changes of ministerial minds. As one might expect, the Board chairmen were happier with the second idea than were the Ministers and their officials. The Select Committee were persuaded that circumstances might change drastically within a year and that a rigid annual policy statement might be too inflexible (655). Thus the Committee concluded that it might not be possible 'to make use of the formal powers to issue general directions' in order to make annual policy statements. 'Nevertheless they believe it would be highly desirable for Ministers to issue periodic statements of policy ... which would have considerable informal authority and for which Ministers would be accountable' (655). In these, 'Ministers should periodically restate their policies for their sectors, together with such further detailed policies for individual industries, or for coordination, as have been decided' (366).

It is important to realize that the 'informal authority' such statements would have does not relate to the inexpediency of a once-for-all annual statement, or of using the power of general direction (because it would be breaking precedent to describe such a general statement as in the 'national interest'). One is far from clear as to whether the Committee realized it, but it should mean that such a statement is a set of suggestions without binding force. Rather informal speeches in which Ministers talk about 'their' electricity, coal or railway policies are not uncommon. If they are preparatory to legislation they may make sense, as they refer then to the Minister's *legislative* policy, but otherwise the pronoun is misleading. In short, Ministers cannot have an electricity, coal or railway policy. Only the electricity, coal and railways Boards can. But there will be informal discussions between Ministers and Chairmen when Ministers will try to persuade the Boards to do what they would prefer them to do. All this should not be so surprising if one stops to consider that, though to some it may seem a

mere legalism and formality, strictly there has been no nationalization and no public ownership if by them is meant ownership by the
state. In a sense, nationalization or public ownership is a myth.
The assets are not owned by the Government, the Crown or by
Parliament, but by the Board. In law, they are the proprietors.[1]

One suspects that the inability to pronounce on general policy
meaningfully in any other way makes some Ministers the more
inclined to go for legislation. But why should the matter not be put
right by giving Ministers the power to make general policy statements? This would, in the context, be meaningless or revolutionary.
If the Boards were to retain their autonomy such 'policy' statements
could be no more than a set of suggestions of suasive force, in which
case a power is not needed and would be inappropriate. However, if
Ministers had a duty and power to lay down general policies for
nationalized industries, then it is difficult to see how the industries
could have autonomy. They must become 'subsidiaries' of Ministers
or divisions of their departments. Thus the dilemma of Board
freedom and responsiveness to the wishes of Ministers would have
been solved by diminishing the first very greatly. But a power to
make the policy statement, if meaningful, is a power to take the
decisions above which will determine the decisions taken lower down.
It cannot mean anything else. Everything else the Board does – how
it can meet its financial targets, determine the size of its investment

---

[1] This was Lord Justice Denning's opinion, as he then was, in Tamlin *v.* Hanna-
ford (1950) which was of key importance in defining the legal status of the public
corporation. The question was whether the British Transport Commission was a
servant of the Crown and therefore bound by the Rent Restriction Act. This depended on the interpretation given to the 1947 Transport Act. Lord Justice
Denning said that the BTC was a statutory corporation of a comparatively recent
kind in British law, having many of the usual powers of corporations and powers
that it could not exceed; but there was the major difference in that it had no shareholders to subscribe capital or to vote. But the fact that the Minister of Transport
exercised control over the Commission did not make it the Crown's agent or servant.
'In the eyes of the law the corporation is its own master and is answerable as
fully as any other person or corporation. It is not the Crown and has none of the
immunities or privileges of the Crown. Its servants are not civil servants and its
property is not Crown property. It is as much bound by Acts of Parliament as
any other subject of the King. It is, of course, a public authority and its purposes,
no doubt, are public purposes. But it is not a Government department, nor do its
powers fall within the province of Government.' (Cited by W. A. Robson,
Nationalized Industry and Public Ownership, Allen and Unwin, 1962, pp. 69–70).
Going further back in history, one feels that the early developers of the notion of
the public corporation would have felt that Lord Justice Denning had interpretated
the law as they would have wished. The Boards which were most influential in
determining the characteristic modern form of the public corporation were
creations of the Baldwin Government in 1926: the Central Electricity Board and
the BBC. In the first case, Mr Baldwin made it clear that he intended a trust, 'a

27

programme, etc. – is conditional on these general policy decisions *ex hypothesi*. Thus the Minister would become responsible for the nationalized industry. The triangular relation between Parliament, Minister and Board is replaced by a linear one with Parliament at the top, the Minister in the middle, and the Board at the bottom.

The logical way out of the dilemma would thus formally be to make a Board a 'subsidiary' of a department, or simply another 'division' of it. Then all the powers and duties would belong to the Minister, who would delegate some to the Board, and the Minister would have as much practical ability to determine Board policies and check on their achievement as would a holding company's chairman. This is directly against recent trends – which have, for example, converted the Post Office from a department into a nationalized industry – and is quite opposite to what the Select Committee would like, since it would wipe out the dividing line by abolishing the (qualified) independence of Boards (not that this disposes of changing the relationships in this direction, as we shall want to examine in *Chapter 13* below).

However, there is another way out of the difficulty.

Board managed by practical men closely in touch with industry on the lines of such an authority as the Mersey Docks and Harbour Board or the Port of London'. In the second, the Crawford Committee on Broadcasting (1925) proposed 'a public corporation . . . to act as a trustee for the national interest'. (See D. N. Chester, 'Management in the Nationalized Industries', *Public Administration*, Spring 1952.) The Royal Commission on Transport, which had been set up by the Baldwin Government in 1928 to consider *inter alia* regulation and possible reorganization in transport, defined nationalization as departmental control and put forward as an alternative to this and to private ownership a 'Public Transport Trust'. The report of the minority on how such a trust might work is almost identical to the forms of words that Morrison himself used to describe the 'Morrisonian Board'; and as well as appointing the London Passenger Transport Board, Morrison, who was Minister of Transport when the Commission reported, was engaged on drafting an abortive plan for 'socialization of transport', which was probably based on this proposal. Morrison did hail the LPTB as a triumph for socialism but, as *The Times* said in a leader at the time: 'Where in fact does the socialism come in? On what point of principle will the new transport undertaking differ from the Central Electricity Board or from the Imperial Communications Company, both of which were created by a Conservative Government?'. Morrison himself, who was trying to win friends for his LPTB, acknowledged his debt to Baldwin in the House of Commons (E. Eldon Barry, *Nationalisation in British Politics: The Historical Background*, Cape, 1965, pp. 288–99). It is interesting to go back to Keynes' 1926 paper 'The End of *Laissez-Faire*' (*Essays in Persuasion*, Macmillan, 1952) where he wrote of 'progress' lying 'in the growth and recognition of semi-autonomous bodies within the state – bodies whose criterion of action within their own field is solely in the public good *as they understand it* [my italics]'. Keynes was not original in this, but echoing a belief, widespread at the time, in the potentialities of the public trust.

Chapter 4

SOCIAL POLICY

As we have noted, the Select Committee divided the interest of Ministers into two spheres: (i) the oversight of the Boards' efficiency and (ii) a more direct concern, so it imagined, with the social aspects of the nationalized industries' behaviour. Indeed, if there were to be a division of labour, the most natural one might seem to be between commercial and social policies, the first being the primary interest of the Board, 'overseen' by the Minister, and the second being the primary interest of the Minister. Most of those appointed to run nationalized industries are businessmen. Unless by a chance a Minister is a businessman by background they will know more of business problems than he does. On the other hand, a Minister should be more of an expert on social policy, partly because he is a politician with an ear to the ground, partly because he is a member of a Government whose business it is to decide these things.

By an irony the historical development of the division of powers has been very different. 'Not surprisingly', said the Select Committee, 'though not necessarily correctly, the concern of Ministers has been almost exclusively confined to those matters in which money is directly involved' (51). Until recently the interpretation of their social obligations has been laid on the Boards as part and parcel of the business of formulating an overall 'electricity', 'coal' or 'railway' policy. Ministers have had plenty of financial powers to give them potential leverage in relation to commercial policies, but they have had few powers which have touched on the social policies of the Boards. The development of social levers for the Minister to operate has been gradual. The Boards have had to ask Ministers for their consent to a number of actions, but this has given limited opportunity to Ministers to develop positive policies. For example, under the 1962 Transport Act, British Railways had to ask if they might close unprofitable branch lines and Ministers were given the power to refuse. Though it did not happen in any definite way, Ministers could have laid down criteria indicating the policies they had formed to govern their decision whether or not to refuse permission

29

in a particular case. If a Minister had said that the lines he was readiest to close were those losing most money per passenger carried, but that he would discount the financial case if the line ran through an especially poor area, or an area judged to be under-developed, this could have influenced the Boards' priorities – it would perhaps have had 'informal authority' – but it could not have determined them. Except in this negative way he had no power to say what social services the Railways Board should run or to say anything about different ways in which they might be run which could be more or less socially useful. This powerlessness of Ministers provoked endless complaint in Parliament and some incredulity there and outside. The Railways Board, some said, was deliberately running down services or running them to miss connections, so as to deter traffic and make a better case for closure. It was also said, often by rank-find-file railwaymen, that the Board was being stupid and extravagant in the way many of these services were run, and that in many cases the services need not have been unprofitable. But none of this was Parliament's business, or the Minister's. By the statutes of the time, this was all part of the 'day-to-day' business of the Board upon which the powers of the Minister did not bear, just as pit closures and the rationalization of gasworks and power stations were. Similar cases can be found in relation to other nationalized industries.

One supposes that this developed because of the priorities people had when the approach to nationalization was being worked out in the 1920s, 1930s and at the end of the 1940s. There was the traditional interest of Parliament in financial matters. Thus there must be certain safeguards to make sure the nationalized industries did not mis-spend public money. That powers relating to this should find their way into the statutes went without saying. Besides, it was quite easy to adapt the financial safeguards of the Companies Acts and of legislation on trusts to fit the public corporation.

The social duties of the public corporations received far less attention. A reader of Robson, Chester and Eldon Barry knows that pre-nationalization thinking extended over more than a century and was extraordinarily complex. No simple account of the motives behind nationalization will do. It is tempting for an economist to overstress the economic and industrial motives, yet, especially in the late 1920s, 1930s, and in the late 1940s when the memory of the Great Depression was still vivid, they were significant; and these were the years when the most important industries were nationalized and when the modern British conception of a nationalized industry was formed. Frequently, nationalization, in many cases introduced

30

by a Conservative Government and in many others not opposed in principle by a pragmatic Conservative Opposition, was a tidying-up operation. The industry was nationalized, not so as to serve social or national ends better, but because some 'market failure' meant it was not serving commercial ends well. In some cases this was because the prides and jealousies of independent owners – coal, iron and steel – prevented their merging and rationalizing to achieve the economies of scale which would have been their rational course of action if they had really set out to maximize profits. In some cases – the public utilities particularly – the cry was against monopoly. In others – London's bus services and road goods transport – it was against wasteful competition. The first meant the opportunity, whether taken or not, to make excess profits from the public. The second meant that the provision of services was bedevilled by uncertainty about price and quantity for the consumer and about employment and wages for the worker. Competition did not settle down in any steady way. In many cases – gas, electricity, the railways, coal – one or other kind of market failure, it was argued, had caused excessively low investment and a failure to re-equip the industries to take advantage of technological development. This could not be profitable without large-scale merger through either private initiative or nationalization. In many industries, private mergers and cartels did arise to realize some of these advantages; but in some cases these, as with iron and steel, raised the problem of control of monopoly – just as an argument for the nationalization of coal, electricity and gas was that if existing entities had spontaneously merged on a sufficient scale to realize the potential economies of scale, they would have become very large private monopolies able to set their own charges to soak the public, and so should be nationalized.

The market failures in many of these industries caused social problems: unemployment and, not to be forgotten, the attempts of employers to cut costs and raise profit margins by cutting wages, lengthening hours and otherwise worsening the conditions of work. Thus one can see why the solution of the commercial and the social problem seemed to many to be the same. The Board of a nationalized industry could cancel the evil effects of monopoly profit by lower prices or better services. Or it could eliminate the wasteful competition and given the consumer reliable public services and the worker steadier employment. It could, because of its size, invest in vast capital works, like the Electricity Grid, which promised high profitability, lower prices and steadier employment, or invest in the mines to achieve more efficient production. As so many of the

31

industries which were candidates for nationalization were basic in the sense that they provided significant inputs – fuel and transport especially – to a host of other industries, lower prices and better quality products would have an effect which would permeate through the economy and increase international competitiveness (and thereby production and employment), as well as reduce wage-cutting and the tendency to let working conditions deteriorate throughout the economy.[1] It is important to remember that the percolation of Keynesian ideas was slow, even after the publication of his *General Theory* in 1936, and the general belief in industry and in all political parties was that if Britain was to pull itself out of the recession in general and in particular industries and reduce unemployment, it would be through increasing the efficiency of individual firms and industries. Thus the economic motives behind nationalization thinking, though complex in detail, had a central simplicity. During foul weather – slump – nationalization was held to be necessary to rationalize the industries and make them efficient. But when they had become efficient, and there was fair weather, nationalization was needed in some cases to prevent excessive profit-making at the expense of the public.

Thus the social aims of nationalization could be achieved by rationalization, for the most part, as Lord Ashfield rationalized the bus services of London or as a succession of Board chairmen rationalized coal, electricity and gas production and, eventually, the railways.

Up to a point, an economist standing back would say that the commercial and public interests in these circumstances would coincide. By becoming efficient, each industry would make a major contribution towards solving the community's social problems, of which unemployment, wage-cutting, long hours and poor working conditions were the most important. But this was not necessarily how people saw it at the time. There were always those who argued that it was efficient and profitable for employers to work their labour force as hard as possible, to pay them as little as possible, and not to spend on frills such as working conditions and safety measures –

---

1 It is worth recalling just how bad labour relations were. 'One has to remember that working conditions in industry as a whole in 1945 were very different from what they have since become. Relations between labour and capital were strained, to say the least. There was little joint consultation; there was little provision for redundancy or for promoting the workers' welfare or enlisting his support in improving productivity and efficiency. By giving their employees a genuine sense of partnership in their public enterprise, the nationalized industries . . . were going to demonstrate that industrial democracy pays off.' (M. Shanks, *The Lessons of Public Enterprise*, Cape, 1963, p. 23.)

even to cause enough unemployment to encourage the others. Nowadays – and it was then a point pressed home by Alfred Marshall in the most widely read economics textbook of the time – we tend to think it pays firms to be good employers and also to deal honestly with their customers. But one did not have to be a Marxist then to argue that firms should be forced to sacrifice some profits in the interest of a fair wage, a decent working week and decent working conditions. If competition made this impossible, then here was a reason for nationalization to secure the 'public interest' as opposed to the mere commercial interest of firms. As the strength of the trade union movement has grown, as there has been legislation to remove the worst anti-social practices of bad employers and as firms generally have found that it pays to be good employers, this reason for nationalization has withered. There is less reason to make a distinction between the public interest and the commercial interest, either of private or public firms on this account.[1]

With this focus one can see why it did not seem odd to lay the primary responsibility for interpreting the social aims of the Boards on themselves. They were best able, given the duty, to decide in detail how to be good employers. The Boards of the electricity and transport authorities were in the best position to decide what was an adequate public service. There were other social and political considerations than the control of monopoly and the elimination of wasteful competition, but this could be achieved by the Minister's talking to the Chairman and not by any statutory formulation, as Herbert Morrison made clear in his 1933 book, *Socialisation and*

[1] Perhaps the most important surviving obligation of this kind are the services provided by the National Coal Board under various Acts and for which they are only partially compensated by the Government (and that only since 1965). The Board argues that these have the effect of requiring it to be a 'better' employer than private industry. The items include: redundancy payments, payments in respect of loss of superannuation and employment prospects, payments to transferees whose place of employment is changed and who therefore move their homes, provision of housing for transferees, and provision of travelling allowances and transport for those whose place of employment is changed. This cost the Board £5 million in 1966–7 and £7 million in 1967–8 after payment of specific Government subsidies. The difficult questions are: how much of the remainder represents the Government's requiring the NCB to be a better employer than is usual in private industry, and, still more fundamental, whether, through more generous redundancy and other provisions, there is a case for putting all industry in the same position in this respect. Why did the Government require the NCB to be a better employer than private and other nationalized industry? A stage of its requiring all industry to go so far? Or, as seems more likely, the reason is that special treatment of coal-miners is justified because they have exceptionally poor alternative job opportunities because of the remoteness of many mines? (*Minutes of Evidence*, p. 131.)

C

33

Transport, which, though little read, is still the source of the pre-vailing ideas on how nationalized industries should be conducted.[1]

What is perhaps more surprising is that Board Chairmen have not taken the opportunity given them to develop Board policies with social content. One might have supposed that a railway chair-man might have arisen who would have had more positive ideas on how the railways could have been used as means to wider social goals, while satisfying the financial criteria. Board Chairmen have not been known for the quality of their thinking as social reformers. Lord Ashfield (and of course Southern Railways) have left an indelible mark on London, but one does not get the impression that his policies for London were meant to achieve conscious physical planning, social, political or economic ends: to help the poor by improving their access to a greater extent than the access of the better-off, or to use public transport as a town-planning tool to achieve a better environment.[2] The duties that Boards have under-taken against their strict commercial interest, but without statutory requirement, have, to a surprising extent, also amounted to cross-subsidization of the rural community by other consumers, though

---

[1] Constable, 1933. On rereading I found it astonishing how many phrases and ideas which are now commonplace in the discussion of the powers and duties of Boards are to be found in this book. While it was written to justify Morrison's setting up of the London Passenger Transport Board, after he ceased to be Minister of Transport in the 1931 debacle and before the legislation had been through Parliament finally, it does embody the philosophy of how national-ized industries were to behave, the philosophy which was hammered out between Morrison and his civil servants and which later was also to dominate the post-Second World War nationalization statutes. It has a claim to have been a most influential book, perhaps even because it synthesized in a lasting form, notions which were not original to it, but which came from a spread of sources.

[2] All such social policies mean giving more weight to the interests of some group than they are ready to pay for. In the jargon of welfare economics they are *redistributive* measures. But it is interesting to note that Morrison defined a public corporation in terms which suggested that they should not engage in redistributive activity. He was reacting against a situation in which he believed private transport undertakings had been the football of sectional interests: capitalist, municipal and even labour interests. Therefore he saw it developing management attitudes which would not give weight to any special interests. It would show its difference from a private concern by the way it behaved in detail. It would be honest, free from corruption and fair. Indeed, this was another reason for regarding the social behaviour of Boards as primarily a matter for day-to-day management. Of course he is right. It would be ridiculous to pay a nationalized board to compensate it for being more honest and consumer-oriented than its private rivals, and it would mean day-to-day interference in management if a Minister were to think it specially his concern that the employees of Boards showed these public-spirited qualities. But this underlines the argument of the text. Our ideas of the social policies of a Board have broadened.

34

why there has been this concentration of interest to the virtual exclusion of other candidates for a subsidy is not clear. Gas and bus companies and the railways have all cross-subsidized country people. So has the Post Office, though it, in providing kiosks and the telegram service (both unprofitable), has shown a somewhat wider notion of public service in providing a standby service for the poor and others without their own telephones. In so many cases there is a probability that the public service argument is an *ex post* justification for continuing whatever geographical network of services it has become traditional to operate, and therefore for whatever deficit has occurred (*Minutes of Evidence*, p. 600). The Board Chairmen could perfectly well answer back that if Parliament had intended them to do more of these things, the statutes would have indicated it – and this is a reasonable answer. The working of the statutes laying upon the Boards the duty to interpret overall policy, gives perhaps the opportunity for a radical, socially motivated policy, providing this also fulfils the financial objectives; but the actual wording used, the references to 'public' or 'adequate' service, are too slender to suggest that Parliament wanted someone to interpret the words vigorously and imaginatively. Until recently the requirement under the 1947 Electricity Act to develop and extend rural electrifications was a rare example of something more specific. One also has to remember that even now the social policies are few for which people tend to think of the Boards as the most efficient instruments. Perhaps the only Board Chairmen who is remembered as having a strong concept of the social duties of a public corporation was Lord Reith, who had a fiercely educational and moralistic view of the role of the BBC. Of course, it is perhaps easier to see this as relevant for the BBC than for other nationalized industries, but it would have been possible within the statutory framework for any Board Chairman to have developed a very revolutionary approach towards workers' participation and control, say on the Yugoslavian model. However, none has attempted this. The statutes do not give them any encouragement. Neither, on the other hand, do they give Ministers the power to develop and impose policies of this kind It is only recently that Government and Parliament have become increasingly concerned with the impacts of policies on particular groups. There seems to have been a convergence of interests. For a long time there have been Government policies for the poor, the disabled children, old people and numbers of other interest groups. As the years have passed the organization of the machinery to implement these policies has become more formal. There has been greater interest in developing criteria. Thus, in a sense, the problem

35

of controlling these policies has become more like that of controlling the nationalized industries *in form*. At the same time there has been greater interest in the non-commerical consequences of what nationalized industries do. Thus their performance has come to be judged by less exclusively commercial standards.

There were several reasons why powers were taken in the 1968 Transport Act to enable the Minister to make grants for unprofitable rail, bus and canal services. The Minister of Power at much the same time was taking powers to be able to pay the National Coal Board to postpone or avoid pit closures, and the Gas and Electricity Councils to induce them to burn coke; and there were a few other examples of this principle which had been advocated by many people for many years.[1] The Select Committee had suggested it in earlier reports and came out strongly in its favour in its report on Ministerial Control, published after the 1967 Coal Industry and 1968 Transport Acts. In its evidence to the Select Committee the Treasury said that it also was in favour, except in cases where the sums of money were too small to make such an arrangement not worth the trouble (Q. 107).[2]

---

[1] If one draws the net wide enough, one can find many early examples: for instance, the agreement by the government not to continue to require the railways to carry members of the armed forces at reduced rates. On the variety of such payments see the Select Committee (706–8, 728–34). London Transport was compensated for delaying fare increases in 1965 and 1967 – an important precedent to which we will return in *Chapter 9*. Recently, BEA have been compensated for being forced to buy British aircraft in the national interest, rather than the the American aircraft which would have been more profitable for them.

[2] The Treasury witnesses to the Select Committee presented interesting variants on this procedure. While there was no direct subsidy to BEA for the 'social' and unprofitable services to the Highlands and Islands, the annual reports have a note on the net loss on these services. As a question of presentation, the difference is trivial. What does matter is whether the cost of the service has been negotiated between Minister and Board so that a view has been taken on the amount of money and scale of service which would serve the social ends the most efficiently, given competing uses for scarce resources; or whether it has been left to the Board to decide what to spend and make a note? The subsidy procedure in practice seems more easily directed towards the first end than does making a note of it in the annual report. The Treasury also defends another alternative: that the target of the Board should be lowered to compensate it for unprofitable social services. To my mind this suffers from two overwhelming disadvantages. (1) A Board's target should be the end-product of deciding what it can earn on its commercial assets and new investment, given its pricing policy and market prospects. From this may be subtracted the losses on 'social' services. But one cannot sensibly calculate such a target until the forecast losses on the social servoies have been estimated. (2) The estimated losses on the social services cannot be calculated intelligently unless there has been negotiation between Minister and Board on their scale and size. Thus, this alternative either amounts

Thus there was nothing new in the principle adopted. There were also strong practical reasons for adopting it. Not only was it impossible to make sense of the nationalized industries' performance without something of the kind, but the industries recognized it as well. This problem could have been met by a slightly different solution. The nationalized industries could have continued to take the responsibility for the social as well as for the commercial decisions, putting a note in their Annual Report when they incurred an expenditure for a non-commercial decision to indicate the cost of this to Parliament. But I doubt if that solution crossed anybody's mind because of the growing and unquestioned belief that, if there were specific decisions to be taken, the function was the Minister's.

Another advantage of going about it this way is that it forced the department and the Minister to decide what any subsidy was for. Again, this was not essential. The power to pay deficit grant allows a Minister, in principle, the right to subsidize a wide variety of activities for an infinite variety of reasons. The decision to go for specific subsidies came from a belief that the Government should make up its mind in advance on the principles of subsidization. Thus, as the White Papers show, a conscious decision was taken *not* to subsidize freight movements. Some arguments for doing this were put forward: one was that it would be in the overall economic interest that more traffic should go by rail, which justified a subsidy insofar as getting traffic off the roads would reduce congestion on them. This argument vanished when it was shown that, on average, the movement of goods by truck to a goods yard, usually located in or near the city centre, plus another truck movement at the other end, implied more time being spent on more congested urban roads than shipment by a truck would which head straight for the periphery of the city and then on to the inter-urban highway system. One could find exceptions but the rule seemed robust.

After much discussion the principle behind the subsidization of passenger traffic emerged as one of benefiting certain groups of people who were poor or for some other reason unable to use competing modes of transport. This generally seemed to rule out the subsidization of long-distance passenger transport. This, and steps like it, may not seem to be very great ones, but they were

---

to much the same thing as the specific subsidy approach and is only a difference in expression, or, and this may be more likely, it will conceal a much cruder set of calculations. If one believes that Parliament and the Minister are right to wish to exercise more oversight over social expenditure, this alternative also suffers in that it would seem to escape the scrutiny of the Public Accounts Committee (740).

37

more important than they may appear. It was clear – and not only in transport – that nationalized Boards were confused about what successive Governments saw their social duties to be. They had an impression that many of the things said by Ministers had not much content, and also that so many things Ministers wanted were very particular and not easily generalized. They also were well aware that civil servants had had much experience in making the particular colourably general by writing it up as if it were a general principle. Indeed, Boards (and sometimes civil servants) occasionally may have hoped they could get away without policy changes by rewriting what they were already doing in a form more sympathetic to the prevailing party ideology of the personality of the Minister. If the Minister had no clear social ideas of his own they could hardly be blamed for this. For years the system had encouraged Ministers not to think through what they meant.

Another influence in favour of greater clarity and precision was the greater concern about public expenditure. A socialist government found itself spending an astonishing amount of time trying to decide public expenditure priorities as public expenditure totals were revised downwards. This sharpened up the competition for funds and it was more natural to ask what particular subsidies were for, so that they could be compared with other ways of spending the same amount of money.

For all these reasons the new approach was adopted. At its strongest the attitude was as expressed in Mr Carmichael's speech described above (p. 24), which saw the relationship as basically a contractual one. The Boards operated purely on commercial principles. The Government and local government decide what unprofitable services they have to pay for. There is a danger that the nationalized industries will take this literally and become indistinguishable from (rather grasping) private enterprise. Although this may be unlikely, one supposes Parliament would not like the Boards' commercialism to be predatory. Some of the old ideas of the Boards that they should not cheat, deceive, knowingly lie in their advertisements, give their customers short measure or be 'bad' employers could be constraints on their ability to make profits.[1] There may be a time when it would be wise to include among the duties of the Boards some subsections which express the ideas of what is good business practice. Also, there is the danger, which the

[1] One wonders what the reaction would be to a statutory duty which required Boards to provide the information about their goods and services which would enable a consumer to make a rational, efficient and economic decision, to attempt the kind of words often found in statutes.

Treasury foresaw, that there may be minor social policies the cost of which does not substantially affect a Board's financial position. Where this is so one would hope the Board might be prepared to yield to the Minister's wish. Certainly, a rigid line that social services are only provided if paid for, might be taking clarity too far.

I do not think that any concerned with the Transport Bill saw the additional advantage which flows from the earlier argument: that for the first time Ministers would have a power (wherever they had a power to make grants) which gave them power and a duty to make a policy for these social services. It goes further than this. The Minister is now responsible for how this money is spent – not the Board – and this means that this money is subject to the scrutiny of the Public Accounts Committee. Unlike the expenditures of the Boards themselves, Parliament can ask all sorts of questions about how it is spent, as they can about other public expenditure.

How important this development is depends on the width of its application, and on the comparative merits of achieving such specific public policy ends through subsidizing public corporations as compared with other means: direct subsidies and taxes, regulations, etc. As far as public corporations are concerned, one of the most interesting possibilities lies in the use of London Transport and the provincial Public Transport Executives established under the 1968 Transport Act, to achieve more rational urban transport and planning policies. The use of roads in cities tends to be under-priced especially in the peak, partly because the costs of providing and operating urban roads are higher, but more importantly because of the social costs of congestion. Because they use more road capacity per person, cars tend to be relatively more under-priced than buses, using the petrol tax here as a measure of the price charged by the community for road use.[1] Thus there is a strong case on economic efficiency grounds for subsidizing public transport to offset the under-pricing of urban road use. Apart from transport, there are some interesting possibilities in planning. The public corporations are, by statute, free from the need to get ordinary planning permission from local authorities. But as a kind of *quid pro quo* in the case of electricity the Minister has the power to approve the siting of power stations, pylons and underground distribution systems.

[1] The congestion argument that urban roads are under-priced has a long history. Its origins can be found in Pigou, but for a fuller explanation see *Road Pricing* (Department of Scientific and Industrial Research, 1964) or A. A. Walters' *The Economics of Road User Charges* (World Bank Occasional Staff Papers, no. 5, Johns Hopkins, 1969). The case for paying London Transport a subsidy to keep its fares down was essentially this one. See p. 113 below.

There are many arguments which could be used for this. In many cases the alternative to the CEGB putting up pylons in one local authority area is for it to route its electricity through another. Therefore, for a good decision to be made on environmental and physical planning grounds it is arguable that this must not only take account of the views of local authorities but that some overall view should be taken by national authorities. New Town Development Corporations are public corporations. It would be possible for them to operate (like the private corporations which have built new towns in the United States) purely commercially to select the most profitable development opportunities. Alternatively, they could be required to temper profit maximization by pursuing certain social ends, either by giving citizens a quality of life which they would not get for the same money elsewhere or by being deliberately required always to accept a proportion of very poor or otherwise under-privileged people and help them achieve standards of housing, health, education, welfare and job opportunities they could not buy with their incomes elsewhere. This raises an important question to which a full answer would take us too far from the argument of this book: Why not give such people an income supplement (whether by negative income tax or in some other way) rather than a sub-sidized environment? The short answer is that higher standards of housing, health, education and welfare, or access to a variety of jobs, including some which will give them a ladder up which they may climb, may not be available in their old environment, or may not be at a price they can afford. It may indeed be cheaper to provide these opportunities in a planned new environment because of the ability to realize economies of scale.

But some of the most interesting cases are outside the nationalized industries and refer to other entities which are, or may become, semi-autonomous. As one widens the scope of bodies beyond the traditional public corporation, there are more opportunities for Government's subsidizing outside bodies to achieve social ends – as they do now: the British Council, the Regional Hospital Boards, the museums and the Social Benefits Commission. Just what balance between commercial and social ends Government wishes to attempt raises tricky problems of policy-making to decide what is to be subsidized and why.

Furthermore, how Parliament is to exercise this power of subsidy and how it is to draw the dividing line between autonomy and control in this respect has hardly begun to be decided.

Chapter 5

FINANCIAL OBLIGATIONS: THE TREASURY'S FUNCTION

If Ministers have no general or residual powers to make policy (except when introducing legislation) and if, until recently, they had few social powers, what about their position where powers and duties are given them by statute? As we have seen, the most useful of these are financial, the most important of which relates – in one form or other since the different statutes alter the wording without apparently wishing to alter the intent – to the approval of capital expenditure programmes. The Minister, in consultation with the Treasury, also authorizes borrowing, but this is not so important since it tends to be contingent on the approval of investment (Q. 55). In some cases, where the industry has had persistent deficits, the Minister has the power to authorize payments to meet these deficits out of money voted by Parliament, but wherever there are such powers and there is a deficit, this also tends to be automatic. In addition, from 1967 to 1969 there were powers under Prices and Incomes legislation to disapprove and otherwise delay price increases.

Once again, for similar reasons, these powers are not given the definite form of criteria either in statutes or in White Papers, though there can be no question that a Minister has the power to do this before, during and after legislation. However, the most important statement of such criteria is in a Treasury White Paper.[1]

In the White Paper which came out towards the end of 1967, in time to be noted and warmly approved by the Select Committee, are to be found:

(1) A discussion of investment criteria which states that these should be in net present value form, and explains how the discount rate is fixed and how one should allow for risk in making project appraisals. It also suggests that special cost-benefit studies should be done by the department to demonstrate the worth of major

---

[1] *The Nationalised Industries: A Review of Economic and Financial Objectives,* HMSO, Cmnd. 3437, November 1967.

projects which cannot be justified financially, yet are thought worthwhile.[1] It is a distillation of recent official wisdom on investment appraisal.

(2) The right pricing policy is set down as long-run marginal cost pricing, and there is some discussion of the problems caused when marginal costs are below average costs. If prices are then set equal to marginal costs, total revenue will be less than total costs and there will be a deficit. The other point discussed is the delaying effect of Prices and Incomes legislation on price rises.

(3) In the past there has been some tendency to concentrate on pricing and investment criteria, but an enterprise can adopt long-run marginal cost pricing and also perform good investment appraisal but still be inefficient because its costs are higher than they need be. It uses labour badly, buys inputs at unnecessarily high prices or fails to take advantage of cost-reducing investment. Thus the White Paper has a section stressing the importance of increasing productivity and otherwise cutting costs per unit of output.

(4) Lastly, it is argued that nationalized industries should be set financial targets. This is to be the logical culmination of the other three. They are to represent what a Board is to aim at. The targets may be expressed as a percentage rate of return on net assets as has been usual, but other forms of target – an absolute amount of profit, etc. – are not ruled out.

There is no purpose in going through the paper in detail. Two points I do want to make. Firstly, an economist can read the paper with sympathy. It is written using the kinds of words he uses, though expressed lucidly and clearly so as not to fox a knowledgeable layman. It is a reasonably sophisticated, brief essay in public enterprise economics. Its main authors show to an experienced eye, by the subtleties of their expression, that they have probably read about as much on the difficulties and nuances of these criteria as anyone. In this respect, and its readiness to use economists' phrases, it is different from the White Paper it replaced, though that must be given great credit for beginning the process of formulating criteria.[2] An economist outside the Government may disagree with it on the way

[1] Financial appraisal of projects usually means the appraisal of projects to determine their profitability to the enterprise: to evaluate what Pigou called their private benefits and costs. Cost-benefit analysis is appraisal to determine social benefits and costs, usually when the project is expected to be unprofitable. By definition, these social benefits and costs, or externalities as they are often called, accrue outside the parent enterprise.

[2] *The Financial and Economic Obligations of the Nationalized Industries*, HMSO, Cmnd. 1337, February 1961.

in which the discount rate is said to be determined, or on a number of other counts, yet he will probably recognize, and be able to amplify, from his own knowledge of the relevant literature, the reasons that have persuaded the Treasury.

But there is a second level on which one can read this White Paper and notice that all arguments are qualified to the point of equivocation. The interpretation of the criteria which he would recognize to be logical and precise swims in a sea of phrases which make it possible to read in many other interpretations of crucial points. Any undergraduate with a taste for logic could prove this in detail. But, for example, there seems to be a clear statement on page 5 that the only case for approving investment projects which do not show a positive net present value at the going discount rate would be because 'they are justifiable on wider criteria involving an assessment of the social costs and benefits involved, or are provided to meet a statutory obligation'. On page 7 the argument is qualified, apparently to cover other possibilities. Apart from 'social or wider economic reasons', 'it is desirable in a few cases to provide services at some direct financial loss'. There does not seem to be here the implication that the only other exception would be where there was a statutory obligation to make an investment – as, for example, the Gas Council has in its distribution network, in the interests of safety.[1] To take another example, paragraph 18 has the most direct endorsement of marginal cost pricing in principle, but the phrase, 'marginal costs', is not used (as it is in the rider paragraph 22). Instead, one finds that 'the aim of pricing policy should be that the consumer pays the true costs of providing the goods and services he consumes'. But 'true' has no special economic meaning. It leaves open the question whether the costs that should be paid are short-run marginal costs – those actual ougoings caused by the consumption in question – or long-run marginal costs which reflect also the capital costs and other overheads incurred in providing the extra unit of output. In addition, one might suppose it leaves open also the dispute between marginal cost pricing of either kind, and full cost pricing or average cost pricing. In this particular statement, which bears most directly on the behaviour the industries are expected to adopt, the language is imprecise. Yet it is very easy on reading to miss the use of 'true' here and to assume that the more exact, but still slippery, definitions of marginal costs used elsewhere (paragraph 21) carry over into the formulation of the

[1] Once one recognizes this style of ambiguity, it sends one back to p. 5 to wonder whether the use of 'or' in opposition to 'normally' was conjunctive or disjunctive: presumably the former.

43

pricing rule as laid down for the Boards. Where it is being pre-scribed for the nationalized industries it is at its least precise; where it is at its most precise, it is not being prescribed.

Why does this White Paper equivocate with weasel words in relation to powers laid on Ministers by statute, in a document which many, even so, would regard as a stronger and more explicit document than usual? One knows it cannot be lack of expertise. The Treasury has quite enough economics-trained administrators, backed by trained economists, to have been more definite. Neither can one argue, as one did of other White Papers, that this is meant especially for MPs and laymen. The language is technical enough anyway to deter people without experience of the concepts. As always, one could argue that the White Paper is ambiguous in order to make it possible to change policies without rewriting the paper; but then, of course, it is not serving the purpose of laying down explicit criteria.

One can always fall back on human factors. The White Paper itself indicates that it was a long time appearing, and indeed the outside world knew it was almost ready for some time. There are internal signs that, in spite of its merits, it was pieced together from several 'sources'. Fatigue could have set in. But these explana-tions are never very satisfactory. Treasury officials, like those in other departments, are more than used to rendering a hotch-potch consistent, whatever their fatigue. It is surely safe to assume that the way that the paper was drafted was meant.

A much more reasonable explanation is that the ambiguity reflects the realities.

(1) *Marginal Cost Pricing.* There is no Government policy on the interpretation of marginal cost pricing. The basic economic argu-ment is well established in economics. If price is below marginal cost then the cost of the service is more than the marginal revenue from it, and output should be contracted until the two are the same. If price is above marginal cost then it would be profitable to expand output until the two are equal. If in one industry price is above marginal cost while in another it is below, it would be a more efficient use of resources if resources were transferred from the second to the first until marginal cost equalled price in both industries. Since the principle ignores all costs already incurred – overheads – short-run marginal cost pricing may well mean a deficit. The French engineer Dupont's example of a bridge was just one of this kind. He assumed that there were no maintenance costs (and no congestion); thus, once the bridge was built the marginal cost was zero. So, to

set a toll was necessarily to set a price above marginal cost, which would reduce output below what was efficient since increasing output did not increase costs. The decision how to finance the bridge could be taken quite separately (in terms of decision as to what was the most efficient method of levying taxes).

A marginal cost pricing policy which meant a deficit might not be popular with the Treasury but, quite as important, it would go against the statutory obligation to break even at least. There was some discussion of marginal cost pricing in relation to the railways. At one stage as is indicated in the Railways White Paper,[1] the railways put forward a proposition which was very much like a request for marginal cost pricing. It was argued that the railways had a large amount of 'standby' capacity, that is, excess capacity. This was the result of past generations of railway investment which was surplus to present normal requirements, but which might be regarded as 'standby' which it was worthwhile for the nation to subsidize through a deficit grant, because it would be available if there were an emergency – a war or exceptionally bad weather, for example, when a big increase in railway traffic might result. Thus it was very much like saying that the railways should meet their marginal costs, but that some proportion of their overhead costs should be regarded as sunk costs and should not be recouped in fares and charges. If this capacity had been accepted either as something worth subsidizing in its own right or as an implication of marginal cost pricing, there might have been a continuing heavy railway deficit (or subsidy). But investigation showed that a high proportion of this standby capacity was not truly fixed. It was possible to reduce excess capacity and tailor the capacity of the line to the traffic. Thus the effect of the exercise was to show that marginal and average costs were much closer than had been commonly supposed.[2] In this case the principle of marginal cost pricing was probably not sacrificed and there was no commitment to deficit financing. It is anyone's guess whether the principle of marginal cost pricing would have been preserved if the facts had defended the old belief that marginal costs were well below average costs.

But a policy of marginal cost pricing might run into difficulties for other reasons. One of the most persistent and troublesome lines

[1] Ministry of Transport, *Railway Policy*, Cmnd. 3439, para. 10 and Annex, para 2.18. See also S. Joy, 'The Standby Concept on Railways', *Journal of Transport Economics and Policy*, vol. 1, no. 3, September 1967.
[2] S. Joy and C. D. Foster, 'Railway Track Costs in Great Britain', Paper presented to the Institution of Civil Engineers Symposium on *Developments in Railway Traffic Engineering*, May 1967.

of attack on the Transport Bill, as on many other recent nationalization proposals, was on the sections which gave various Boards powers to manufacture and provide services: to sell the output of their workshops, to set up petrol stations in their car parks. Many, noting the success of European nationalized industries in expanding their operations in new markets and in building up conglomerates, have wondered why this has never been allowed for British Boards. The proposals that went into the Bill were much narrower; they did not allow the Boards to move into entirely new lines of business, as a private company might. Even so, the opposition was formidable. The Opposition required, and obtained, reassurance that the price charged should cover all the costs attributable and that there should be no 'cross-subsidization' of these activities by the Board's business as a whole, which would mean they undercut private competitors. This too can be squared with one interpretation of marginal cost pricing.[1] The prices of these outputs must cover the marginal cost of producing them. But it would not square with another which would allow the Board when it had invested in the necessary equipment, which might be a once for all investment, to charge down to short run marginal cost, if this were more profitable than stopping its activity.

There is no simple definition of marginal cost pricing which is compatible with all the statutory obligations, let alone with the interpretations put by the Boards on their powers. The actual working out of marginal costs can be very complicated, requiring a sophisticated simulation of the system.[2] The principle is only the beginning of what is needed. When London Transport asked the Select Committee for its advice on how to interpret marginal costs in some of their trickier pricing decisions, the Committee shied away

[1] It did allow them to charge down to short-run marginal costs where there was a temporary fall in demand.

[2] Mr Silberston, an academic economist and part-time member of the British Steel Corporation, gives a poignant and enlightening account of his difficulties as a clarifier of marginal cost pricing. He wrote that one could only find how decisions were made in determining marginal costs 'by spending as many hours in (presumably) smoke-filled rooms as each working party had to spend, hearing all the arguments expressed and inferring those that were not . . . given the necessary complexity of the whole operation and the amount of specialized knowledge involved, it was not possible for those Board members not directly involved to do more than approve broad principles and to ask searching questions. In reply to these, the experts' answers were very convincing though at least one Board Member was left with the impression that 'commercial considerations' were probably not in fact always as pressing as they were thought to be by those on the commercial side. But how is one to tell who is right?' ('Surveys of Applied Economics: Price Behaviour of Firms', *Economic Journal*, no. 319, September 1970.)

from such detailed involvement. But it is the case that the interpretation of marginal cost pricing is more often than not a very detailed matter. Is there a case for pricing peak power (or traffic) more than off-peak? The answer depends in part on the marginal costs of the peak as well as on the marginal costs of having a differentiated fare system.[1] Neither in practice is it possible to make a clear distinction between short-run and long-run marginal costs. There are many lengths of 'run'. It is hardly surprising that most of those nationalized industries which are in competition (most of transport, aviation and a few others) tend to regard market pricing, pricing what the market can bear, as a reasonable approximation to marginal cost pricing given that degree of competition. It is far from clear that Government would have the power to deflect them into another interpretation, given the duties of the board to conduct their business with efficiency and economy.

(2) *Discounted Cash Flow.* The Treasury White Paper comes nearest to an order in its request that investments should be put up in discounted cash flow form. (It does not in fact insist.) Discounted cash flow has been recommended by the Treasury for many years now. It was one of the measures that was written up by NEDC many years ago in the hope that its adoption by businessmen would mean higher average returns from investment in British industry because of fewer mistakes. The good sense of the principle is undeniable. A pound is worth more to me today than in one year or ten years' time because in the meantime I could reinvest it and earn a return. If I can invest at 10 per cent then the value of a pound coming to me in one year's time is $0 \cdot 9$ of its present value – in ten years' time is approximately $0 \cdot 4$ of its present value because of the years foregone during which I cannot earn 10 per cent on it because it is not mine.

DCF is in many ways the perfect recommendation of a non-interventionist Government. Apart from the insight just mentioned, its desirability does not require any knowledge of the facts. It is perfectly general, and one can, short of arrant cheating, tell simply by looking at the return given on an investment whether it has been discounted or not. The Treasury goes one step further than this and selects the discount rate at which public expenditure and Board

[1] And on calculation of the elasticity of substitution between peak and off-peak. Both in power and transport much of the disagreement between managements (who generally do not want to differentiate charges for the peak) and economists (who do) turns practically on disagreement over the magnitude of the elasticity, and on the difficulty of measuring that is normally caused by the problem of distingusihing between price-inducement and other influences on revenue.

expenditure is to be discounted. Broadly speaking, it is fixed in relation to the returns that private industry is making at the margin. So this too requires no knowledge of the facts about a specific project or industry. Indeed, with a set of tables and a discount rate, anyone can sit down and do the necessary calculations to come up with the net present value. (The calculation of an internal rate of return, defined as the discount rate which equalizes the present value of the revenue and cost streams, is more laborious but no less mechanical.) It is true that serious mistakes can be made by any-one who is too impatient to sit down and work the present value out, or to get the data which makes it possible to work out an intelligent present value on the basis of forecasting cost and revenue streams.

Thus it is all the more extraordinary after all these years that so many projects still come up to Ministers and the Treasury without net present values having been calculated. The only Chairman who gave evidence to the Select Committee and claimed that just about all his projects were appraised in this way was Sir Anthony Milward of BEA. All the rest, and the departments who dealt with them, said that a high proportion, sometimes more than half, of their projects came up either with a first-year rate of return only, or in many cases with no return calculated at all. The Gas Council and the National Coal Board said that it had the Treasury's approval for some of the methods it used instead of discounted cash flow, and it is said that there is one nationalized industry which has considered discounted cash flow and has rejected it.

What is the explanation of this seemingly strong resistance all these years after the Treasury first took the initiative? One explan-ation is that, by and large, the Boards take discounted cash flow much less seriously than the Treasury and regard its preoccupation with it as academic and remote from reality, almost an eccentricity – and there is something to be said on their side. Discounted cash flow is a way of arranging figures rather mechanically, as we have said. What matters are the figures and, some would say, what one knows about the characters and aptitudes of those who have produced the figures. If one is reasonably happy about both, then the actual working out of the DCF is a matter for clerks. If it shows anything strikingly different from what a first-year rate of return does, then someone should point this out. But many Board Members and senior Board officials will say that they usually expect returns to be so much greater than costs that that kind of error should not matter except for very large projects with very long lives.

But while I would agree that the arithmetic of DCF is not a profound experience and can be delegated, I would also judge those wrong who think that projects usually show benefits so much in excess of costs that discounting does not matter. In practice, one all too often finds that discounting does substantially alter the worth of a project put up undiscounted (occasionally to its advantage). Therefore it is simply prudent that a DCF calculation should be done; but the Boards are right to think that this is not the most important act in appraisal. As my then colleague Mr C. P. Scott-Malden told the Select Committee, if all projects came up with DCF returns attached and one believed the figures, there would be nothing to worry about (Q. 1502). But the more important point is the second one: it is the figures and the people responsible for the actual figuring that give one confidence in a project. The DCF is secondary.

But this gentle cynicism about the value of DCF is not the main reason why so many projects turn up without a DCF rate of return. One can hardly suppose that the Boards would deliberately create ill-will by refusing to go through the mechanics of this calculation. True, there are some accountants who have a rather different intellectual difficulty in that they say that they learned about discounting, probably in their first year as accountants, when they also learned all about the difficulties of finding the correct method of depreciation. If anyone can tell them, by which they mean persuade them, which is the correct method of depreciation, they will take the matter more seriously. Meanwhile they regard the doubts about depreciation as creating such errors in the calculation as to make it a waste of time. Sometimes one can sit down and persuade them they have missed the point; sometimes one cannot.[1] But this only refers perhaps to some who have not read the latest accounting textbooks. More often, accountants, like businessmen, tend to think that discounting is something they have known about for a long time, and if economists (by which they mean the Treasury but not only the Treasury) should have just been fired with passion for it they cannot see why they should put this god on their high altar, instead of in a side chapel.

[1] The value of an asset is defined by its earning power. As time passes its earning power (and the discounted sum of its expected future earning power) probably declines and the asset depreciates. All the *ex ante* conventions used by accountants – straight line, reducing balance and the rest – are at best approximations to the truth and none of them are right, except by chance in a particular case. But the method of depreciation is irrelevant to DCF. What one is asking is whether the discounted stream of benefits or revenues over its expected life exceeds the discounted stream of its expected costs. If it does, the prediction is that it will produce a positive gain; if not, a positive loss. The method of depreciation is immaterial, as is depreciation. The problem is in the choice of discount rate which, in Britain, is solved by the Treasury who select a rate for the public sector to use. See, for example, A. J. Merrett and A. Sykes *Finance and Analysis of Capital Projects*, Longmans, pp. 47–9.

The main reason that so many projects do not show rates of return of any kind or in first-year form only, is more fundamental: the inability of the Boards to produce the figures required. A large part of the investment which does not have a return calculated on it is often referred to as replacement investment, although this is in some respects a misleading description. For many Boards it is a large proportion of all investment, more than enough to determine the profitability of the enterprise even if all other investments were to promise a satisfactory return (which they do not).

It is worth going back for a minute to the industry which has solved this problem, at least for about half of its activities: electricity. In some brilliant work done in the Électricité de France in the 1950s, there was theoretical matching of the essential technology and economics.[1] By this I mean that the economist-engineers and mathematicians penetrated behind the textbook cost curves of more or less arbitrary shape and were able to produce mathematical models which showed the costs of increasing output (and the effect on costs of changing the costs of inputs) more realistically. These were used to estimate whether it was preferable to generate additional electricity using 'conventional' power stations, hydro-electric methods, nuclear power or some mixture of these, and gave a technically meaningful and reasonably precise meaning to the marginal cost of increasing output (overall, in a particular place, at a certain time of day or season, and in other contexts). It followed that a fairly definite answer could be given to the question: what would be the effect on the net revenue of Électricité de France (or CEGB) of replacing one or more power stations. In effect, one could model the network of power stations as a system. Thus, following up this pioneering work, one is not surprised to find Sir Ronald Edwards of the Electricity Council saying that DCF returns are always calculated on power station projects (though not on the considerable investment in distribution (Q. 435)).[2]

Unless there are also social returns to be considered, at the very

---

[1] See J. R. Nelson (ed.), *Marginal Cost Pricing in Practice*, Prentice Hall, 1962; and P. Masse, *Optimal Investment Decisions*, Prentice Hall, 1962. Such reconcilations are still rare. There is an excellent basis for one in A. Maass's *Design of Water Resource Systems* (Harvard UP, 1962), but it does not seem to have been used, perhaps reinforcing the argument that such developments are more likely to catch on if they arise from within.

[2] Why then have so many of the profitability estimates on generating stations gone horribly wrong? Because of poor cost control and over-optimism at the possibilities of technological improvement. But without the models, better cost control and technological realism would not by themselves have achieved profitable investment.

least one is concerned with the effect of an investment on the net profitability of the enterprise. The more technologically interrelated the parts of an enterprise, the more difficult this is. If one has an enterprise composed of plants producing output more or less independently of each other, one can usually calculate the return on an investment in one plant in terms of its effect on the output and net revenue of that plant alone, though even then it may affect the output of the firm's other plants through competition. But in a firm where the plants add up to a production process with intermediate products passing from plant to plant until they emerge as final products for sale, investment in one part of the process may have quite profound effects on the profitability of other parts of the process, relieving or causing bottlenecks. Thus, the more complicated the technological relationships of the parts of an enterprise, the harder it is to calculate a meaningful rate of return which reflects the net effect of a change on overall profits.

I would imagine – though in many cases I could not prove – that there are many nationalized industries which, for this reason, would find it easier to calculate meaningful returns than is the case with electricity generation. Perhaps this was why Sir Anthony Milward was able to say that they always calculated a DCF return in British European Airways. Some industries, like coal, are probably in an intermediate state,[1] but there are others where the problems of calculating a return seem to be more intractable than in electricity generation. The most exacting would seem to be telecommunications and some transport industries. The reason is similar. All are complicated networks. Putting a new telecommunications link between London and Birmingham will not only benefit callers between the two cities but, through rerouting and reduced congestion on other links, between other points as well. In principle, a rather complex mathematical model of the telecommunications system is needed to predict, and then evaluate, the effect on the whole, and the net revenue position of the whole.

A good example of the emergence of the problem is in the port industry. To work out the return on, say, spending money to improve the handling facilities at a port (or on a productivity agreement), should be a fairly straightforward calculation. One is spending money to cut costs. It is probably unlikely that such an

[1] Calculation of marginal costs in coal has attracted considerable attention: see I. M. D. Little, *The Price of Fuel*, Oxford UP, 1953 and W. G. Shepherd, *Economic Performance under Public Ownership: British Fuel and Power*, Yale UP, 1965. For a discussion of ambiguities in marginal cost pricing see the last, pp. 42–5.

51

investment will have a significant effect on the total traffic passing through the port; and even if it does divert traffic which would otherwise have gone through rival ports, there may be no harm in regarding this as a bonanza from the standpoint of the investing port, a stimulus to do better to the surpassed rivals. Thus, to calculate the effect on the whole port industry of installing a new crane at Grimsby, was (and is) a waste of time. But the massive investment required for a container port has changed all this. Allowing one port to become a container port can have a very significant effect on the profitability of its rivals. Allowing too many ports to build container facilities may keep them on a par but may make them all high-cost operations because of the low ratio of traffic to the facilities involved; so there could well be a tendency for them, particularly on the East Coast, to lose traffic to Rotterdam, the cargo going to and from the big ships at Rotterdam in small vessels. Thus there is a need now to estimate the *systems* effect of the kind of really large investment in a port which is represented by the installation of container berths.[1]

The relevance of all this to the status of the Treasury White Paper on DCF is twofold. Firstly, it stresses again, as with marginal cost pricing, that both the actual interpretation of principles like marginal cost pricing and discounted cash flow, as well as the ability to interpret the principles, is often highly specific to the technology of an industry; and that this is particularly true of some of the nationalized industries which have had the most unsatisfactory performances: the railways, telecommunications. Thus any attempt to try to write a document which will state these principles in general terms applicable to all nationalized industries is bound to fail. Secondly, it indicates that what is necessary in many industries to get discounted cash flow investment techniques working, and therefore financial control, is something that cannot be adequately described as the adoption of a principle. It is a breakthrough in the ability to model mathematically the salient characteristics of the industry – not that all industries require a great sophistication here, but some do.[2]

---

[1] The first development of such a model was reported in the Ministry of Transport's *Portbury* (HMSO, 1966). There have been later refinements.

[2] One of the most heartening features of recent years – I would almost say the most heartening – in transport policy has been the thorough recognition by British Railways, the National Freight Corporation and London Transport – that they both have the skills and the need to apply economics and mathematics, sometimes called operations research, in this way to illuminate their *strategic* decision-making.

(3) *Constitutional Position.* Quite apart from the impossibility of writing a tight White Paper on these matters for all nationalized industries, which would lay down criteria with anything approaching the clarity the Select Committee would require, there is another and equally fundamental reason for the White Paper's ambiguities. The statutes only give the Treasury a secondary role in relation to approval of expenditure and borrowing. The statutes require that they be consulted, and even their consent gained, on a number of issues (*Minutes of Evidence*, vol. 3, pp. 8 f.). The truth is that the power to settle financial criteria, so far as it exists, belongs to departmental Ministers.[1] If departments have doubts on the practicality of the criteria as they affect their Boards – or the Boards have doubts and are able to persuade their sponsoring departments to reflect this – the Treasury are peculiarly vulnerable. They would find it hard to resist amendment of a point of substance since there would be an inconsistency in Government policy if what they wrote did not reflect the department's views as they actually operate the powers. This is something more than the ordinary tact and good manners of bureaucracy, which will normally lean over backwards to accept an amendment of no, or of only marginal, importance if this will persuade someone to give their support. For example, the Treasury is probably least vulnerable in relation to taxation where it can make almost no concessions to the wishes of departments, even if it wants. On national economy policy there are a few other departments which have a right to have their views taken seriously on a number of points, but in relation to this the Treasury still has the prime role, provided it has the support of Ministers. However, the same is not so in relation to the expenditure of nationalized industries. The prime role belongs to the departments. Hence the greater vulnerability. Thus, one cannot expect such a document to be a management document. It is the highest common factor of agreement among those responsible, and the fact that it has gone as far as it has is a tribute to the educational role of the Treasury over the last ten to fifteen years.

Thus, both because the criteria could be stated more specifically

---

[1] The Select Committee stated (233) that in their opinion, so far as the department's policies on pricing were '. . . at variance, the Committee believe that the Treasury should be held responsible. They are the department responsible for taking the lead in developing and formulating for the Government new economic and financial policies. But the Committee fear that the Treasury themselves were handicapped by indecisiveness at certain vital points.' The Committee does not seem to have perceived that a possible explanation of the Treasury's 'indecisiveness', or ambiguity, is that they did not have the responsibility in this context to be decisive.

in relation to each Board and because the statutory powers belong first to the individual Ministers, the place to expect greater clarity in deed and thought is not in the Treasury but in the sponsoring departments themselves.

Indeed, there is a sense in which the framing of these criteria, even so, is the most positive action the Treasury takes towards what can be described as a management policy for the nationalized industries. This is because the Treasury does not operate managerially in a coordinated way towards the nationalized industries.[1] The mystery of the actual role of the Treasury has unsettled some of the Boards considerably. The Select Committee asked Chairmen whether they would like to see the Treasury face to face. All said they would on occasions. Some said that they and their officials had never met the Treasury officials. Some said they had asked the sponsoring departments if they could, but it had never come to anything. Others had been, but not very often. Some sponsoring departments seemed perfectly happy that the two should meet, but did not see why the Boards were keen. But, quite apart from the feeling that one sometimes met among the senior officials of the Boards that the Treasury officials were worth meeting because of their legendary brilliance, it is quite easy to see how the Boards could form an impression of the Treasury, moving and deciding mysteriously behind the scenes – and deciding without taking verbal evidence from them. They did not really know whether it was their pieces of paper that were forwarded to the Treasury or some encapsulation of them. In their worst moments they might see the Treasury as a judge which habitually heard one side of the case. But at others one felt they suspected that departmental officials who used the not infrequent phrases, 'I must speak to the Treasury about that' or 'I must get that cleared with the Treasury', were using the Treasury as a convenient sleeping partner to delay or take the blame for an opinion which was their own.

The tradition that, if a Minister is a conglomerate, then the Treasury is a super-conglomerate, is pervasive; and, in a way, documents like the White Paper tend to reinforce this by their very existence. It is anyway the natural analogy that occurs to an executive

---

[1] It is interesting to note the reply when the Committee asked Treasury witnesses about their strategic role. 'We know how much in a way to allocate to the nationalized industries' sector of industry as a whole. Coming back to our test rate of discount – because it is basically that which telling us – if an investment is properly appraised and the pricing policy is sensible, we are saying that if it passed the test rate of discount, it could not be invested for a better return elsewhere in the economy' (Q. 51). But, while so many projects do not show a return, there is something lacking in this control.

in industry. Yet, when these meetings happen, the representatives of the nationalized industries may go away feeling that they have had a 'useful talk' or a simulating afternoon, or even hope that the Treasury officials were more sympathetic and reasonable to their point of view than the departmental civil servants. But they are unlikely to have come away with a clear idea of how this conversation fitted into the decision-making process as it affected them.

Although the main financial powers belong to the departments, one can see how the Treasury might have used its influence to have developed a powerful position as the nationalized industries' ultimate financial controller. But it has not worked out in this way – as it has not for public expenditure generally – principally, one supposes, because it would have meant a degree of centralization that nobody wished. The Treasury's financial interest in the Boards seems somewhat fragmented. There is the White Paper. There is the role as a clearing house and coordinator should any department show any signs of wishing to change the traditional duties and powers of the nationalized industries in legislation. There is, I believe, for I was never more than dimly aware of it, an army of correspondence passing on various matters connected with the terms of borrowing, details of the accounts and other housekeeping. There is the machinery that combines the nationalized industries' investment programmes and grants to go through the machinery of Government. But a system has never developed by which the Treasury itself collects the investment programmes and profitability forecasts of the nationalized industries, and recommends how investment funds might be reallocated between them in order to achieve a higher return on the whole (or for political reasons). Until very recently it would seem that nationalized industries were supplied with what funds the industries themselves thought they needed at the going interest rate. Provided that in general the industries expected to be sufficiently profitable, the Treasury's main interest has been how it was to be financed. Thus, it was because nationalized industry borrowing from the market was making management of the money market difficult, that in 1956 the Boards were required to borrow through the Treasury.[1] But this was no check on the flow of funds. The interest in financial targets seems to have started because the Treasury wished the ratio of prices to costs to be such in the power industries that those Boards would achieve a substantially greater degree of self-financing and so reduce the pressure on the bond market. From time to time and especially in the second half of the

[1] W. A. Robson, *Nationalized Industry and Public Ownership*, Allen and Unwin, 1962, pp. 301, 302.

sixties there have been attempts to cut back on Board investment. These were made as part of general policies to restrain public expenditure, not because the Treasury felt that the particular returns were too low to justify as much investment – though naturally the Treasury would hope that the projects cut out were marginal.[1] If the Treasury were interested in knowing the actual projects elimi-nated, this again was because they were anxious that they should be real and not 'paper' cuts, because of criticism in Parliament and elsewhere that much of the postponement was an illusion. Projects which would never have been started or which had slipped in time for some other reason, often in a way which was predicted, might be put up nominally to satisfy on paper the need for cutback.

Besides this, the Treasury does take an interest in some investment projects but, as it told the Select Committee, not in a systematic way. When the nationalized industry first indicates the proposals it expects to be putting up the following year, the Treasury indicates an interest in seeing a proportion of those the Ministry asks to see, because they involve either very large sums of money or some point of principle. Its purpose is not to get a view on the worthwhileness of a Board's total programme. Some of the interest is in seeing whether the criteria have been applied. But this approach grows out of the traditional civil service approach, sometimes called 'candle-ends', to be described in the next chaper. As we shall see, it is more an inspection, or control through inspection, system than anything systematic.

[1] This is the explanation of most of the investment cuts, especially in the power industries, which have been reported (except for those aviation projects cut or interfered with for non-financial reasons, which we will come to in *Chapter 10*). For example, the 1957 cuts in railway investment were defended for *national* reasons – not because of any inadequacies in the railway modernization plan. See Select Committee on Nationalized Industries, *British Railways*, HMSO, 1960, p. xix. For an analysis of more recent experience, see Select Committee on Nationalized Industries, *Ministerial Control*, Report, pp. 222–4. Though in the present state of financial control inevitable, the procedure is largely irrational since it does not discriminate between public industries whose marginal projects are profitable (or socially desirable) and those that are less so. Not seldom, a cut is followed by a rather arbitrary increase so that, for the most part, projects have been delayed, not abandoned.

Chapter 6

FINANCIAL OBLIGATIONS: THE MINISTER'S FUNCTION

The powers of a Minister, and by delegation of his department, are greater than those of a minority shareholder but less than those of a majority shareholder or holding company. The metaphor of the Minister or Government as a shareholder (Q. 650) or holding company (Q. 567), though often used, is seriously misleading. The assets of nationalized industries are not vested in the Minister (or in the Crown). They are their own proprietors. The Minister's powers are more like those of a merchant banker – a simile also often used (Q. 954) – with the differences that, while a private firm may change its merchant banker and a banker may switch his investments, the Government is the sole channel of long-term funds for a Board; and also that a Minister does not use his powers as a merchant banker would.

Among the papers submitted to the Select Committee are various memoranda which could be described as statements of investment criteria. While several are excellent expositions of the principles laid down in the Treasury White Paper, what they add is not more explicitness particular to the individual Boards. What is added is mostly some description of the procedure by which projects are to be selected for examination. One reason for this has already been given: the empirical difficulty of being specific because of the complexity of the operations of many Boards. But the real point is that we have now come into a world in which financial powers are exercised more by examining and approving projects than through statement of criteria. (To the point of whether this is right we will have to return.)

Nothing was more astonishing to me on entering the Ministry of Transport than to find that no railway investment project had been turned down in spite of (i) the large deficit the railway had run for many years, and (ii) the widespread feeling, shared by many officials, that a very large slice of that railway investment had been digging

B.R. deeper into the red since the mid-fifties, though some projects may have been modified and others discouraged.[1]

One came to understand why (and evidence to the Select Committee suggests that this was the rule in relation to all Boards – projects were seldom, if ever, turned down) (QQ. 448, 489, 894–8). Though the statutes gave the Minister powers to control investment funds and borrowing, the fundamental feeling seems to have been that even these were secondary to the Board's responsibility to Parliament for its overall financial position. It is quite clear that the statutory powers would have enabled a Minister to act more like a merchant bank and interpreted his 'oversight' of the Board's efficiency in a more decisive manner. The Boards made it plain that they saw the duties of the Minister in this respect as falling far short of a system of financial control which would affect their independence. While that itself might have been inconclusive, when a Board states categorically, as it has been known to do even publicly, that in its opinion some investment is more or less essential if it is to discharge its statutory financial responsibilities to Parliament, this puts the problem of conflicting powers and responsibilities nakedly. A Minister who then denied the Board these funds because, in his judgement, based on the advice he had received from his officials, the investment would not produce a sufficient return, is giving the Board an alibi against a failure in performance – one more fact to be brought forward by the Board when it says that it did not do better than it did because of the interventions of Government. Indeed, it is arguable that a Minister who was to deny funds in a major instance where his financial judgement conflicted with the

1 'For many years now the railways have been investing at a rate of more than £100 million a year. The famous Modernization Plan which was authorized in 1955 has cost the nation some £1,700 million. One has to conclude that the average return on this investment and other railway investments over the past ten to fifteen years has been zero. The principal evidence is the record of their profitability over these years.' Mr Carmichael (in a speech to the Management of Transport Workers Conference, June 25, 1968) went on to point out that that was after assuming that social grants had been paid retrospectively to meet the cost of social services, including their capital charges, as defined in the 1968 Act. But 'this does not imply that it is impossible that BRB could invest £100 million a year wisely in the future, only that under previous managements they have misused a large part of their investment funds in the past'. Some of the projects they invested in may have been profitable, others clearly were not, though we will probably never know which were profitable because of the difficulty of disentangling the data to get a clear picture of the costs and revenues attributable to projects. But one of the legacies is that, by channelling so much money in certain directions, they did not invest in other ways which one could have had more confidence would have been profitable. See also C. D. Foster, *The Transport Problem*, Blackie, 1964.

Board's was in some sense taking over *the* responsibility of the Board.

Moreover, in many cases where the commercial returns were doubtful, it might seem to the officials, as to the Boards, that there were social or national reasons for saying Yes without their being able to say how far the poor commercial results were the effect of social obligations and how far of inefficiency, because no analysis had been done to disentangle the social from the commercial or even clarify the main objectives.

Indeed, if one wants an analogy for the traditional relationship which departments regard as normal, it is much more like that of a lawyer administering a family trust fund than that of a merchant banker. One of the members of the family for whom the trust is administered visits the trustee and asks for capital from the fund as he is entitled to do under the terms of the trust. The trustee must satisfy himself in general terms that there is no conflict between the purpose for which the capital is wanted and the terms of the fund. But the expectation is that, if the client is over the age of twenty-one, he would not have asked for the money if the purpose had not been legitimate. If he is known to have been a little reckless recently, the lawyer may talk to him a little longer and try to probe his mind. He may even in the odd case try to dissuade him. Apart from that the lawyer is not too interested, except possibly by way of friendship, in knowing why the money is wanted. Thus he expects to give his consent on almost a minimal assurance that the purpose is a respectable and legitimate one. The parallel is not exact but it is nearer the tradition than the analogies of shareholder, holding company or merchant bank. It picks up the quality of the consent which a civil servant would most like to, and often does, give (and for which he may feel his expertise is most fitted). It also picks up the quality of the consent a Board would most like to receive.

But in recent years the idea has been growing that Government has a greater duty to secure oversight of efficiency than this, especially when a Board is in persistent deficit. The question is how to do it. One way is for the Minister and his officials to act as a pressure group and try to persuade Boards to use criteria. One might do this without altering the traditional power relationship, especially if one can separate discussions about criteria from the examination of investment programmes. But, as we have seen, the pressure has not been outstandingly successful. DCF is not universally employed and sometimes cannot be particularly meaningful until Boards have the economic and operations research expertise to look at their activities more systematically. For the same reason it is difficult to say whether any Board is practising marginal cost pricing and what it would mean if it were – and, until recently, Ministries have had even fewer people who could be helpful here than the Boards have had. Thus, at the level of knowhow and expertise at which discussion takes place, of how one translates abstract criteria into meaningful analysis, the departments were in no better position to be effective educationally than the Treasury – and for them to have intervened very far to gather the necessary information would have seemed impertinent to the Boards.

If education was not enough, what did one do? Did the Minister and his officials shuffle off the role of trustee and adopt that of a merchant banker, with the sense that the funds were first his (or the nation's) and only to be used by the Boards if they could show they could use them profitably? Did the officials sometimes contemplate the possibility of having to say No? One reason they didn't, born of experience over a long period and not the most important, may have been a lack of confidence that Ministers would uphold the officials' recommendation if they advised turning down a project.[1] Though he might come to share the officials' doubts, many Ministers in the end would prefer to go along with a Board on management questions rather than with the civil servants, in spite of what he knew of the overall performance of the Board. (In some cases he may even have been influenced by the thought that if he turned something down, the row would blow up in his own time, while the results of bad investment would not bear fruit until somebody else's time.) After all, a Minister may be keenly aware of his own lack of relevant experience should a Chairman urge that a project is commercially necessary. Also, he would have a greater responsibility than a merchant banker would who turned down a project because the client could always go to another

[1] The Labour Government came to power in 1964, assuming, one supposes, that the Tory Governments had done passably what they would think of as characteristically Toryish things. Among these may have been a belief that a business-minded Government with a rather high proportion of businessmen in it would have a rather efficient system of public expenditure control. It seems to have been a shock to find that thirteen years of Tory rule had given this question almost no attention, and had shown almost no interest in the application of modern management methods to Government – at least not to the extent of getting anything fundamental done about it. Thus it was a Labour Government – hard pressed to trim public expenditure because of economic troubles – which stimulated officials to develop the beginnings of a more efficient system of control. As far as one can tell, the Tory Ministers before 1964 had no better record in simply turning down unprofitable projects, or projects without sufficient evidence that they were likely to be profitable. Concorde and the more infamous weapons projects were but the tips of the iceberg.

merchant banker to try his luck. Turned down by him, the Boards could not borrow from anybody else.

The professional diffidence of the administrator would have been at least as great as that of the Minister. He is not a businessman and knows it. Neither is he an expert in the affairs of a particular Board. Thus he would be likely to bend over backwards to try to make sure that the Board had a good case, despite first appearances; and even if he could not make sense of it in the end, he might be reluctant to assume that no sense could be made of it. Thus he would have to discuss and think hard for a long time before going so far as to say No to an investment submission; and this was farther than in the end he was ready to go. So, finally, the Minister gave the benefit of the doubt. His juniors who have advised him may be able and penetrating but, in the end, is he to pit their, and his own, intellect against the apparently unanimous mass of a Board?

So if on reflection it is not surprising to have found no investment project turned down, neither was it surprising to find that the civil servant was not a rubber stamp. Most of those projects which raised no doubts in his mind, he approved at once. But where there were doubts, the technique used was to question the Boards. First there is a general annual investment programme in which the Board sketches the projects it wishes to invest in during the following year. At that point, Ministry and Treasury tend to decide what projects they want to have a look at in more detail. The remainder are more or less approved *de facto* since the Board does not have to put in a report on them. What is looked at is a small selection, in most cases, of the larger projects. Some time later the submissions on each of the projects to be selected will arrive at the Ministry, where the practice used to be for the sponsoring division and the Finance Division to give their views (though if any other division had an interest it might be given an opportunity also). If there were doubts, there would be a written reply to the Board raising questions: If there is no figure of financial return, why is the project said to be 'necessary'? Why does it have to be done now? What are the demand forecasts it depends on? There may then be a meeting; possibly followed by more questions, and more answers; perhaps at successively higher levels in the Ministry and Board hierarchies if the case is contentious; even, exceptionally, a meeting between Minister and Chairman. Thus the ambition of the doubting official is to persuade the Board to go away and think again. Can he do this? Always. Several times, if necessary. But can he persuade them to change their minds? Not often on a major point.

The technique used is a development of the traditional one used by the Treasury and Finance officers in Government, sometimes called 'candle-ends'. Within the Government there is a multitude of letters passing in which people are asking approval for all sorts of expenditure. While much expenditure does not have to be approved by the Treasury, it is surprising how much does; and there are rules and conventions to make sure that the odd case and a fair sample of the routine cases come to the Treasury's attention, but not so many as to weigh them down. When an administrator gets such a letter, he will look at it to see if there is something 'wrong', something which does not 'stand up'. It might be something at odds with an earlier letter on file, a figure that does not seem right, or merely an awkward or inept way of presenting the argument. These may indicate just carelessness, or possibly the flicker of something which should not be. When he finds a lapse, he asks a question to which the convention is that he must receive an answer promptly. If the defence is quick and robust, he will probably be satisfied. He has found a simple mistake or clumsiness in expression. If not, he will go on asking questions until he has bottomed it and made a case, or been satisfied.

But the interesting thing about this is that it is fundamentally a logician's approach. What gives the clue is an inconsistency in argument, more often than not, and this is as likely to be among the explanatory words as among the figures. Its best practitioners develop a tremendous nose for incoherence in argument, and a sense of for how long it is worth pursuing a point. Its protagonists claim that there is a high probability that the method will unearth something really wrong. It is a method which one might well have expected to have developed, as it has, among people of high intelligence and logical ability, but without great specialized knowledge. (Of course they come to know a great deal about their industries, from even the relatively few years they spend in post, and also from hearsay. But they generally end by being more aware than the outsider of the limitations of what they know.)

It has something in common with the cross-examination technique of a lawyer who is also probing the witnesses' defences to see what he can find. But whatever its merits within Government – and I would argue that, for reasons of economy in highly trained manpower, there is a case for finding more systematic methods of financial control – it is much less successful when used to probe the investment submissions of a Board. The cross-examination approach breeds a race of Board representatives who are skilled at the soft answer that turns the edge of a question and who quite naturally sally into technical language and detail which the administrator does not easily follow – and the Board representative's intelligence is likely to be different from that of the administrator. Within his own organization he will be less used to logical arguments setting out a case explicitly. He will be able to assume a common knowledge and sets of assumptions. To some extent, what a ports man thinks about ports or a railwayman about railways is something he has absorbed on the job and never learned explicitly. Thus, he is less likely to be impressed by logic, or dismayed when the illogicality or incompleteness of what he has said is pointed out to him. He is more impressed by someone who, he believes, shares some of the craft mysteries that he does. Also, quite apart from this, he knows that, though he may not feel as agile intellectually as the civil servant who is questioning him, in the end – he may have to play it long – he must win, because of the final lack of self-confidence the administrator has in his ability, or his right, to say No.[1]

The virtual certainty that in the end they would get approval did not make the process any more popular with the Boards, as is shown in copious evidence to the Select Committee from the Boards.[2] They

[1] The most elaborate exercise to co-ordinate investment policy was at the then Ministry of Power; of this, visible outputs were the 1965 and 1967 Fuel Policy White Papers. In this case (unlike transport) the different enterprises produced fuels that were close substitutes for each other and for oil for most consumers. The sheer magnitude of the investment involved meant that any attempt to let competition decide the winner, and in particular the reaction to natural gas, would have meant substantial excess capacity at a very high cost to the nation. Here then, if anywhere, was the case for national planning to provide a more efficient solution than the free play of market forces. For a number of reasons the forecasts on which the fuel policies were based have not turned out well. But the points I should like to stress here are: (1) Although under the Ministry of Fuel and Power Act of 1945 the Minister is given 'the general duty of securing the effective and co-ordinated development of coal, petroleum and other . . . sources of fuel and power in Great Britain . . . and promoting economy and efficiency in the supply, distribution, use and consumption of fuel and power', this general duty is not reflected in any specific power in relation to the nationalized fuel undertakings or, of course, petroleum. (2) Coal, gas and electricity made it clear to the Select Committee that the Minister, in forming his fuel policy, had not in fact asserted his will in relation to their investment programmes (which is what one might have expected if the minister had been decisive in predicting or demanding a change in fuel policy. (3) The then Minister was at pains to explain to the Committee that the Minister's job was to apply influence, bring the industries round a table and 'ensure that the arguments are discussed backwards and forwards between them' in the belief that 'they can usually be convinced if there is a good argument' (QQ. 1260, 1261).

[2] (QQ. 522–3, 526–8, 633, 1300–1, 1443, 1819, 1970.) Youth – and sometimes economists – took the rap. For example, Sir Ronald Edwards spoke of 'young and enthusiastic members of the Civil Service' (Q. 187).

resented the time the process sometimes took (though the departments were able to prove to the Select Committee that the causes of delay were, as often as not, on the Board's side). Board members were often irritated by what they regarded as the triviality and irrelevance of the questions. Someone who starts with a great experience of an industry prides himself on immediately asking the two or three questions which will get to the heart of the matter. But an administrator who does not have this advantage fires more questions, expecting that some will hit a target. Indeed, he is often likely to discover which of his questions were the most pertinent by the answers he receives. But in asking questions, some of which are patently pointless to the experienced representative of the Board, he may in some cases lose the latter's respect, which is quite unfair. Also, the fact that the candle-ends method works from the particular – looking at cases, not strategies – to the general – though sometimes never reaching the general – is likely to make it seem trivial, even petty, to Board Members who have learned a quite different approach to financial control, an approach which they believe is more strategic. Thus the Boards, almost without exception, complained of too detailed an intervention in their affairs by the officials of their Ministries.

Neither were the Ministries happy. The officials were as aware of their professional weaknesses as of their strengths; and, almost more to the point, of the weaknesses and strengths of having to operate within the traditional notions of the rights and duties of officials in such matters, especially when, as with Boards in deficit, the situation seemed to require more than this. Some, perhaps, hoped the difficult times would pass and the old trustee relationship would be restored. Others may have felt that the movement of Government and the mood of Parliament was towards more financial control, even with industries not in deficit. Others perhaps saw no alternative: it was the only possible relation between department and Board, apart from doing nothing – but surely that would have been immoral, indefensible before Parliament, given that so many national resources were at stake and that the records of very few Boards were spectacular by commercial standards. In the case of the railways, such a record would have had the sharpest reaction from a minority or majority shareholder, holding company or merchant bank. But whatever their feelings, they knew that any good influence they had was only educational, since, as we have seen, they did not say No. But one could not blame the civil servants. They were doing as well as able men could, given their particular expertise and the conventions of the system.

The difference made by the economists who joined the Ministry of Transport in 1966 and were posted to work with the nationalized industries' side, was to strengthen the administrators' appraisal of investment submissions and, backed by strong Ministers, to reach a confidence where Boards were occasionally told No. The co-operation on this work between the two was immediate and stimulating. The economists' analysis was quickened and forced into being more robust by the administrators, who punched away at any weaknesses (particularly at the common weaknesses of the professional to throw light on only a corner of an issue, in a way which does not always help to form an opinion on the whole).[1] The economists' commercial and financial background and slant helped to make the questions more pointed and, one might hope, more like the questions that an industrialist or merchant banker would *first* think of.[2] The submissions as they came in were now sent to the two or three economists, who worked on appraisal and provided an investment analysis section of the kind that many top managements have to help them take investment decisions.

The second thing the economists had to offer was some knowledge and experience in the use of discounted cash flow techniques; but this was not especially important because many of the administrators concerned happened to know these well also and, as we have seen, so many of the projects came out without a discounted return

---

[1] By the time one is a don or even a research student, one never hears most of the penetrating criticism of one's work because it is behind one's back, either as one don talks to another or in the essays of students and their tutors' comments on them. This is not always the case: there are seminars where some of the audience may gather their thoughts quickly enough to offer useful criticism; there are book reviews; and articles are written which dive into a controversy so that the author knows quickly enough at his peril what a number of other people think. But conceiving and writing academic work is usually a solitary occupation, which is perhaps as it should be. Working as a professional in Government is very different. One finds oneself explaining what one is going to do before doing it, during and after, all very rapidly, to people with keen minds who have high standards of logic, clarity and relevance. If both sides agree that what is being discussed is important it is rather like going back to a tutorial again, and is bracing. If the professional in Government does not find himself locked in this close relation with the administrator, something is awry, and the chances of his doing anything useful are small.

[2] Like other Boards, the Railways gave the Select Committee an example of the excessive intervention they condemned. But while accepting that in general the Ministry of Transport was intervening too much, the Committee conceded that 'judging by the answers ... nearly all (the questions) appear to be relevant to a decision on this application. They are also detailed. Clearly British Railways should have asked and answered most of these questions themselves. But had they?' (vol. 1, p. 222).

E

anyway. The third thing the economists contributed was, to my mind, by far the most important. As we have seen, the instinct and expertise of the administrators was to detect weakness in the coherence of the argument presented to them. Since so many submissions were incomplete (in that they were not coherent, did not stand up) this meant asking the Boards for figures to complete the submissions. The first task of the junior economist who received an investment submission from the Board was to try to reconstruct what the complete justification of the proposal must have been. If too many pieces were missing, this was impossible; but on the basis of what else was known about the industry it was often possible to build a tentative 'model' of the proposal. Sometimes it was a very simple construction, hardly worth dignifying with the word 'model'. (For example, if the project were to show a positive return when discounted at 8 per cent present value, then there must be an increase in expected demand of x per cent, or some cost reduction we do not know about.) On rarer occasions the construction was substantially more elaborate, and occasionally the mathematicians who arrived in the Ministry at the same time were brought in to build something refined. It was also possible to test the sensitivity of the 'model' to changes in some of its parameters. (For example: What would happen if labour costs rose by p per cent rather than q per cent? What would happen if the predicted demand did not build up so soon?) This made possible more meaningful discussion with the Boards on their submissions. They would be asked if the missing pieces had been guessed aright. And where the assumptions did seem optimistic there was a basis from which to probe their judgement. The purpose of a good appraisal system is certainly not to check figures (which is what some Boards complained their departments seemed to be doing) nor to force those down the line to support every assumption with hard evidence. It is in the nature of statements about the future that there is much in them that cannot be proved. Judgement is needed: the aim of good investment appraisal is to get assurance that what could reasonably be quantified, has been; and that those identified with the investment submissions have really stretched their minds over a project, and in the end have genuinely made a best, rather than a casual, capricious or overcautious, judgement. Besides their expertise in investment appraisal, the senior economists on this side were also able to contribute because they had had experience of appraisal in commerce and industry.

It would have been too much to have expected the Boards to have welcomed the change. Some, especially the Select Committee, represented it simply as more intervention of the old tiresome and time-consuming kind (though, in fact, projects took no longer to go through the Government machine). Others saw it for what it was, the first attempt to impose a financial discipline that bit, and while some – as individuals and perhaps as taxpayers – welcomed it, others did not.

So the combination of circumstances, Ministers, administrators and economists in the Ministry of Transport – the combination of the last two not duplicated in this context elsewhere in Whitehall – meant a modest step towards using the Minister's financial powers as a basis for some financial control and for saying No. The normal position was not this, but one in which the prime financial responsibility was seen as the Board's, as derived from their powers and duties, to which the Ministers' financial powers were secondary. Therefore, Ministers and officials should stalk warily round this like cats, lest too many traces of this responsibility brush off on to their coats.

Chapter 7

THE POWER OF APPOINTMENT

While on some of the earlier Boards – like the Mersey Docks and Harbour Board and the Port of London Authority – many of the Members were otherwise appointed, the common practice since the Second World War, which is followed in all the major public corporations, is for the Chairmen and Board Members to be appointed by the Minister. Many have argued that this is not only the most important, but also the most influential power a Minister has, indeed, even that as long as Ministers have this sovereign power they have the control they need and that other powers matter less. Therefore, in spite of what we have found in earlier chapters, the statutes may still secure effective ministerial control.

Herbert Morrison seems to have believed that the most important thing was to choose the right man and then let him get on with the job. One still finds this echoed in the evidence to the Select Committee by one or two of the Board Chairmen and also by academic witnesses. It was argued, as it has been many times before, that Ministers, having chosen the people, should let them get on with it; and if it should happen that they lose, or never had, trust in them, they should not meddle but should replace them by people they do trust.

This does not describe the present position in many respects. First there are doubts whether the best people are appointed. Nationalized industry Board salaries tend to be lower than those in private industry with fewer fringe benefits; and the pension arrangements are less generous than in private industry. While this deters some from accepting appointments, others would say that more important is the reputation of intervention by Ministers. One of the ambitions that many businessmen have which drives them towards the top, is the wish not to be a subordinate. The choice they have to make near the start of their careers is often whether they should go into a small concern, where the probability of their getting on to the Board is higher but the scope of their power is limited by the size of their firm, or should toil upwards through a large organization with the dazzling prize that if they do become Chairman, or even a Board Member, their power is very great

68

indeed – none greater, some would say, in the Western world. Of course, except in some of the giants, this is tempered by the market and by shareholders. Nevertheless, the reputation of Government intervention which the Select Committee and the Boards deplore, persuades many that, not only would they be sacrificing salary in going to a Board, but also power; and though we will wish before long to draw a distinction between freedom from intervention and freedom to act, there is undoubtedly something to this.

But there is quite another difficulty. It is a legitimate criticism of the traditional system that a Minister and his officials do not often go to the trouble a good firm does in making its senior appointments. A high proportion of the senior appointments in a firm will be of people from within, whose abilities and characters – especially the difference between their public and private faces – will be known to the top management from long experience and because of personnel records. A large part of the time of the top management, perhaps even a third to a half of their time, is taken up assessing the suitability of those below them for promotion – one way or another. When a firm considers appointing from without it is very conscious that it knows much less about any outside applicant and will go to great lengths to make up for this; but, whatever people write in praise of the outsider, he will have to be substantially better to offset the fact that the insider is known in the round. These days a firm will often go to personnel consultants – firms that have a knack in knowing the reputations of people throughout management and great experience in asking testing questions. Then the firms can supplement their own judgement. But whatever the exact procedure, one can only be impressed by the thoroughness of the thing in the best cases (and by how the number of instances where someone gets a key job because he was met on the golf course, is diminishing).

Under the traditional system the Minister and his officials are in no position to be so thorough. They have to rely on the Chairman's opinion of those who are suggested for promotion to the Board from within; and though they will have their own opinions of individuals from past acquaintance, they may find it difficult to agree or disagree when the Chairman says that X, who may be unimpressive at meetings or occasionally puts his foot into it in public relations, has nevertheless other qualities which the Ministry has never had any reason to know anything about. Thus, if a Minister decides against someone a Chairman recommends, he may be putting too much emphasis on rather superficial public qualities. The only other thing the Minister and his officials can do is to agree pretty much with the judgement of the Chairman because, although over the years they do get to know most of the more or less senior Board managers to some extent, the arm's-length relationship prevents intimate knowledge: the knowledge of how people act in a crisis, how they behave to their own subordinates, how much they are talkers rather than doers, and the psychological weight they will carry on to the Board.

In making outside appointments one might suppose the Minister is in no worse a position than the Board. But he may have a hundred or more appointments to make in a year – though it is true that no more than ten are likely to be of the first importance. Indeed, Mrs Castle told the Committee that during the coming year she had to make some 1,000 appointments, paid and unpaid, and that while many were formalities, a large number were not. Over the next three years there were 25 first-class, full-time posts to fill and 160 important part-time posts (Q. 1597). One can hope, with Professor Robson, that 'if Ministers are not fitted to make such appointments, for what tasks are they likely to be fitted?'.[1] But even though many will have had little previous experience of making such appointments, the sheer volume of appointments to be made, given all the other claims on even an excellent Minister, can explain a procedure which is not always as thorough as it might be.

Even if he gave enough of his time to make half a dozen of these carefully, he could easily spend a quarter of his time doing nothing else but sifting and weighing suggestions, making contacts and conducting interviews, if he were to be half as thorough as a Chairman should; so he would have to be a lazy man in almost every other respect in order to do this job well. So would the Permanent Secretary. It would, of course, be wrong to think that much effort and searching does not go into the appointment of suitable outsiders; but there has been some tendency to fall back on names put up by the Boards themselves, names the Minister or his senior officials have heard of, or names sent along by the Civil Service Department. These last, which tend to be the most comprehensive, are, not unnaturally, mostly the names of those who have served Government on commissions and committees. They are seldom younger than in their late forties and are mostly older than this.[2] If they are

[1] W. A. Robson, *Nationalized Industry and Public Ownership*, Allen and Unwin, 1962, p. 220.
[2] While it would be wrong to assume that, because civil servants have a promotion system which tends to mean that men are not promoted until they have reached a seniority – a system which is perhaps defensible given the particular conditions of the civil service – this is why young appointments are very rare, yet Board appointments do tend on average to be of remarkably older men than are to be found promoted to similar positions in private industry.

eminent they are usually happy where they are and unlikely to be reached by the salaries that can be paid. Also, it has to be said that the reason a few of them are serving their country is because they have come to a stage where they are serving their firms less well. But even so, after the toiling and moiling to find someone who is both suitable and wants the job, it is surprising how many capable people are prepared for the challenge.

While I was in the Ministry of Transport, Ministers realizing the inadequacies of the old methods made many attempts, some abortive, to make the process less wearing and capricious. One need was for job definition.[1] One could argue that the nationalized industries should have done this themselves, and internally it is possible that some did, but in general it was not a habit, though by now it may be. One wanted a careful description of what the function of the Board Member ought to be, and of the character of the person needed. For a Minister to make an appointment without a detailed description of the job is foolish. One sometimes suspects that the reason able people sometimes were not as successful in a Board as they had been before was because the system they found, if they had been, say, financial men, and the traditional role of financial heads were both so different from what they had known that they were ineffective. They had not perhaps the leverage nor experience to fashion anew, nor the versatility to make as good a thing of what they found. But, as probable as a square peg in a round hole not being efficient, is the possibility that a carefully chosen contrast in personality alongside and beneath him would be the best corrective. (Is the number two labour man a hothead, instinctive rather than intellectual, but with a gift for getting on well with the unions? Then there may be a case for topping him with a planner. Or is the problem that, while there are clever men below, they have argued themselves into an impasse and need galvanizing?) Now it is just these questions, which are so important, that a Minister is unlikely to take into account because of the constraints on his time and the limited degrees of freedom he has in choosing people. His most difficult task is to compare the Chairman's notion or candidate with what he believes is necessary, and then to find someone who provides the corrective, without antagonizing the Board. But on a number of occasions, though there are happier instances, it would seem

[1] One has heard from a number of Chairmen that, while they are often asked to recommend names of those who might succeed them or be appointed to their Board, it is extremely rare, if not unknown, to be asked for job definitions. The practice of asking for such definitions was introduced by Mrs Castle and was an important innovation.

71

Ministers have provided people who are different, but abrasive, or people who are perhaps a little too like those already there.

Given the pressures on Ministers and senior civil servants, one wonders what else can be done to improve the situation, besides closer job definition. In my time at the Ministry of Transport, personnel consultants were used. There were various consultations with a number of experienced people. For a time there was one special adviser. But the great difficulty was always the same: that the Minister and his officials were at one remove from the Board whose appointments were at issue, and thus, rationally, to a large extent could only act as a broker between the Board and expert advice, weighing evidence, pushing candidates, but inevitably with less decisiveness in this matter than one would expect the Chairman of a holding company to have. In the end it is rare, if not unknown, for a Minister to make an appointment against the wishes of a Chairman. A Chairman may not always get the man he would have liked most, but he has, in the interests of Board harmony, something like a practical right of blackball.

However, more relevant to our argument than the strengths and weaknesses of the present system of appointment, is that it is one which is dominated by management considerations. No doubt a Minister would like to appoint someone who had all the management requirements *and* was politically sympathetic, but for the Labour Party at least this seems to have been a rare conjuncture; and one can hardly think of a case where a socialist was appointed because he was a socialist, though a less able manager than a right-wing rival. One also gets the impression that, although most Conservative appointees will vote Conservative, as most managers do, political loyalty or overt political sympathy is not an important criterion. Indeed, except where they are striking, the candidate's political sympathies may not be inquired into. Such is the strength of the Morrisonian tradition that it is good managers who are being looked for. As well, there may be another tradition: quite exceptionally, and not so often as in most other countries, one gets the unexpected appointment of someone from a quite different and less businesslike background. Britain seems to expect promotable people to have had experience in the field in which they are to be promoted, and in this context, as in several others, relevant experience is held to be relevant management experience.

What about part-timers? Even here it seems commonplace that a Minister most wants someone whom he knows he cannot find a place for, or persuade to serve, full-time, but who will bring financial or other management qualities to bear. While a Chairman may be less insistent in opposing the appointment of a part-timer because he does not feel he would fit well into his team, than he would the appointment of a full-timer, yet again it is exceptionally rare for a part-timer to be appointed against the wishes of the Chairman. A number of suggestions have been made on altering the nature of the part-time membership and making them more the Minister's men – for political or other reasons. The Report of the Advisory Committee on Organization, appointed by the Coal Board – the Fleck Committee – argued for the importance of the Board as a united and compatible team, but also suggested a special position for the part-timer.[1] They should not merely turn up to Board meetings. They ought to put in work between times. They should have a personal right of access to the Minister. They should act as his representatives on the Board and as his watchdogs. They should also advise him on full-time Board appointments. Some would go further and suggest that the Minister should have regular meetings with some or all of the part-timers and that they should state his views at Board meetings. To be a logical possibility, it should follow that part-timers should be appointed or reappointed by each Minister on taking office. They should offer their resignations and the Minister should decide whether they have his confidence for this purpose or whether he wishes to appoint one or two others who are closer or more sympathetic to him. While a Minister may well lunch a part-timer very occasionally and ask his views without the Chairman's being there, the present position is very unlike one in which the part-timers are his close and regular confidants. This could be made to come about, but two questions need to be answered. The first is whether the disadvantages are as substantial as many would argue. These would say that a Board is a team and that the prime responsibility of Board Members *qua* Members is to that team. The others should not feel that one or two have influence behind the Chairman's back. Many would argue that it would divide the Board if some members did have such a primary responsibility outside the Board itself. Even without this there is a tendency for the full-timers to see more of each other and to meet formally or informally as a management committee, just because the part-timers are seldom there; but if the part-timers had a special allegiance, such a division would be more likely and there might be more of a tendency for the most controversial and confidential business to be agreed by the full-timers before a full Board meeting. The second question is whether in any case, even if a Minister were to make

[1] 1955.

part-time Board appointments with a political or other motive to help him effect his policies, they would have much leverage.

More influential than the appointment of Board Members is the appointment of the Chairman, who will be in a far stronger position to alter the policies of the Board he heads. But even the power of a new Chairman selected to carry out the Minister's policies, though infinitely greater than that of any individual Board Member, will be conditioned by the Board he confronts (and by the number of Board memberships he is quickly able to advise the Ministsr to fill with people to his liking). One has the impression that the reason some able, and even brilliant, appointees have not been as far-reachingly successful as they should have been, has been that they, too, found it difficult to exert enough leverage. Boards come to have a collective and inherited character, which has much to do with the interpretation they put on policy. Beneath the Board and beyond the Minister's reach are management layers sharing this character. Chairmen promoted from within a Board will have had their characters and predilictions influenced by that Board. Chairmen appointed from without, as most have been, may have the will to make profound changes – even possibly to effect something as specific as the Minister's policies – but will have to win the confidence of their Board and practically come to some accommodation with them before making a real difference in policy; and, of course, the shorter the time they are with the Board, the less likely they are to be able to make a significant difference; the longer they are with them, the more improbable it is that they can be identified with the current Minister's policies. Changing a Board's results and attitudes by a consistent appointments policy is difficult. Even if a Minister were to move more actively than is usual to make appointments of people to execute his policies – whether these are primarily new management (more efficiency) or social policies – the potential of his power of Board appointment on their policies is limited. It is perhaps not quite as difficult as it is for a US President to change the complexion of the Supreme Court, though not so different. A Minister is unlikely to be in the same job for more than three years. During that time he is lucky if two or three vacancies arise on any one Board. If he forgot every other consideration, did not promote anyone from within, and so on, the leverage he could exert would be small. One or two on a Board, or even a new Chairman, will not be a majority.

The Committee slips into the view that the ultimate sanction of the Minister in relation to ends more legitimate than most of the pressures we have had in our minds, is this power of appointing, of not reappointing – Board Members usually have five-year terms – or, *in extremis,* of actually dismissing a member. As the Chairman of the Prices and Incomes Board (himself an ex-Minister who had fired a Chairman) told the Committee, 'the act of firing is one which it is very difficult to do; it is not utterly impossible, but it is not easy' (Q. 2265). The ability of a Minister making an appointment, whether following a dismissal or not, to secure prior agreement from the candidate that he will follow some 'policy' or other of the Minister's – legitimate or not – is slender. The most he is likely to get is agreement that the industry must become more efficient and that it has social obligations. Once appointed, inevitably the Chairman or Member's main relationship is with the Board; and one must also remember that when a Minister has appointed someone, his ability then to dismiss him (or the probability that his term of office will end while he is still Minister) is negligible.[1]

---

[1] One is not here questioning the legal right of a Minister to dismiss Chairmen or other Board Members. While, as a matter of law, it does seem doubtful whether a Minister has this legal right except where a Member has embezzled, gone bankrupt or mad or become incapacitated, it is usually thought that, in practice, a Chairman or Board Member who is known to have lost the confidence of his Minister will simply resign. (One of these days, such a Member may have the rashness not to do so, but of course the more he resists, the less are his prospects of re-employment elsewhere.) Neither is it sensible to question the moral right of Ministers to dismiss Members. The classic statement is that of Aneurin Bevan, who defended a Conservative Minister against the charge that he had irresponsibly dismissed the Chairman of the Iron and Steel Corporation on the grounds that the Minister must be presumed to have a greater right to judge the national interest than a Chairman.

The Minister must have the supreme power, in the interests of democratic control. 'Oh, it is excellent to have a giant's strength, but it is tyrannous to use it like a giant.' The limited information a Minister normally has and the limited opportunity he may have for replacing a person dismissed by someone who will in fact do better, should make a Minister think long before doing something that runs the risk of being arbitrary and arrogant. Very careful inquiries are needed to corroborate the first evidence that a Board Member is unsatisfactory enough to be dismissed, not because dismissal is a wrong thing, but because wrongful and unjust dismissal of a man, based on an incomplete appreciation of him, is both unjust and inefficient. It will have long-run repercussions on morale and also make it difficult to attract an able successor. To take a recent example, the Minister for Posts and Telecommunications of course had the moral right to dismiss Lord Hall, but did he do it after giving himself a long and deep enough opportunity to understand the workings and needs of the Post Office, the functions that Lord Hall performed well, and those he performed badly, and the kind and availability of a Chairman who would do better? While I have no evidence to suppose that Mr Chataway was not profound and perceptive in his inquiries, it is important to avoid any suspicion that a Chairman's dismissal was sudden or arbitrary, or based on the mere fact that Minister and Chairman did not get on well together, irrespective of the Chairman's merits or demerits as Chairman.

75

All this is to say that the recipe of an academic witness to the Committee, 'that the more you can get to a situation where the Minister gives the nationalized industries its marching orders, and appoints the right people to run it, and leaves them to get on with the job, the more healthy the position of the industry would be, and probably the more satisfied Parliament will be in the long run', is an impossible ideal as things now stand, at least if it is meant to describe a situation where appointments are an important method by which a Minister achieves his policy (Q. 1862).

Deciding that a Chairman or Board Member should go must be a most pains-taking procedure. In this particular case, one feels that, whatever Mr Chataway's case, it is imprudent to have a Minister who has little else to do in life except oversee the workings of this corporation (as well as the BBC and ITA, from which he is necessarily more remote), especially with a staff which was brought up to regard his predecessors as effective heads of the Post Office, when they were Postmasters-General before the Post Office became a public corporation. Not having a greater span of command is an incitement to duplication which it may be difficult for an energetic person to avoid.

Chapter 8

CONCLUSION: A PRACTICAL INDEPENDENCE

What has been described in this book so far amounts to a very great practical independence for the Boards. To recall the main points:

(1) Contrary to what is widely thought, Ministers do not seem to have the power to lay down the general policy within which Boards work. Ministers construct legislation for approval by Parliament and may recommend a Board's powers and duties in it. But for a number of understandable and inescapable reasons the statutory description of those powers and duties – that is, those not expressly laid on the Minister, the Treasury or someone else – could not be anyone else's but the Board's without jerking the dividing line between autonomy and ministerial authority to the other limit. That would mean practically abolishing the Board's independence and making it subordinate to the Minister. Except in promoting legislation a Minister may try to persuade a Board to follow his interpretation of their policy, but he may not instruct it (*Chapter* 3).

(2) There has been a growing feeling that the non-commercial policies of a Board were more peculiarly the (public) interest of the Minister; and this has been shared by the Committee. These non-commercial, or social, policies have been thought of as those expected to be unprofitable (excluding profitable policies with social benefits in addition). But this is a new approach since, in the past, the social aspects of the Board's policies have been seen as their responsibility and as derived from their responsibility for general Board policy. This is what one might have expected from the way in which Herbert Morrison and others since him have interpreted the social policy of Boards. They have not seen it as covering much, and what there is of it they have seen as intimately entangled with the detailed management of the Boards' business – as a difference in style and integrity from private industry, rather than in policy. As a consequence, Ministers had been given relatively few duties

77

and powers relating to the social or public interest activities of Boards. But the recent granting of power to Ministers to make grants for social purposes, is a very important departure, though largely undertaken from quite different motives concerned with the financial viability of Boards. Since the Minister has power to spend money for these services, both he and Parliament have more right to say how and on what it is spent. While this may be an inroad on the practical independence of Boards it is too early to be sure it will. The powerful tradition of independence may assimilate even this (*Chapter 4*).

(3) While the Treasury has some financial powers, these are secondary to those of the sponsoring Minister and are exercised as such. The Treasury does not behave at all like the Financial Controller's Office of Great Britain, Ltd. Its White Papers on the financial and economic obligations of the nationalized industries are not management directives. They are the highest common factor of Government (and to some extent of Board) agreement, and represent an achievement in persuasion so far as they go. But they are crucially ambiguous. In this they recognize the realities of power (*Chapter 5*).

(4) Sponsoring Ministers do have statutory financial powers which could be interpreted by them to mean a firm financial discipline exercised by them over the Boards. But it seems they have not developed a tradition of using them in this way. This is partly because they see that even those powers are secondary to the prime (financial and management) responsibility of the Boards to Parliament, but also because, in the past, this appears to have been what was expected. As a result, the relationship between a Minister and his officials and Board has been more like that between a trustee and the beneficiary of a trust fund than that between, say, a merchant banker and his client. Ministers have not been passive in face of Board losses, and have in general – both Conservative and Labour – felt some need to stimulate the Boards to greater efficiency; but they have used persuasion rather than authority. In the end the Boards have mostly had their own way. While this seems to have been the normal Whitehall position, some attempt was made in the Ministry of Transport to move towards a more definite financial discipline. It is open to question whether it will last and whether it can be improved on (*Chapter 6*).

(5) Neither does the Minister's power of Board appointment give him much influence over Board policy. Not enough places will fall vacant for him to appoint his own majority; and even if he could, his power of influence on them would be one of gratitude or respect on their side since his ability to dismiss someone he has appointed

is negligible. Besides, he will be under great pressure to appoint people for qualities which probably have nothing to do with policies he wished to promote; and even if he were to break with this tradition, the more radical or unusual a person he appointed the less his leverage on the Board would be likely to be. This is almost as true in appointing the Chairman as in appointing an individual Board Member. Although appointing a Chairman is far more significant than appointing any other Member, the practical power it gives a Minister is exaggerated (*Chapter 7*).

At the beginning of this Part, it was shown how the Select Committee attempted to analyse what I described as the triangular relationship between Parliament, Minister and Board, by making a distinction between policy and execution, and how this was an illogicality. One cannot hope for any great light to be thrown by an illogicality. So it has proved. It has not illuminated one issue we have discussed. Its effect is generally to overstate the power of Ministers, as the right to make policy seems to imply the essential power a Minister would wish to have. Couple with this the habit many Ministers have formed of suggesting their sovereignty by using words which refer to Board policies as if they were their own, and it is easy to come to the conclusion that if a Board fumbles or fails, it is the Minister's fault – he or his predecessors have not exercised sufficient ministerial control. Many Ministers have therefore pretended to more powers than they have; and some of them have therefore been blamed for failures which are hardly their responsibility.

If one penetrates the myth – and the reality is consistent with the statutes – one finds a better guiding principle in the so-called Morrisonian notion of the autonomous Board. Even where Ministers have powers in relation to these Boards, they have tended not to develop them so that they could use them powerfully. Not by the exercise of formal powers then, but by other means does a Minister tend to exert his most important influence. We shall see that in general this does not reverse the impression of practical independence, though it modifies and constrains it. Taking all these together, the actual dividing line between Minister and Board has therefore been drawn to leave the Minister very little power, much less than the outside world and the literature assume. Yet this practical independence co-exists with what Sir Ronald Edwards has called 'almost intolerable' and Lord Robens 'quite intolerable' intervention. We must explain this paradox.

Part II

THE PERSUASIVENESS OF MINISTERS

Chapter 9

PERSUASION

There is wide agreement that the quanity of intervention by Government and Parliament in the nationalized industries has increased over the twenty-five years, much of it in search of information. The most public of these interventions is the Parliamentary Question. The MP asks the Minister and the Minister asks the Board for the necessary information to answer the MP. But by a tradition which is fairly well established, Ministers do not answer questions in Parliament on matters of detail about the nationalized industries. Since many of the local and practical questions which most interest MPs are detailed, they are not silenced but instead write directly to the Boards. Though they do not have to, the Boards tend to reply, presumably because they think it polite and politic. Parliament also debates nationalized industry affairs from time to time, and Ministers who have to defend Boards then require information from them as briefing. These one may call the traditional forms of intervention in search of information which Boards expect to be heir to. They are expected as a price of democracy.

But from the beginning there have been various forms of inquiry into Boards, also largely after information. The number and frequency of these have grown. Since its foundation, the Select Committee on Nationalized Industries has inquired into the major Boards and also into general problems affecting all Boards, such as this one of ministerial control. As a glance at any report will show, the Boards write copious papers by way of information and their top management gives evidence, which also means preparatory work by the Boards. Perhaps this also is coming to be accepted as part of the price of democracy because its inspiration is parliamentary – and it is to Parliament, of course, that the Boards are responsible. For a number of years during the life of the Prices and Incomes Board, they also had to give it information as a basis for its report-writing. From the beginning, there have been independent and ministerial inquiries into organization and Board policy. While the Railways in 1959 were responding to the Select Committee, they also were being investigated by the Stedeford Committee, whose inspiration was the Minister. While the Railways were responding to various Price and Income Board inquiries in 1966 and 1967, they were also undergoing, by agreement between Minister and Chairman, the investigations of the Joint Steering Group under Mr Morris, then Parliamentary Secretary to the Minister of Transport; this was a more fundamental inquiry than any before and required more Board work to provide the relevant management information. Other industries, of course, have had their inquiries too. There is an expectation that the Boards will co-operate in starting and serving such inquiries, but their reports may also influence the possibility and detail of new legislation. How much Boards welcome any particular inquiry depends mostly on how far they feel they can influence the legislation, how much they feel there are problems which must be solved through legislation and, of course, whether they like the directions the Minister is taking.

Still other interventions in search of information do not relate to the Boards' own policy and behaviour, but to wider Government interests. Information required for the 1965 National Plan was one example where the Boards were felt to be under some moral obligation to be more forthcoming than private industry. But to pick on the National Plan is invidious. Hardly a week passes, it would seem, but Boards are asked for information related to some Government proposal – from draft legislation down to the hunch of a Minister first turning over in his mind something he may in the end decide to drop.

Some of the less important statutory powers of Ministers will also mean paperwork. Boards will be asked to report on their research or training programmes, even though Ministers then have no further power to take action on them, and the exercise of financial statutory powers, as we have observed, also means a flow of information from Board to Minister: capital investment programmes, individual submissions, replies to comments on submissions, replies to the comments on those, and so on.

One cannot be surprised that the Boards become restive as the demands build up or that those coming into Boards near, or at, the top find this the most striking difference in their lives. Private industry does not give shareholders anything approaching this volume of information. While a holding company may require more, or more systematic, financial information from subsidiaries and also information on other major areas of top management interest, there tends to be a clearer line between what top management does and does not want to know. Because Ministers and members of Parliament understandably, given their job, interest themselves in a wide variety of issues, many local and particular, the Boards are not able to shuffle off the burden of answering to a special 'consumers' relation' department. Much will be delegated, but a Chairman has to be brilliant to decide just what he can safely delegate, just what letters to Ministers he may sign without scrutiny, just what briefings for Ministers to answer Parliamentary Questions he may only initial, trusting his subordinates. More often than they care, Chairmen and Board Members are drawn into such matters, to an extent which they complain distracts them from management. (One may note that it affects (i) the qualities needed to be an effective Board Member and (ii) the kind of people interested in becoming Board Members.)

However, information is not always the ultimate purpose of interventions to gain information. The MP may hope that the question he asks alters the behaviour of a Board. Plainly, the demand for information by Ministers either directly, through their officials, or through inquiries is meant to start an interaction which it is hoped will change Board policy and behaviour. The discussion of criteria is one of these. The Boards write papers setting out their criteria; but the process, however much at times they would like it, does not end there. The process of investment appraisal, as we have described it, is intended, at least in its traditional form, to give the Minister and his officials a chance to persuade Boards to change their minds, and vice versa rather than a chance for the Minister to make up his own mind to the point of saying No. The discussions between Ministers and Chairmen and between Board officials and Ministry officials, which are mentioned so frequently in the literature, are also mostly intended to be opportunities for reciprocal persuasion.

What give the Minister and his officials their opportunity are what Herbert Morrison, who certainly seems to have seen the role of the Minister as persuasive rather than authoritative, saw as 'the respectful relations' between the two.[1] Yet the nature of the relation

---

[1] 'Just as a shipping company treats the President of the Board of Trade with respect because he is a Minister of the Crown and the Minister who deals with shipping, so would the Board of the National Transport Corporation have respectful relationships with the Minister of Transport. But they would be franker relationships than between the Minister and the private railway companies, because both the Board and the Minister would be public servants. Every Member of the Board would know that he had been appointed by the Minister [sic] and that the Minister looked to the Board to make a success of the undertaking. . . .

is such as to give Ministers, if they are not careful, a manner more that of a teacher or Nanny, than of a supreme commander. The opportunity and the right to persuade is not a power to command obedience. Except insofar as they could be doing things other than listening (or writing papers giving information), this is no infringement of their practical independence. They may be persuaded; but it is their decision to be persuaded. In many of the most important areas persuasion seems to have worked very slowly and – it could be argued – only over things which command *consensus* beyond party. As we have seen the Treasury campaign to improve Board investment appraisal – let alone the campaign to get Board pricing policies to reflect marginal costs – has not succeeded yet. Some campaigns waged by politicians or officials – for example in relation to the Boards' use of their purchasing power – have perhaps deserved to fail, though those politicians in favour would not think so; but one cannot assume automatically that the campaigns succeed which

---

Somebody must be answerable in Parliament, if not actually for the Board, as in the case of direct Government administration, then at any rate *about* the Board and its administration. . . . The answers to the questions, the material for debate, must often be obtained by the Minister's officers from the Public Corporation concerned. If all went well the Minister would give the answer or explanation on the basis of the information supplied by the Board. Where, however, the Board was pursuing a policy which was tending to get into conflict with legitimate public criticism, the Minister might have to say, "I do not think that is a very good answer, or explanation, or undertaking, but if it is the best you can give me I will inform the House accordingly; you will not, however, expect me to defend your point of view as if it were my own because, quite frankly, I cannot do it." The Board will, therefore, wish its policy to be so sound and popular that it can be defended by the Minister in Parliament. It is quite likely when, in certain cases, it is about to make a decision which involves ticklish policy in relation to the general public that the Chairman will have an unofficial talk with the Minister in order, not to receive instructions, but to ascertain his views and to keep his mind fully informed in readiness for any public or parliamentary discussion which may arise. By such means the Minister may exercise an influence where it is proper and legitimate in the public interest that he should, without in any way interfering with the management of the undertaking; and indeed often at the desire of the Chairman of the Board or the Board itself' (*Socialisation and Transport*, pp. 172–3). I quote this at length because it is a perfect picture of the traditional conception and because there is no mention of power but a considerable reliance on persuasion. What happens when the Minister explains the Board's position in Parliament without being able to defend it? Rather than put up a lame defence which will seem to implicate him in the Board's inefficiency or misdoings – in spite of his constitutional position – a Minister may be inclined to collaborate with the Board in making a more effective defence to Parliament than the facts warrant – just to avoid the retort 'what are you going to do about it then?' when there is nothing he can do.

86

should do so, because they represent the will of Parliament or well thought out Government policy.[1]

It would be wrong to think that a situation in which persuasion is so important does not have its advantages. Ministers and their officials must recognize the strength of the Boards' traditions. The development of a feeling of continuity is perhaps the most positive aspect of the Boards' practical independence. It commands loyalty at all levels. In confers a style. It makes the whole stronger than the men, even the top men. The fact that Chairmen and Board Members have been appointed from outside has hardly affected this, for they too have to reckon with it. In many cases its roots go back to long before nationalization. Superimposed on the Board traditions is the Morrisonian tradition of the public corporation. The benefits from this are great, both to itself and, in many ways, to the service it gives the public. It would be for the worse if the traditions went; but they do reduce the effectiveness of, or delay, persuasion.

There are other costs. The right to freedom of speech is usually held to imply the right of everyone else not to listen; but the 'respectful relations' between Minister and Board deny the Boards the second right. They must listen. The costs of this to the Boards, the expenditure of top management time, will not be inconsiderable. As well as having to listen they are expected to reply, since they do not have the further freedom to listen and say nothing. The Boards would say, often enough, that they give in not because they are persuaded, but because the Minister and his civil servants are indomitable and show perseverance in repeating and amplifying the Minister's views. Because worn down, they will frequently concede points they do not think vital, but not, they would say, the vital ones.

It is tempting to think that the natural response of a Minister frustrated by his lack of powers and unable to persuade a Board to do what he believes important, would be to legislate. Yet while the effect of legislation is not wholly persuasive, much of it is, especially in an area like this where legislation defines powers and duties as we have seen them defined. There is a cynical school of political scientists, many of them American, who would think that the influence of legislation in altering Board behaviour is minimal. This is closely allied to the belief that greater control cannot be

[1] One example is said to be that, after the then Minister of Fuel and Power, Mr Aubrey Jones, publicly endorsed the recommendation of the Herbert Committee to decentralize the organization of the electricity industry, the new Board went and centralized. But there are many occasions when Boards have not been persuaded and have used their practical independence to go their own way, just as, of course, there have been occasions when they have been persuaded.

achieved by altering, or clarifying, objectives because words do not confer power. If a Board is able to interpret a set of unclear objectives to its taste, there is often nothing in logic to stop its conferring the same interpretation on a clearer, more self-consistent set. Plainly, many objectives are of this kind. If a Board used to be asked to provide an 'adequate public service' and is now asked 'to pay due regard to the rural users of electricity', there may have been little gain, unless the Board paid no attention to rural users before. If a Board used to be asked to break even but is now asked to become profit-making or profit-maximizing, there is no necessity for it to change its behaviour (even if it was making a loss before). Especially from outside, one cannot prove that there was some other policy it could have taken which would have been more profitable, without taking over and running an experiment. Some objectives are more definite – for example to require a Board not to do something which they did before – but the cynics would say that, even when there is a change which cannot without violence to the language be treated as merely semantic, the power to change behaviour and change motives by Act of Parliament will be very slight. Agencies do not always see the need to obey.

One reaches a belief like this mostly by *a priori* reasoning. It is a position which is hard to prove true or false. Does it prove the Boards care because they go to a lot of trouble to react when legislation is pending? No, because there are other things in legislation besides matters which affect, or are supposed to affect, their behaviour. Would it prove this false that there have been Boards unable to interpret their statutes viably – that is, so that their behaviour was in contrast with what they are supposed to do? No, that some Boards have been able to stay in deficit so long could itself, though it need not, be a measure of their practical independence. Even if one were to accept that the Boards would rather have conducted their affairs so as to show this, and other signs of, efficiency to the outside world, surely it must have been possible for them to have taken quicker and more effective action if they had really tried. Of course, one keeps on coming back to the British Railways, the Coal Board, the Port of London Authority and the one or two others whose deficits were visible signs of inefficiency – while knowing that there were many reasons why equal inefficiency in other Boards (and large private concerns) would not have had equally visible results.[1] But the Railways could have closed their

[1] The inevitable tendency one has to say more about industries in deficit, is itself a consequence of practical independence. Much more sophisticated techniques are needed to determine the comparative efficiency of electricity, gas,

loss-making services down fast enough to have broken even before 1962, and since then there have been other things they might have done, though they could not close down branch lines freely (things like cutting their freight services and rationalizing their track). But while one explanation of deficit may be that the Board was struggling to reconcile its financial duty with its interpretation of its social duty, there are other explanations equally as plausible. One is that there has been an influential body of opinion, even until recently, which has hoped that the decline of traffic was temporary and could be reversed – by various measures, mostly implying massive investment. (Similarly, the Coal Board could have taken more drastic action than it did, but there was the same optimism for many years in the National Coal Board.) Another is that, even if they had decided to reduce their scale of operations to become less unprofitable, as Beeching and Robens did, they may not have had enough management information or analysis to know what to prune to reduce costs more than revenues.

Yet, to assume implacable independence in the face of a clear expression of the will of Parliament, also seems an overstrained *a priori* position. One's hope is that Boards are slowly persuaded by changes in the objectives given them by Parliament, though they may try at first to assimilate it to what they have always been doing. The changes are likely to be put into effect by those a little more responsive or sharper, or less defensive or, in some cases, a little younger or more recently appointed. One suspects here that a Board is more likely to recognize, albeit slowly, a difference between the old order and the new, if there is one, and to accept the change, even against their own inclinations, if it has been well thought through and argued at length and, most of all, if it bears the authority of Parliament. In the end, I think, one says that one does not believe that the Boards have been so disillusioned with Ministers and Parliament, or are so arrogant, that they take no notice and claim an absolute independence, secretly or openly (though some of the more determined will claim such an independence against the non-statutory forms of persuasion which they resent most).

What is one of the most impressive functions of the British civil service – the great lengths it goes to in order to relate new legislation to old and make all consistent – may in the end be itself persuasive. There is an expectation that the clauses applying to one Board will

the airlines (given the direct and indirect subsidies they receive), the BBC, the British Transport Docks Board and others who may find it easier not to make a loss and still not be as efficient as they might be.

have a strong family resemblance to those applying to another·
When a Minister wants to make a substantive change in an objective,
duty or power, this is not something his department can decide by
itself. It would have to be cleared all round Whitehall as affecting
'general' nationalized industry policy, and unless it was quickly
shown that the change was genuinely particular to the industry and
did not raise an issue of general principle, it would probably have
to come to Cabinet, unless the sheer complexity of procedure had not
already persuaded the Minister of the relative unimportance of the
innovation. But while all this is a conservative force, it is arguable
that, when there is a change, the ground has been better prepared
for it. No one is likely to mistake a change of substance for semantic
juggling; and the change will be related to what has gone before.
But outside Whitehall the significance of such changes may not be
picked up. A Minister can reckon on a Board's feeling under some
obligation as public servants to alter their behaviour according to
the wishes of the Minister as confirmed by Parliament; but will also
tend quite naturally to assimilate new ideas to existing practice if it
can. Thus, merely to change the wording of a statutory objective
is not enough. A statute is seldom looked at by even the most
senior of those operating under it. A Minister needs to make an
impact, writing the changes up in a White Paper, debating and
speechifying. Then, provided the transition from the old to the new
has been thought through thoroughly enough – which has not
always been the case in recent legislation – one may hope that the
general recognition that there has been a change in objectives will
be translated into a change in behaviour. One suspects that there are
not too many Ministers with the patience, perseverence, thoroughness and touch of perfectionism, as well as stamina, that are needed
to achieve a profound change.

But there would seem to be no easy tests of propositions of this
kind. A stronger test than any in the past may be what notice the
Boards take of the changes in their objectives and management
philosophy which are incorporated in the 1968 Transport Act and
1969 London Transport Act; these embodied a change in the
Morrisonian conception which, although evolutionary, was in many
respects, more significant than any before.

But if the Boards do prove to be unresponsive when Parliament
is beginning to require more and different things from them, the
Boards will be tempting Ministers and Parliament to do what they
certainly can do in legislation: a statute can empower a body to
do some things and prohibit it from doing others. It can give and
it can take away; it can specify an organization in detail; and while

a change in organization does not necessarily entail a change in Board policy or behaviour, it may make it too difficult for things to stay just the same. At worst, it will mean unnecessary effort and distraction from more important things. From time to time Parliament and Ministers may want to do these things on their merits. The danger is that they will come to do them – as one sees signs in the United States – because of frustration and powerlessness, as some kind of costly discipline on a Board and an indirect way of making the Boards politically and financially responsive.

How does this picture of very considerable Board autonomy, tempered by persuasion and the influence of Parliament through legislation, relate to the views of the Select Committee? As we saw, the Select Committee's views were not fully consistent and could be interpreted in both a more and a less interventionist sense than in present practice. But the spirit of their recommendations was to agree with the Boards that there was too much ministerial intervention (while they had almost nothing material to say about ministerial power).

It may be helpful to construct something like a model of how the Select Committee would like to see the working relation between Ministers and Boards. Because of the lack of complete consistency in the Committee's views and because of compression, it is bound to be a simplification, but not a violent one. Besides, it represents a view held by many outside the Select Committee and is in many ways the touchstone of our argument.

In this model there are 'normal' and 'abnormal' times. The Boards are efficient enough in *normal* times. Their top management will be acceptable. Most of it will have been promoted from within but Ministers will, in their turn, have improved the balance of the Board and stimulated it by adding some outsiders. There is no reason to suppose that management below Board level will not be good, though this will be no concern of the Minister until he reviews names for promotion to the Board. The Board will have a first-class system of financial control. One result of this will be persistent self-imposed exercises to cut costs, but from time to time there will be efficiency studies in areas fixed after consultation with the Minister. These studies will normally be carried out by management consultants. Another result will be a Board rolling-investment programme for up to five years ahead. This will show a financial return (in net present value terms) against every project intended to be profitable. Where there are important unprofitable services retained for social reasons, there will have been an exercise to work out their cost-benefit return on lines previously agreed with departmental officials. In general, the Board will be paid the marginal cost of running such unprofitable services. Thus, from time to time, possibly once a year, there should be a special review between Minister and Chairman, or between their officials, when they should agree on what these services are to be and how much should be spent on them. There will also be periodic discussions of what the Board's financial objective should be (which logically should derive from its pricing and investment criteria), as well as discussion of past performance. In some cases there would be co-ordination of financial policy. The Select Committee seemed to accept, though not without some questioning, the Minister of Power's argument that it was his duty to see that there was not substantial over-investment in the fuel industries by trying, after consultation, to exert some persuasion to influence what should be the future market share of each industry.

While the discussion on social policy (and, where relevant, on co-ordination) might be informal, the hope seems to have been that the Minister's and officials' role on investment could simply be to approve the programme. Financial control would become an administrative control of a fairly routine kind because all commercial projects promised to be profitable and had financial returns which exceeded the minimum required by the Treasury. Approval would mean little more than formally ticking projects, since it would be pointless for Boards to put up projects that would not pass on this basis. At all costs Ministers and officials should avoid discussing particular projects with Boards. Instead, they should occasionally discuss and revise criteria, if necessary. The Boards would also want to listen to what departmental officials had to say about the national economy.

However, if for some reason a nationalized industry was inefficient, the Minister and his officials might alter their behaviour for a time, though they should return to normal as soon as possible. In these *abnormal* times the Minister's officials would again discuss criteria with the Board to discover if there were any mistakes in the application of these criteria which were a cause of the inefficiency, on the grounds that if the criteria had been correct the results should not have been bad. The Minister and his officials could call for more information to improve their understanding. They might suggest a deeper, wider efficiency study. (They have not had the power to demand one.) They further might consider what they might do when Board Members came up for appointment or reappointment. But even in abnormal times they should avoid getting down to particular questions relating to their efficiency, and they should avoid going through their investment programmes (or their revenue budgets) in detail. The Committee concluded that the more professional exercise of financial discipline by the Ministry of Transport – itself a response in part to a feeling that the Boards did not anywhere near approach the Committee's ideal – was wrong: '. . . the form of detailed scrutiny that the Ministry have developed has been mistaken. The emphasis appears to have been on the *ad hoc* examination . . . of the merits of a wide range of projects . . . If the examination of projects is to proceed in this way, with projects looked at separately, and with regard to the individual merits, by both the Boards and the Ministry, then the Committee see advantages in having as much detail spread before the Ministry officials as possible . . . But the Committee would prefer to see the officials concentrating their attention predominantly on the techniques used by the industry in appraising the projects, rather than on the merits of the projects as such. Scrutiny of this type would probably involve much more general, informal discussion at an early stage of the appraisal of a major project, about the methods to be used, and less formal scrutiny of the outcome of the appraisal after it had been completed. In other words, the Ministry should concentrate on methods rather than results' (564, 565).

Implicit in this is a certain innocence about criteria and the pleasures of persuasive argument, as if the Committee had not tried to imagine (i) just what might be expected to go on when there was one of these discussions of criteria and techniques of appraisal of which they approved, and (ii) what would distinguish them from the discussion over projects that occur now. The Committee seem to have believed that the first would be less resented. I wonder if this would always be true, even of the most innocent form of these discussions that one could imagine – when backroom talks to backroom – and this is treated as something to be left entirely to the professionals. As we have seen, one has to go deep into methods of analysis and, in some cases, build sophisticated models, if one is discussing how to use discounted cash flow analysis or what is meant by marginal cost pricing, for instance. This does mean having professionals in the Ministries capable of such discussion; and if it is not to be only a beating around with words, the professionals on both sides will have to know the business. Inevitably they will learn more about the economics, profitability and technology of the industry than they do now. One can suspect that many Boards will be wary of letting departments in on this information and, indeed, will see discussion of criteria as an example of detailed interference in management, both because of the fine detail it must descend to *and because, quite simply, it must question what management is doing now* (if it is not to be pointless, academic and hypothetical).

Boards do not normally draw a distinction between discussions of projects which they resent and of criteria they see as innocent and legitimate. One can think of cases across Whitehall where discussions of criteria and technique were no more easily accepted than discussions of the worth of projects. One came before the Select Committee. As the then Permanent Secretary of the Ministry of Transport, Sir Thomas Padmore, told the Committee, 'the case that Sir Stanley Raymond (then chairman of the Railways Board) was particularly outraged about was precisely one of these cases . . . where there was a very genuine difference not yet finally resolved between the Ministry and the Railways Board as to the applicability of these techniques of appraisal' (Q. 1501).[1]

A discussion about criteria is one way of trying to alter the behaviour of management – a fulcrum for Government as a pressure group. There is a closely related reason why Boards may not appreciate the subtlety of the Committee's distinction: because what they seem to be approving may get close to 'candle-ends'. It is not an uncommon administrative technique to initiate a discussion of

---

1 This was the coaching stock case referred in the footnote on p. 65. There were many millions involved and, in a sense, it was very relevant to the whole future of the Board's mainline passenger services. For some considerable additional cost the Board could have new coaches with air conditioning and many other costly features. The increased cost would mean a considerable increase in the fare unless demand was expanded. Refurbished coaches could reach a high standard of comfort but without some of the trimmings. They would not imply a fare increase. The question then was whether the additional expenditure would generate a profitable enough rise in demand. The Board originally offered their opinion that it would do so. Evidence from foreign railways was conflicting and indicated that it depended on particular circumstances. The questions of technique at issue were: (i) whether any market research could be done, and (ii) what market research should be done, to whose results both sides would agree. It was a question about criteria because the conception of a satisfactory investment criterion implies that it is one whose demand forecasts are believable. As the footnote on p. 65 shows, the Select Committee accepted that the questions asked by the Ministry were to the point, but did not accept that it had a right to ask them. The Board should have asked and answered them themselves, without intervention. But what a department is to do when a Board does not ask and answer such questions either in a particular case or commonly, is just the kind of question of *power relations* where the Committee does not give guidance. Presumably, they might in the end refer to the Minister's power of appointment, reappointment and sacking, but even if this were a credible power – which we have seen it is not – one simply cannot imagine an issue of this kind or even a succession of such issues as the basis of a crisis in confidence. It is not the sort of thing where a Minister could justify extreme behaviour to Cabinet, Parliament or Press.

principles, criteria and methods when what is going on in some part of the machine is particularly obscure. Papers are called for in which the laggards, or recalcitrants, explain their criteria, that is, the principles on which they make their decisions. They may then be asked in more detail *how* they go about it, and for further illumination they are likely to be asked to give *examples* of projects to show the methods at work. Thus the scrutineers may feel their way to an understanding of what is really going on.[1] In this way a discussion of criteria may not be innocent and divorced from management, and there is scarcely any reason for a Board to resent it any less than a more direct approach. (They may dislike it more because it represents an oblique, devious and abstract approach which does not correspond to the more concrete way in which they are likely to be used to looking at things.)

But more important and characteristic even than this – and what is underlying it all and is really remarkable – is that the Committee considers the whole question without discussion of *power*. Except insofar as the Minister wants to put the consultants in – which, as we have seen, he has not the power to do without the consent of the Board – and except in relation to appointments, the Committee would seem to accept the model of the Minister and his officials as a pressure group which relies on the power of its reason and, of course, on the splendid position it is in to catch and hold the Board's ear. Even then they would seem to want it to be less active, making fewer interventions. (They do not seem to realize that if one has not power, one has to use more words.) They do not come to the conclusion that a Minister should always stop short of going beyond persuasion, but they do not give guidance; and hence, in the end, the tendency of their argument, the weight of their opinion, is to reinforce the fact of practical independence, as well as to encourage Ministers to increase the quantity of their interventions in order to persuade.

Why should a Parliamentary Committee – made up of politicians – be so interested in criteria and the application of techniques and so uninterested in power relations and, in effect, in the substance of the question they set out to answer: the dividing line between the

---

[1] It is not in my view an effective technique because it can be met so easily by the production, by those being inquired into, of a sample of projects which fit the criteria admirably and display the use of admirable methods. What one really wants to know is how the ordinary average decision is taken – indeed, how all decisions of consequence are taken – and to find out one needs a more comprehensive approach. To do that would, by present style, presume on the autonomy of Boards *vis-à-vis* departments, or of departments *vis-à-vis* the Treasury, and would go beyond 'candle-ends'.

95

freedom of the Boards and the authority of the Minister? The contrast could hardly be more complete between the ways in which Parliament and the Congressional Appropriations Committees act, which must be a large part of the explanation. One only has to appear before a Congressional Committee, or even to read its proceedings, to realize how totally different is its approach to a financial question. All the emphasis is on examples and results. Even when criteria and methods are relevant, as in discussion on programme (output) budgeting, they are not interested in discussing criteria and methods as such. Any abstract discussion – which the Select Committee in this, as in its other reports, frequently enjoys – would make Congressional Committees impatient, even rude. Rather they want to know: When was a method used? By whom? What difference did it make? Could it be applied to this problem? To that? Would the witness care to consider the applicability of what he is saying to a particular expenditure item the Congressman has in mind? If not now, then later in writing? Congressional Committees never get far from particular cases, and, if they feel like it, will put departmental and agency representatives through the wringer on a particular project or item. To discuss criteria would seem like a dereliction of duty, and an agency which tried to explain its criteria rather than get down to cases might be treated as if it had something to hide. In this they are more like businessmen than MPs are (though there are marked differences between their approach and that of businessmen, which do not all have to do with the publicity of congressional procedures).

Parliament of course behaves differently. The Select Committee (and the Estimates Committee in relation to departmental expenditure) does not see it as its job to uphold, cut back or increase moneys appropriated or lent to the Boards. They seem to regard it intrusive to spend time on a particular case, preferring to remain at a hypothetical level. To take sides in a dispute between a Minister and a Board, even when most of the relevant facts were before them, they would see as improper. When on occasion a Board does raise a detailed point, even on the application of criteria – as London Transport did with its escalators – its habit was to pass quickly on.

One suspects that the cause of this is that Parliament is a more purely legislative body than Congress. Its job is legislation (and expostulation: a safety valve for protest and opinions, an important way of letting Ministers know how the country feels and so the most important pressure group of all). In enacting laws, it is, in effect, laying down criteria of a kind. But then its interests tend to cease. It is for others to interpret and execute those laws. In general,

96

questions of power and authority in relation to those laws do not concern it. In *Chapter 11* I will argue there are strong arguments against Parliament's learning to behave like Congress in these respects, but Congress would never make the mistake of not perceiving that the key question which Government has to face up to on behalf of the nation, is one of *power* when persuasion fails or when the costs of persuasion in terms of time, money, energy and ill-will become too great: how then does one get results?

There is another aspect worth noticing. So far we have treated as irrelevant the distinction attempted by the Select Committee between policy-making and execution. Its mischief is that it tends to obscure the truth and to vitiate many solutions to problems of control, drawn up as if the distinction were useful. But here we have a collision between two ways of regarding the relationship between Minister and Board which is arguably much more mischievous since it tends to lend too much reality to the fake picture where it matters most – in Parliament. From the beginning, the House of Commons found it difficult to limit the scope of Parliamentary Questions on the nationalized industries; and so they fell back on the distinction between questions on policy – which were allowed – and on management detail – which were not. On this basis, one is not surprised to find difficulties of deciding at the margin whether particular questions were allowable. But more important, the distinction has tended to reinforce the myth of overall ministerial responsibility for the Boards: a Minister stands up and answers as if his were the responsibility. Often no distinction is made between cases where what he reports relates to his own powers and cases where it does not and he is only the mouthpiece of the Board. Hence the Minister becomes more identified with the Board and the Board with the Minister than is the case. Yet the fact that the Board has to use the Minister as its mouthpiece does give the Minister some leverage over the Board (though Parliamentary Questions rarely relate to the strategic policy questions with which we are mostly concerned).[1] That a Minister must stand up in Parliament as if all the answers were his, means he often feels a right to secure a wording he would prefer to defend.[2]

[1] An MP has small chance of being incisive with a PQ. The question must be fairly short. The answer is usually short. The member may follow up with quick supplementaries to which the Minister will make quick answers from his brief. Because the follow-up is limited, the process cannot be searching and therefore, though useful in some circumstances, it is not useful in the policy issues with which we are concerned.

[2] While one can hardly expect the House of Commons to reconsider what is by now almost an old tradition, two modifications would seem logical. The

G

Like many other paradoxes, on examination, that between the practical independence of Boards and the growing intervention by Government, turns out not to be one after all. The two are compatible. For a number of reasons Government has increased its interventions, as has Parliament through the Select Committee. One reason is the strength of the practical independence of Boards. Governments particularly have wanted to find out more about what was happening within Boards. Given their powers and the traditional way of exercising them – the relation we have called the practical independence of Boards – their natural response and the response of their officials is to have tried more persuasion. All this tended to increase the intervention by, though scarcely the power of, Government. What the Select Committtee does not seem to have seen is that the growth of intervention has not been an exercise of power (except in the very limited sense of having the authority to get some, but not all, of the information one wants and the right to be listened to), but an alternative to the exercise of power. Neither does the Select Committee seem to have realized that, by themselves side-stepping the question of ministerial power, the relation they seem to encourage would itself increase the interventionism they tend to deplore. Of course, much of the interventionism is related to other ends of MPs and Ministers, some serious, some whimsical – and no doubt it would be possible to reduce greatly the volume of intervention, if thought democratic, that does not touch on Board efficiency or on social policy. Even so, the Select Committee's approach is one which is unlikely to discourage intervention as an alternative control, because it is the increasing volume of interventions that fills the power vacuum. It is not an effective substitute for control and is likely to be most effective in relation to the spasmodic initiatives of Ministers. It is not an efficient way of achieving sustained financial control or social policy.

---

first would be to allow Ministers to answer questions which bore only on their own powers and use this in the place of the distinction between policy and management. The second would be to adapt the more realistic convention of the Canadian Parliament in relation to the Canadian National Railroad, a nationalized industry. On questions which relate to the Railroad's responsibilities, the Minister has little to do with framing the answers and is known to be a mouthpiece. If the first is thought to give the nationalized industries too much immunity from question, the second might be preferred. This should help bring home to the House of Commons the extent of Ministers' powers. If, as apparently with railway closures, it had been dissatisfied, it would have had an earlier incentive to change the law to its liking.

Chapter 10

PRESSURE

We ought to step aside to notice a view of the matter which sees much of what we have said throughout as beside the point. Why all this talk about *powers* and *duties*, the letter of the law, as if Ministers and Board Chairmen were lawyers rather than politicians? Why all this talk about persuasion, as if one could always assume that Ministers and their officials, or Chairmen for that matter, relied on reason to get their way? All have to be something of politicians to survive – as does the Chairman of a private company. Surely Ministers can get their way through informal means, except insofar as they are stopped by the political skill, or occasionally firmness, of a Board?

The Select Committee were well aware of this possibility. Again it is closely related to their belief in clear policy statements and having things as far as possible in writing. Like a school of thought between the two World Wars, they have a belief that the public good will be better served if there is 'open diplomacy'. Moreover, their belief that Boards should have a primary or residual independence – after all, specific powers have been allotted to Ministers as Parliament decides – is also connected with this. It is much easier for open statements to become the norm if Boards have a primary independence. If the Boards were to be the responsibilities of Ministers, Parliament could not be sure that Ministers were not using their then almost absolute power to do things that Parliament would not approve of, or indeed were contrary to the statutes. Parliament might also have less trust in public statements. At present, neither Minister nor Board can make a policy statement quite opposed to the truth since the other has the independence to protest and reveal.

Some will still feel this to be an argument about shadows. Even if a Minister has not the formal power to impose a 'gas' or an 'aviation' policy, surely the formal and informal powers he has are sufficient for him to impose his will. One can see from its questioning of Board witnesses how the Select Committee fears that this may be so. One suspects they may have been reading some of the many

American writings which analyse politics in those terms, as well as listening to rumours in Westminster.[1] The Board Chairmen reply that the pressures are not too great and it is very important for them to be able to request a published instruction from a Minister when he wants them to do something against their interpretation of their statutory duties and own best interests.

But one can almost hear the members of the Select Committee hoping that this is the whole truth while finding it rather hard to banish their suspicions. A Board Chairman who complained of informal pressures to the Committee might seem to be in an odd position, for if he was subject to them, why did he not demand a public instruction? If he asked for one and his Minister dropped the matter it would be odd if the Minister tried him again and again on other matters. On the hand, if a Board Chairman had succumbed, he would be unlikely to tell the Committee about it. Therefore, can the Committee be sure that the reassurances of a Chairman that he has not been forced, cajoled nor wheedled into acting against his judgement – that these very reassurances – have not themselves been forced on him by insidious pressures? As a Treasury witness said, '. . . if you have got a strong Chairman . . . he is going to insist on the fact that he is being asked to act uncommercially being brought out into the open anyway, whether it is by general direction, or by statement in Parliament, or by something in his annual report, or what have you. If you have got a pliable Chairman, the sort of man who will take persuasion at lunch parties to act uncommercially, and to do nothing about it, he will not ask for a general direction. That is the difficulty' (Q. 340).

The Select Committee also condemned this possibility in many of its earlier reports. One of its most effective Chairmen, Lord Aldington, reflected that 'in each of the inquiries we did we were greatly impressed by the additional influence which Ministers had over the policy of the nationalized industries by their frequent and informal discussions with the Chairmen of Boards'.[2] Mr Albu, another member who later became a Minister, said more strongly that 'Ministers . . . have increasingly practised a system of arm-twisting of Board Chairmen, while resisting Parliamentary questioning and any serious degree of Parliamentary control'.[3] Professor

---

[1] It is interesting, however, that it is a committee of Parliament which is the most anxious to depoliticize political behaviour in this instance. All that one has read about Congressional Committees suggests a contrast.

[2] The Select Committee on Nationalized Industries, *Public Administration*, Spring 1962.

[3] In M. Shanks, *The Lessons of Public Enterprise*, Cape, 1963, p. 91f.

Robson has observed the tendency of Ministers and their liaison officers to admit more influence as the years have passed. 'The evidence tends to show that Ministers . . . are interfering with the corporations a great deal more than they are compelled to do by statute.'[1]

There seems to be a tendency to confuse two forms of intervention which ought to be kept distinct. Some would seem to want the relations between Ministers and Boards to be as formal as possible. They would discourage the frequent informal chats which even Morrison thought desirable and necessary. This would give Boards a practical independence which would be almost total since they would be free from persuasion. But persuasion need not be the same as arm-twisting. In a given case it may be appallingly difficult to distinguish the two. Did a Minister in getting his own way rely on persuasion and perseverance, or did he go further than this and twist arms? Of course a skilful Minister with a silver tongue can persuade a Board Chairman, like a lot of other people, to do something they would never have thought of doing and which they may later regret. Whether a Minister and his officials get their way through persuasion depends, in a sense, on their competence. Broadly, one can say it is persuasion when a Minister is relying on reason and perseverence to get his way. If what he wants conforms to his and their own statutory duties, well and good. If it conflicts with them, and is genuinely persuasion without coercion, it is hard to escape the Treasury witness's conclusion that the Chairman must be culpably pliable, weak or out-manoeuvred. But by arm-twisting one does mean coercion. There must be a bargain by which one party causes the other to do something, or not to do it, by doing a favour, or not doing a disfavour, in relation to something else. Unlike persuasion, as we have used the word so far, arm-twisting is an informal exercise of *power*.

How common is arm-twisting? Is this type of intervention also on the increase? It is hard to say anything on this which does not sound sententious. The successful arm-twister may do it invisibly. The only outward sign in the other party is a sudden inexplicable change of mind, perhaps not even that. Thus, to say there is not much arm-twisting might merely mean that one has not seen it. What there is, and what one sees, may depend on the Ministers one has served. I formed the impression that this is much exaggerated as an essential element in the relationship, and that the popular belief to the contrary may have been based on little irrelevant

[1] W. A. Robson, *Nationalized Industry and Public Ownership*, Allen and Unwin, 1962, pp. 142–4.

101

evidence – perhaps even on American contemporary history, on memories of reading Macchiavelli or the Chartreuse de Parme, or even possibly on generalizing too much from the way that politicians relate to each other and the nature of the relation between them and semi-autonomous bodies like the Boards – but whatever there may be does not have too much to do with policy in the sense in which we have been using it. Whether Ministers wished it or not, informal exercise of power of this sort is not a major way of determining Board policy or their social policies, or of establishing effective financial control. There are safeguards in the British system. A Minister has about as much privacy as a patient in a general ward. The busier and more energetic he is, the less privacy he has. From early in the morning to late at night, every minute will be accounted for by meetings of one kind or another or by time spent in the House – when civil servants, messengers and others will be dropping in and out. A private secretary has a perfect right to fit a meeting into a blank in the diary without first asking permission. Of course, if a Minister wants to see a Board Chairman, or anyone else, alone, late in the evening, without his private office knowing about it, it can be done, but it is a devious procedure and the chances of a Minister's doing it very often without being found out by a chance phone call, the casual entry of a messenger or an official into the room, are small. Even a moderately diplomatic Board Chairman who wished to avoid such a meeting could easily do so. The Minister will hardly ever be alone at any meetings, lunches, dinners or other engagements. The private secretary will be there if no one else. None of this, however, can prevent a determined Minister from lunching alone with a Board Chairman, or sending officials out during a private chat, if he really wants to, one supposes, he could put the screws on. But that there is no habit in Whitehall and Westminster of *tête-à-tête* probably diminishes the frequency of arm-twisting.

But quite apart from the limited opportunities that Ministers may have for the sustained effort and privacy that arm-twisting requires, one wonders, looking back over all that has been written on the subject and especially at what the Select Committee has unearthed, whether there were many issues where Ministers would have especially wished to do this. Moreover, *with two major exceptions* explained later, the kind of thing on which Ministers may wish to get their own way tend to be rather particular and isolated; and in relation to these, it is arguable that Ministers – in contrast to American politicians – have few favours they can perform with which they could buy consent where the Board did not wish to give it. From time to time with all Governments, a Minister or another influential MP bridles because, against all evidence, he believes that the prospect of a pit or railway closure may lose an election, or because the proposed siting of a power station has caused strong feeling in the constituency – or he may feel that the siting of some new factory, office or depot, will help win an election. If the constituency is a Minister's he may feel that taking a decision against his constituents will be thought not a sign of impartiality, but a lack of Machismo. In many of these cases a Minister has powers which bear directly on the decision. This presumably is why many of the consents which are required of a Minister are written into statutes. Of course, one supposes that Parliament did not give these powers to the Minister in the first place so that he could refuse consent if he thought the effects would damage his party in an election. But if a Minister refuses closure for that reason, as is sometimes suspected, there is little that the Boards, or anyone else can do about it.[1] The social grant procedure described in *Chapter 4* should help to stiffen Ministers against outside pressures. For example, it would be odd for a Minister not to refuse consent to a railway closure but then refuse to pay grant for the line. But if he pays grant for the line, his department can be questioned by the Select Committee on Estimates about it. If a decision to keep a line turns out, after a few years, to be flagrant, very much at odds with the run of other decisions and the policy statements he has made on the subject, his Permanent Secretary as Accounting Officer may be seriously criticized. The possibility of this will give the Permanent Secretary a better position to resist decisions which will embarrass him. Also, it may matter to a Minister that, while giving or not giving one consent does not affect the number of others he can give, if he spends money on one thing, then the chances are high that he will have less to spend on other things he will want to do.

More difficult for the Ministers would be cases where they tried to get Boards to do something where they have no powers bearing directly on the issue. Of course the traffic is not all one way. Boards have been known to have pet (unprofitable) projects they try to

[1] It is easy to think such manoeuvres pointless because of the lack of evidence that this kind of thing influences elections, even when they are pending immediately. All the evidence is that they do not. A seat is scarcely ever lost because a railway line is closed, or won because a Minister persuades his colleagues to locate a decentralizing Government establishment there. One supposes that Ministers have a feeling of duty on behalf of their constituents and recognize this in other MPs; and also like to be liked by those they meet when they go to their constituencies. Perhaps, too, something of this kind is an immediate and visible sign of their power, while so many of the things they do are not.

persuade a Minister to accept on some grounds that they think will appeal to him. Looking for examples of things a Minister wants to press on a Board, one thinks first again of things which could conceivably affect elections, rather than more personal greeds and ambitions. Suppose there is some works a nationalized industry wants to close which does not require the Minister's consent. Or, to take something more disinterested, a Minister may -have representations from unions, constituents or perhaps from private businessmen, acquaintances or cronies, that a nationalized industry is handling something badly – it may be giving very bad service, or a particular local manager may be abrasive or incompetent. Or a Board may have a power of acquiring undertakings which does not require the Minister's consent – this could certainly be exercised in a way or at a time which could create severe political difficulties. Realpolitik might suggest that Ministers could use their undoubted, but unrelated, powers to get their way. Similarly, one could imagine a Minister using his power to approve or disapprove power station sites, or the siting of pylons, to his electoral advantage. One wonders how often it has been done.[1] One might have supposed that the most

---

[1] It is interesting to note the words used by the National Coal Board in a written submission to the Select Committee. Pit closures were probably the case where a Board complained most strongly of extra-statutory pressure. 'The degree of interference in the Board's affairs which can result from extra-statutory pressures can be very great and quite contrary to the underlying philosophy of the relationship between a nationalized industry and the Government, as established by Parliament. An example of such informal, unpublished pressure arose in 1965 over the Board's closure programme, when the Minister required to be informed of the programme in detail and insisted on the publication of lists of collieries, categorized as either A, B or C according to their likely prospects' (*Minutes of Evidence*, p. 130). In evidence, Lord Robens told the Committee how arm-twisting took place – it would seem a mixture of persuasion and possibly something more. 'It takes place in the meetings that you have and the discussions: "Surely you could close more pits? For example why don't you close this pit?", and you go on and on and on until in the end you are having to explain all about the pits you know so well, and the people you are talking to have never seen. You get to the stage when you say, "Well, we'll have another look at it". If the capital reconstruction you want is dependent upon that, or it is implied, then you have to go back and make a judgement as to whether you will start all over again, on your capital reconstruction ideas, or whether you will say, "Well, let's see if we can satisfy the Ministry by these extra closures". ' (Q. 520). While there is perhaps at first sight a more sinister insinuation here than one has heard of anywhere else, one must be careful since two issues may be confused. For a Minister to require a particular pit to be closed, may be extraordinary (and of doubtful political value). But for a Minister to worry about the overall financial position of the industry – in this case a deficit – to ask whether the business could not be contracted faster and so lose less money, hardly seems trivial. If indeed it is extra-statutory (because it concerns disinvestments, not investment)

important of these levers are (i) financial considerations and (ii) board appointments and reappointments.

(i) As we have seen (*Chapter 6*), the most important financial powers are the approval of capital expenditure, and borrowing. But a Minister would find it difficult to use them to do a trade with a Board, for instance, to insist that unless the Board keeps a plant going, he will refuse consent to a particular investment. Many discussions of financial points and investment decisions will begin and end without his ever seeing the papers. Officials will often decide points which they feel need not concern the Minister or on which he has given instructions. By and large, any project which promises a positive return at the going discount rate will never be seen by the Minister; and many others will be resolved lower down. He will only see the ones that are thought to be especially important because they are very large, or because they raise questions of social policy, or because he is being advised that some of his officials think he should turn a project down. Such cases are rare. Very large ones are likely to have been worked on carefully, and for him to use his consent here, or rather the possibility of his dissent, to advance something he wants, would require uncommon courage. The social questions will probably involve his interests anyway and are less likely to be crucial to the Board. As we have seen, suggestions that he might turn a proposal down are rare. Thus the chances of something coming up that he can use to work his will on a Board, are likely to be small. All one can say is that, although a really determined Minister could find the time to push through the mass of paperwork and find an issue of a kind where he could misuse his powers to get his own way, it would be practically difficult for him to do so[1] –

---

then there would seem to be a case for reconsidering the powers of Ministers so that they can deal with a strategic question of such importance. (See *Chapter 15* below.)

[1] How the necessary routines and emergencies of the day – Cabinet, Cabinet committees, attendance at the House of Commons, delegations, Parliamentary Questions, speeches – fill the day from early morning to late at night of even a moderately relaxed Minister, has to be seen to be believed. An exceptionally energetic one will have the day filled to overflowing, to a degree one would not have thought possible. Neither is delegation a simple answer. Many of the things Ministers do are their statutory responsibility. The delegation of other things would mean delegation from the political to the administrative level, which may raise many questions. The industrialist who delegates whatever is needed to enable him to think and act on what he believes important, finds many constraints on his ability to do so in public office. And while the present relation cannot be the best, trying to change it involves very important constitutional questions about the relations of Ministers, civil servants and Parliament, which are not easy to resolve. Neither, fortunately, are they directly relevant to this book.

quite apart from his trying to do this in an environment which would quickly see through what he was doing and would give him little support. This kind of thing is antipathetic to civil servants and would not receive their respect.

(ii) Board appointments we have discussed, and we show how limited an opportunity they give to a Minister to influence policy. Certainly, for an incoming Chairman to be bound informally to do some particular favour for a Minister seems most improbable; and for him to feel bound to carry it out thereafter seems unlikely, since once he is appointed it is difficult for a Minister to resist. More important is the improbability of a reappointment or new appointment coming up when a Minister might be tempted to do a deal. Plainly Ministers could occasionally use the power of appointment or the fear of no reappointment in this way.

In conclusion, it would seem that the informal pressures, as opposed to persuasion, a Minister may exert to get his own way are more limited than the cynical would expect. There are certain particular acts of closure or investment where he may be anxious to exert influence because of the effect these are thought to have on elections; and to some extent the consents required of him in statutes reflect these wishes. But, what is more to the point in this discussion, the kinds of matters which Ministers would like, and may be able, to get decided in their favour, are not likely to be the issues of general policy, which are too subtle and slippery to be fixed in this manner. The counters a Minister has to help him get his own way through striking a bargain are rather few. In particular, the use he can make of financial powers and of appointments to achieve his ends is limited. Therefore their comparative inability to misuse their powers does limit severely the ability of Ministers to influence the mainstream policy of their Boards.

Two exceptions to this generalization have made many wonder, wrongly in my judgement, whether both are the only visible examples of a far larger and as yet invisible species. But even if I am right in arguing they are *sui generis*, both are important and raise central questions of principle.

(1) Over the years BOAC and, more recently, BEA have been forced against their will to buy British aircraft when it would have been more profitable for them to have bought American. In its 1960 Report on the Air Corporations the Select Committee noted what they held to be the excessive and non-statutory interventions by Ministers to achieve this, although they also then felt that the Air Corporations

seem to have been easily persuadable.[1] The 1964 Report on BOAC revealed the influence which had been used to persuade BOAC to buy the VC 10, also against its commercial judgement. There had also been a six months' delay while BEA had to delay ordering the De Havilland DH 121 for BEA because the then Minister of Supply wanted the order placed with another firm. In 1966, Sir Anthony Milward told the Select Committee, he had asked the Board of Trade permission to buy American aircraft. Two months later the Minister had announced to the House of Commons that they were to buy British (Q. 955).

One presumes that the reason for Ministers' believing that there was a divergence between the Boards' commercial interest and the public interest could be based on a combination of three factors:

(i) a wish to subsidize the British aviation industry either in the belief that it would eventually break even or because, even if unprofitable, it was necessary to the defence of Britain; or more simply, a wish to subsidize that industry without any further public aim;

(ii) a wish to help make all the other public subsidies to the aviation industry pay off by creating a demand for those aircraft; or put more favourably, a belief that it would have been wasting all the subsidies if there was not a further subsidy, this time by an air corporation, to expand the market for the aircraft;

(iii) a recognition that the pound is overvalued at the official rate of exchange and that therefore the nominal price of the American aircraft is less than their real price.

It is difficult, after the aviation policy of the last twenty-five years has reached one crisis with the collapse of Rolls Royce this year (1971), not to be cynical about these manifestations of aviation policy. To have made the air corporations shoulder part of the costs of subsidizing the aviation industry in this way was bad for the financial discipline and control of the air corporations since it muddled their commercial duty and social obligations.[2] It was also bad for the financial control of the whole aviation subsidy programme since it helped split up the subsidy into several elements falling on different parties; and made it difficult to bring them together for an evaluation of the costs and benefits of it all.

[1] *Report from the Select Committee on Nationalised Industries: The Air Corporations*, May 1959, H.C. 213, paras 215–18.
[2] This seems to have been realized by Mr Mulley when Minister of Aviation in 1966 when he announced he would compensate BEA for forcing them to buy British, by reducing the target rate of return. There is some doubt whether this would be equal to the adverse effect on BEA's net revenues. Some have called it a phoney compensation. One hopes, even so, for no return to the previous practice.

But the question which interests us most here is whether this proves that a Minister can get his way without statutory powers. Sir Anthony Milward made it seem obscure: '. . . we had a directive. I know that there is a legal connotation for a directive which may not apply in this case, but nevertheless it was a directive to "buy British" . . . I am told that the Treasury does not regard that as a directive. All I can say is that I do . . . this was the first directive we had had in BEA's history, very nearly, I think, to do anything which was contrary to our commercial interest.' Plainly no general direction was issued in this or in any of the other cases. Before 1966 the Government had no powers to 'approve' capital programmes for the air corporations as they had for most of the other Boards. A Board of Trade submission to the Select Committee hints that before then they were resting on Government powers to control borrowing.[1] When the Select Committee took evidence on Ministerial Control, the Board of Trade had by then the power to approve capital programmes, so its representatives were asked the 'blunt question', 'would you use the control of investment procedures as an attempt to prevent one of the corporations' buying a foreign aircraft if that were the policy of the Board of Trade at the time, or would you only use the Minister's direct veto or directive power?' (Q. 1224). Without being as blunt, the answer implied that they would not use a general direction – if that was meant by veto or directive power – but that a question of this sort would be considered in the review of an investment proposal.[2] Therefore it seems a fair deduction that

---

[1] 'To the extent that capital expenditure on these aircraft had to be financed by Exchequer borrowings, it was obviously sound for the corporations to assure themselves in advance that the Government were prepared to finance their intended programmes' (vol. iii, p. 128). If control over borrowing is meaningful, this seems tenable. The power has been reinforced for other Boards, and since 1966 for the air corporations, by a separate power to approve capital programmes. The first would not cover investment internally financed, the second not the source of funds as such—e.g. whether domestic or foreign.

[2] Because the answer is not as decisive as one might have wished – at least for our purpose – here it is: 'On something that is really sizeable the corporation would make an investment proposal to the Minister. On this investment review, what normally happens with an aircraft purchase is this. Let us say a corporation decides the time has come to buy thirty X-type aircraft, none of which will be delivered for years to come. They will make this proposal in order to place an order. However, the investment review which will be looking at it and which covers a period of five years will show very little in the way of payments in the first year or so; then gradually progress payments will mount up. Whether these should be included in the five-year programme will depend on whether the final decision taken was, "Yes, you can have those thirty X-type aircraft".' It would seem reasonable to infer that the answer to the Committee's question was, Yes.

the power to 'approve the lines of BOAC's capital investment' (and before 1966 the power to approve borrowing) was the basis for the Government decisions, though whether this was said in correspondence we do not know (and this might explain Sir Anthony Milward's apparent confusion). As a result it is probable that these Government interventions were not examples of non-statutory pressure.

Are these improper uses of the power to approve capital expenditure (or borrowing), the use of a power intended for one purpose to secure another? The answer is not as simple as it might seem to businessmen (or the Select Committee), who tend to assume that the purpose of capital expenditure approval is to secure a sufficient return, and that this power is to be identified with the Minister's oversight of the efficiency of Boards. However, the statutes do not specify the reasons for approving capital expenditures; to Ministers and officials it may seem as sensible and proper to disapprove investment proposals for what they regard as the public interest, as to insist on its being profitable. There is a difference between a policy developed and pursued over a number of years, indeed by both Conservative and Labour Governments, and a sudden impulsive abuse of these powers by a Minister. On this argument, what has happened with aircraft may appear a proper use of a statutory power which did not specify that the purpose of Ministers' financial powers was exclusively financial. We have here yet another example of the confusion between the financial and social powers and duties of Ministers; and it is for this reason that one would think it worth the while of the Select Committee and Parliament to clarify the scope of these powers. To follow the precedent of indicating the scope of powers, rather than to attempt to define them rigorously, would be to add to the statutory description that Ministers have the power to approve capital expenditure programmes 'in the interest of the efficient and economic use of resources' by the public corporation. Otherwise the possibility of abuse, which would erode financial discipline, is immense. If one can use what appears to be a financial power intended to help Ministers 'oversee the efficiency' of a Board for a public purpose which in fact damages that efficiency, why could one not use the same power for any other public purpose which affects Board efficiency? To amplify the description of the power would imply that Ministers must use another power (preferably entailing compensation) when forcing Boards to act against their commercial interests.[1]

[1] It is remarkable that this aviation policy has been perhaps the most decisive known use of ministerial financial powers.

(2) The second way in which Ministers have intervened presents far more complex issues and is of greater importance: it is to affect prices and sometimes wages. The general position is that except during the period of Prices and Incomes legislation under the Wilson Government, Ministers have had no statutory powers over the prices of the nationalized industries. Even this generalization has to be interpreted with care. The interventions here have been almost ceaseless, and the locus for intervention seems to have been one or other of the following:

(i) Boards refer all significant price and wage increases to Ministers. This appears to be agreed by all Chairmen; and the Select Committee refers to the 'well-established and publicly acknowledged practice that Ministers are consulted in advance and have the opportunity to comment, before final decisions are taken by the Boards, on proposals to increase charges on a significant scale. Ministers may ask industries to refrain from increasing prices, but under nationalization statutes they have no formal powers to enforce such requests' (374). The history of this practice indeed predates nationalization since its origin was the so-called Gentlemen's Agreement in the coal industry which began in 1939 as a wartime measure. It was carried on through nationalization and was imitated for other Boards.

As it stands, this is no more than an opportunity for the Government to exert (non-coercive) persuasion as described in the last chapter. The Board puts up a case for the increase. The department is able to reply, and to delay the increase. Just as the traditional methods of investment control lead often to prolonged exchanges of questions and answers, and so irritate the Boards, so may similar exchanges over prices. The Select Committee received evidence of how much revenue some Boards had lost because of these delays and of how they had jeopardized their financial position. These, more than the delays over capital expenditure approval that Boards also complained of, could affect their financial position seriously, though in the Select Committee's opinion the increases asked for were usually granted in the end (380, 383). It seems as if Chairmen were more pliable or Ministers more persuasive in the fifties than in the sixties, since the Select Committee appeared to think there had been a greater willingness to agree among Ministers in recent years. As they reported, 'It was not easy for Ministers to ask in one breath to achieve financial results and to deny them in the next breath the means of doing this', though it had happened (383).

(ii) There used to be various Tribunals who had a right to refuse or modify price increases which had to be submitted to them by Boards, and in some cases Ministers had similar powers on appeal from the Tribunals. The most important was the Transport Tribunal. With the disappearance of its price-fixing role, this kind of control over nationalized industries' prices and wages has almost disappeared.

(iii) Where Ministers pay grants for services, as they do for branch railways, it follows that they are able to determine the fare paid by users of such an unremunerative service. It is in effect determined by the size of the grant in relation to the costs of providing that service. This is what one would expect, given the purpose of the grant, and in one case a Government has compensated a Board for delaying price increases. It was a deliberate policy of the Labour Government to subsidize urban transport so as to introduce a fairer competition with the motor-car. London Transport was compensated for keeping down fares as an intermediate step towards the longer-term solution made possible by the 1969 London Transport Act.

(iv) Under the Wilson Government's Prices and Incomes policy, major price and wage increases proposed by the Boards were referred to the National Board for Prices and Incomes. This again meant delay while the NBPI investigated to determine whether in their view the increases were justified; and besides delay it meant the provision of information by the Boards so that the NBPI could write its reports. This the Boards disliked intensely. It seems as if the increases asked for were almost always granted in the end and that the effect was therefore much the same as it had been under the Gentlemen's Agreements. The NBPI in its reports often criticized the efficiency of the Boards and suggested modifications in the way any given increase should be achieved; it was this interference in managerial discretion that was hotly resented, rather than the delays themselves, though these were complained of, as they always had been.

(v) Lastly, the Minister of Transport issued a general directive to the British Transport Commission to keep down prices in 1952. This method seems to have been more popular with Conservative Governments since it was not used again until 1970 (against the Post Office), and then again in 1971 (against the British Steel Corporation). In this case the reason given must be that the proposed increase is against the public interest.

Therefore there is a mixture of pressures and powers that Ministers have used to delay or reduce price and wage increases. However, no straightforward opinion on which is most desirable can be given

111

because of the variety of reasons for which Ministers have wished to control prices and wages.

One of the chief reasons for nationalization was to prevent the abuse of monopoly power, both where this existed before nationalization and where nationalization was intended – through rationalization and merger – to create the possibility of monopoly power, which could then be abused. The Morrisonian view appears to have been that Boards would themselves interpret the public interest in this respect, but would discuss with Ministers what they were doing to avoid abusing their monopoly potential. This meant an almost complete trust in the efficiency and public-spiritedness of such Boards (defined here as their keeping down of prices, according to some marginal cost or similar rule). Since Parliament and public opinion were perhaps not always so willing to have perfect trust in the monopoly Board's public-spiritedness, and the Ministers would have to defend such price increases, one is not surprised to find the emergence of the early warning system of the Gentlemen's Agreements. The system remained an imperfect one. One suspects that a Board never recommended a price increase in order to increase already existing profits so as to raise them above the break-even level. Nationalization in itself was enough to prevent such monopoly profits. So the criticism was rather that Boards used their monopoly position, not to make profits, but to be lazy and inefficient, so letting costs creep up unnecessarily and thus make a case for raised prices. While many nationalized industries have effective competition, others do not. The control of investment in its crude form of stating a target rate of return on capital is not a sufficient financial discipline for the power industries or for steel, since these industries more or less can raise their prices to achieve any predetermined return on their capital. So the concern over price rises became one of concern over inefficiency, and in this context the notification of price and wage increases under the Gentlemen's Agreements lengthened into the pattern of question and answer we have already described. The intervention of the National Board for Prices and Incomes took the process a stage further, since the Board had the power to get information and write a report on the efficiency of a Board which, in practice, was not always closely related to the price or wage increase itself.

Monopoly and a derived interest in the efficiency of the Board as such were not the only motives for attempts to control prices and wages, whatever the form in which they were expressed. Sometimes it has been alleged that price increases were delayed to help win an election – a commonly quoted example is the delay in allowing the National Coal Board to increase prices until after the 1955 election. Here one has what most would regard as undoubtedly an abuse of the use of the Gentlemen's Agreement to delay an increase for a convenient period.

In 1952 when the Churchill Government used a general direction to alter price increases, even when they had been approved by the Transport Tribunal, one of the objections was to the pattern of fare increases. The Government was insisting on a different pattern from that determined by the British Transport Commission in its commercial self-interest. One would now hope that any Government concerned about differentiating prices to achieve social ends would take powers to compensate a Board for performing an uncommercial service, or else rely on its powers [of [persuasion. (If the Board thought the pattern the Government wanted was seriously against its commercial interests, they would require compensation. If the financial effects were trivial, they might allow themselves to be persuaded. But to use a general direction to force a Board to behave uncommercially would be a clear case of muddling a Board's objectives.) More recently, as we have seen, the Government has used persuasion and compensation to achieve social ends in keeping London Transport's fares down, which would seem a perfectly defensible and coherent expression of policy. This has been formalized in the powers under the 1968 Transport and 1969 London Transport Acts to grant aid services, which implies a power to fix fares, provided Government meets any resulting losses.

A more important explanation of many interventions to prevent price and wage increases has been the various policies to slow down inflation which several Governments have pursued, especially since the 1961 pay pause, first through the Gentlemen's Agreements. This was the principal justification of the Wilson Government's legislation enabling Ministers to refer increases to the Prices and Incomes Board. In this form it was intended not to weigh more heavily on public than on private firms, but because of the old feeling that Government must be seen to be enforcing their restraints on 'their' nationalized industries, many fewer price and wage increases slipped by uninvestigated in the private than in the public sector. The Conservative Government since 1969 have abandoned a Price and Incomes policy: but they have continued a different kind of restraint on price and wage increases by nationalized industries. In some cases – electricity supply and the Post Office are the most obvious examples – they seem to have persuaded those nationalized industries voluntarily to resist wage increases, while at the same time appearing publicly to claim that Ministers were 'requiring'

H

the industries to behave in this way and set a good example to private firms. In one case—the British Steel Corporation in 1971—they have been stopped by issuing a general direction.[1]

The main reasons for Ministerial interventions to control prices and wages would seem to be: to check inflation, to keep prices low for reasons of social policy, and occasionally for electoral advantage. If the Boards are compensated, there would seem no economic or financial reason why Ministers should not 'buy' a Board pricing policy they believe to be in the public interest. A Minister who delays price increases to help win an election, can hardly be stopped from this while Gentlemen's Agreements continue, Since their essence is to give him power to delay, he can always find plausible reasons for this, even if his real motive is to secure electoral or some similar advantage.

This happily is not a Ministerial intervention. 'Our opinion is that these increases are unnecessary because there is inefficiency or monopoly power in the industry which could be reduced instead.' These arguments or excuses tempt Ministers to be superficial and often act as alibis for other motives. A Minister may believe it no bad thing for a Board to absorb £x million increase in costs without raising prices. He may argue *a priori* that Boards being monopolies and nationalised industries, are by their nature less perfectly efficient, and therefore he will be doing them and their customers a service by forcing them to increase their productivity. If they fail to do this he may take this as further evidence of their inefficiencies. At worst the Board's profitability may fail and there may be a deficit. But he may prefer to accept a deficit in the future rather than a price rise now. If he rejects a price rise, he may always hope for public approval. A deficit he can blame on the inefficiency of the Board. These are exceptionally crude, suspect and incompetent methods of attempitng an increase in Board efficiency. One fears nothing much more profound happened in 1971 when Ministers issued a direction ordering the British Steel Corporation to cut back their proposed price increase by half. In this case there was said to have been a special inquiry by civil servants into the Corporation's financial position before the decision was made. One only hopes that it was thorough, though many Boards would doubt the competence of civil

[1] It was widely thought the Post Office was given a general direction to reduce their price increase proposals in 1970. This was not so. The Minister sent the Chairman a formal letter expressing his view that the proposed increases should be reduced to agree with some recommendations made by the Post Office Users' Council. The Chairman accepted the letter which was referred to publicly.

servants to carry through such an inquiry unaided.[1] In part this seems a return to the Wilson Government's policy of using a special efficiency study to monitor a price increase, though in that case it was the Nattional Board for Prices and Incomes which was used, and that Board had more resources and different kinds of manpower from what a Government department as now staffed has. Any sustained belief by the Boards that such inquiries were being conducted by people not fully competent must lead to worsening relations between Boards and departments, without any assurance that in the end a just and efficient answer had been reached. The use of the NBPI for such a purpose also raised serious objections. The Boards and others were suspicious of the infrequency of their sallies into the affairs of a particular Board; this was widely criticized as leading to superficial reports. More important, to try to appraise Board price policy without looking at the financial position of the Board as a whole is inevitably superficial. What is wanted for a Board is a financial control system which shows the interrelation between output, prices and costs. If a Board in a corporate plan can point out in some detail the effects of holding prices, and stand up to attacks that it can absorb costs by producing data which show its productivity and cost-consciousness, then only does it perhaps have a hope of making its case for price increases credible to a Minister (whatever his motive for holding back prices). So a Board may be able to persuade the Minister – and the world through statements in their published accounts – of the extent of his responsibility if he forces Boards to hold back prices or wages to an extent which is inefficient. Keeping prices down where marginal costs exceeds marginal revenue may increase demand but reduces net revenue. Keeping wages down over a long period drains away some of the better quality labour, so that a Board may be left with a lower quality labour force than would be most efficient for it. On the other side, a Minister ought to feel morally able to insist on keeping prices and wages down in the interests of 'efficiency', only if he has the financial evidence to justify such an assertion of superiority: financial information which, in the normal way, is not now available to Ministers or their departments. This is far from the only reason for proceeding to a system of *strategic financial control* (to be outlined in *Chapter 16*), but it is a powerful one.

Where the main motive behind a Minister's wishing to restrain prices and wages is inflation, the position is much more difficult.

[1] The 1966/7 Railway and London Transport Inquiries could not have gone as deeply as they did without the resources of outside businessmen and management consultants. But see *Chapter 17*.

Ministers often maintain that it is in the interests of Boards to resist wage demands or not to pass on cost increases; but this is often very doubtful. Normally in an inflationary period, it is in every individual firm's interest to concede the lowest wage increases consistent with avoiding a serious strike. A serious strike will cut revenue more than it cuts costs and reduce profits. It will also reduce liquidity and possibly increase borrowing at a time when interest rates will normally be high and a firm would be striving to increase its liquidity. Many of its orders will go elsewhere and be lost to it forever. Therefore, on rational grounds, a nationalized industry, like a private firm, may be wise to avoid a serious strike. If, as with the Post Office in 1971, it stands a long strike the chances are that it will be financially worse off at the end even if it avoids conceding the wage increase demanded. This therefore is a case where the public interest is not the same as the interest of each firm separately; and therefore, on the grounds of equity, it is often argued that a wage freeze, or some other anti-inflationary policy, should apply to public and private sector alike as far as possible. If one believes that this is impossible because such a policy either cannot be generally applied or should not, for some reasons of doctrine, and if one further believes that public firms ought to show a restraint which other firms should copy also, then there is a strong case in equity for compensating the nationalized industries for any disproportionate effort they have made for the general good. This should be treated as a social duty of a Board to be compensated in the same way as any other social duty described in *Chapter 4*.[1] The more private firms follow the example of nationalized industries, the less financial losses will be felt by the Boards since inflation will slow down rapidly; and all will be suffering roughly similar losses through strikes. Therefore, the Government would have to compensate the Board less. Thus, the more effective the policy is of forcing the Boards to lead the economy against inflation, which is presumably the hope of Government, the less compensation they would have to pay to back their judgement. But what is clearly unfair is that the Boards' financial position should be jeopardized because they are made by Government to shoulder these special obligations. In short, the Government should underwrite the risk that the Boards make themselves worse off, rather than better, by taking the lead in resisting wage demands on behalf of the nation. Unfortunately, it seems that if a Government decides not to impose a wage or

---

1 One remembers Sir Ronald Edwards' query (p. 25 above) on what he would feel his duty if he believed a general direction prevented him from meeting his statutory financial duties to Parliament.

income freeze equally on public and private sector, but to use the public sector as shock troops while exhorting the rest, it would seem impossible for a Government to be open on the possible risks to a Board to the point of offering it compensation. For such a policy to be successful a Government must seem to believe, and must persuade others to believe, that the commercial interests of the Boards coincide with the public interest in restraining prices and wage increases. To admit the possibility that this need not be so by being ready to compensate Boards for putting the public interest above their own financial interest, will appear to deflate that presumed identity of the two and might seem to give the game away to the private sector.

Yet when inflation is persistent and such a cure is attempted, this is likely to be the single most important reason for muddling the objectives of the Boards, for relaxing their financial discipline and for landing them in losses which will appear to be their own fault, but which will not be. One cannot expect to persuade a Government that this erosion of the financial discipline of Boards is not a price worth paying for the ending of inflation; but one can hope that Governments might realize that it is a substantial cost of such a policy and to be borne in mind. Perhaps all one can hope for is that Ministers and Boards – if they had the financial information which they do not now have – might be able to agree privately on the probable effect on their net revenue position of Boards' acting in this way in the public interest.

Therefore there are two areas in which Ministers appear to have intervened regularly without explicit powers. In the first – where the air corporations have been made against their will to buy British aircraft – it would seem not to have been arm-twisting as we have defined it, but the use of an overtly financial power to secure an end which is arguably in the public interest but against the financial interest of the corporations. In the other case, the Minister's right to intervene had more or less voluntary beginnings in the Gentlemen's Agreements; and so far as it rests on them, the Boards must be pliable or persuaded, though in fact the costs of delay itself are often heavy. But more recently Ministers have used other powers, as well as that of the general direction, in a way, however, which might not stand up if tested in court – if one were ever to imagine a Chairman's following the lead given by Sir Ronald Edwards and questioning whether his statutory duties to at least break even had priority, even over a ministerial general direction when the two were in patent conflict. However, for Ministers to use general directions as a method

117

of requiring Boards to act against what they believe to be their commercial interest, does suggest a greater strain in the traditional relationship between Minister and Board than almost anything else could. It cannot be an effective substitute for long-term financial control. If, for the reasons described in *Chapter 6*, Ministers and civil servants under present arrangements and with their present staffing have not normally had the experience or the confidence to turn down investment proposals, then imposing a price freeze or otherwise going against Board judgement in restraining prices, which has an even more powerful effect on a Board's financial position, must be too arbitrary unless Ministers develop the capacity to exercise a just and efficient strategic financial control. At the worst, as in the case of the direction to British Steel, it may appear to be not an exercise of financial discipline at all, but an attempt to use British Steel to subsidize the rest of British industry without compensation; a policy which, unless proved to be untrue, must ultimately have the worst implications for financial discipline and efficiency. However, episodes like this appear rarely in the history of ministerial attempts at price control which, for the most part, have been more like the essays in persuasion described in the last chapter.

Reflecting on the last two chapters, one sees the critical question to be whether practical independence, tempered by persuasion and the responsiveness of Boards to legislation, as well as an occasional more decisive intervention by a Minister, is satisfactory. Those who feel that it is, are free to think this. I hope I have drawn out some of the implications of their position. In the next part a number of alternative developments are considered. They are policies which would alter the balance of power between Ministers and Boards, or raise up other forces to help secure some of the ends willed by Parliament for public enterprise.

Part III

ALTERNATIVE DEVELOPMENTS

Chapter 11

THE POLITICIZATION OF ADMINISTRATION

I have described how it seems to me that the backstairs influence of Ministers on Boards was less than the Select Committee may have feared, and that their powers, including those of appointment, gave Ministers less opportunity to effect their policies than is widely thought. To some people to whom I have talked the answer to the problem of control seems obvious: they would say that what is wrong is the length of the arm's-length relation between Minister and Board. The present relations are fairly formal. This is not to say that day-to-day relations are not informal, normally friendly and unlegalistic; but in the background controlling the relationships are ideas on what is appropriate, suitable and, though the phrase would scarcely ever be used, constitutional. To Ministers this may seem a very considerable constraint on their power, and the obvious solution might be for them to get into a position where their relations with Boards were more political: where they could use their powers on one matter to get their way on another without feeling they were climbing mountains of disapproval to do so; and where Board appointments were normally political, that is, their own appointments. When there was a change of administration, there would be an expectation that Board Members would offer their resignations. Some would be accepted; and some of the Minister's men would be appointed.

Such a trend might also seem to have been the way Ministers have been pressing over twenty-five years. They and their civil servants have been increasing their persuasive interventions and, in one or two other examples, like aircraft investment and pricing, they seem almost to have reached a position where powers are being used for one purpose which were generally thought to have been given them for another. From here there could be a movement towards a greater politicization of relations between Boards and Ministers.[1] By politicization one means a situation in which the conventions of politi-

[1] To use another vocabulary to express the same sense: a tendency towards greater pluralism within this area of Government.

cal behaviour weaken and the statutory framework is interpreted ever more laxly, so that it is hardly any restraint at all on Ministers: when the outcome of any tussle between the parties is decided almost entirely by whoever has the greater strength and wiliness. Politicization is therefore a newish name for an old state of affairs which some thinkers have always believed existed behind the front of a constitution: where in this instance neither statutory powers nor Morrisonian or post-Morrisonian conventions channel the wills of Ministers and Boards; where the Minister is one pressure group and a Board is another and on them both act all manner of other pressure groups, which change their strength and position so that in the extreme it is no longer sensible to describe the relationship as one of any consistency. In such a situation it would be pointless for the Select Committee to report on ministerial control, since this presumes on a certain consistency in policy in which there is development and from which there are occasional departures. But the Minister in office, who feels that the conventions are too strong and that the framework of statutory powers confines his will rather than helps him to act – and that therefore he does not have the power to do that which he wants and which he may believe is his expectation, especially as the strength of the tradition may have been hidden from him until he took office – may be strongly minded to help ease the relationship towards a greater politicization.[1]

Suppose first a Minister were to say to a Board that he intended to cut its investment appropriations by half unless the Board put in a management information system which gave better information on the causes of its profits and losses; and suppose he was to be supported by advice on this. One might expect at least two reactions. The first would be that it was interference in day-to-day management; but, if the Minister were to persist, he could argue reasonably enough that since he had a power and a duty to approve capital expenditure, he did not feel he was doing his duty by Parliament

---

[1] Some Ministers do not see a problem, because they either do not try to do much, or are happy to go no further than attempts at persuasion, not caring much whether they succeed and sometimes hoping that immediate failure may be outlived by eventual success, perhaps in someone else's time. Others may not be so concerned for the opposite reason: that they were so skilful and persuasive and perhaps also had changes in mind which fitted in well with the tradition while making an advance, that they succeeded and cannot see why lesser men tumbled nor waste sympathy on them; yet even they may sometimes wonder whether the effort was not disproportionate and whether they would not have done more with a little more personal power. The cost, of course, would have been that, with fewer obstacles, their policies would not have been as well thought out, and not so many interested parties would have been persuaded of its virtues, so that they would have risked another kind of failure.

unless there was better information to increase the probability that given capital expenditure would yield the promised return. For a Minister to do this in relation to any Board would be revolutionary, but it is arguable that it would be well within his formal powers to do so. The Morrisonian notion that Boards are to be left freedom to conduct day-to-day management, while Ministers look to policy, is a convention, not something laid down in statute. As we have seen, the difference between policy and execution (day-to-day management) is not logically drawn. If a Minister should say that the installation of better management information is for him a policy question, he can hardly be stopped from his opinion. However it is not the kind of question a Minister often gets down to, one suspects; and even if he did he is likely perhaps to say in general terms that this is what he thinks is necessary and not get down to the detail of what the management information system would be. If, however, he were to appoint consultants to go into the matter and make detailed recommendations, it might not seem unreasonable for him to do this insofar as the management information system bore on his financial powers. If he had sense, he obviously would rather do this with the co-operation of the Board and would hope that any recommendations of the inquiry would be agreed to by both Minister and Board. But if the recommendations seemed to him to be sensible and likely to mean that public money was better spent, while the Board disliked the suggestions for reasons which he thought were over-conservative or merely resentful of interference, it would surely not be unreasonable for him to say that he would reduce the Board's investment appropriations until they did what he, and the inquiry, believed the situation required. Then he might run into the second argument: that the installation of such a system would be likely to take several years, even if every effort was made, and to cut investment appropriations meanwhile would be a damaging thing to do. This is a familiar situation in handling which he would have to use his best judgement. But to feel that it would be improper for a Minister to be forceful and impose such a sanction, would seem to imply either an extreme belief in the right of a Board to independence or an equally extreme distrust in the ability of Ministers to come to a right decision on a financial question.

But to take another example, suppose a Minister were to be told, and were to have enough evidence to believe, that a Board's pay structure was thoroughly inefficient and inequitable, much resented by the men and counterproductive. The difference is that this does not bear directly on any power of the Minister. (Indeed, in the British system all labour questions tend to be referred to the Ministry of

Labour, the Department of Employment and Productivity and the Department of Employment – as it has successively been called – and not to be regarded as of any concern of the sponsoring Minister.) But though it would not bear directly, it could quite colourably be argued to be affecting the return on investment or the achievement of the Board's financial target. One can imagine a Minister trying to persuade a Board to do something about it; but what if he were again to threaten to cut investment appropriations unless what he were to regard as his policy were executed by the Board? One can imagine situations in which this might be unreasonable. But, as in the last case, the position of the Minister would be very much stronger if there had been some kind of inquiry and he had, as a result, some expert opinion to back him up. Again one would hope that all this could be done with the agreement (even reluctant agreement) of the Board. If it were, not only would the Minister's case seem to be stronger, but there would be some protection for the Board and for Parliament. It would be clear that, if the Minister had in the end to impose his will (for example by cutting or threatening to cut investment appropriations), he would be doing it for the reasons stated: because of the case made by him with the backing of the results of the inquiry. Even then, he would be sensible to weigh up the benefit to the situation from realizing a new pay structure, against the cost of the resentment the Board might feel at being overruled.

But to take a case at another extreme. Suppose a Minister were to insist on a thorough management overhaul at a mine before authorizing a capital expenditure project elsewhere in the business – the two having no necessary connection. This might not be as trivial as it would seem. He might know – and be under considerable political pressure to recognize – that the management was inefficient and the mine was as a result doing so badly that men were being laid off unnecessarily. If he could not persuade the Board of this, he might try again to strengthen his position by a special inquiry into that mine, and then, if it confirmed his view, insist on action or withhold funds.

There have been inquiries on matters of the first and second type, but not on the efficiency of specific operations. It has not always been easy to achieve the setting up of such inquiries since they tend to be assumed to require the Board's consent. What would happen if a Minister felt very strongly, and with good evidence, that an inquiry was wanted into a particular Board and the Board refused to co-operate? It is not a situation which has been tested. (At least, one has no public knowledge of anything of the kind. One fears that a

Board might be able to kill the notion of such an inquiry stone dead and in such a way that a Minister would see no point in making his failure public.) But once there has been such an inquiry, usage would seem to suggest that it is up to the Board for the most part to carry out, modify, or not carry out the recommendations. Of course, there will be consultations between Ministry and Board; but I do not believe it ever to have been the case that a Minister has used his financial powers by withholding funds to enforce the recommendations of such an inquiry. This does not mean that the Minister is quite powerless. Imminent legislation could, one supposes, in some cases force the hand of a reluctant Board.[1] But it does mean that financial pressure has not been used to enforce change as a holding company might use it.

However, what has been outlined so far can hardly be described as a politicization of the administrative process, except by the most enthusiastic believers in the practical independence of the Boards. But in the back of people's minds there are bogeys which may in part be responsible for the fact that the Boards' practical independence is interpreted as it is. One is that Ministers might use their financial powers to impose their will without much evidence to justify their position, or to achieve ends which are wholly political. (This, one can argue, has begun to happen with aviation investment, though there the end was a policy which was public, albeit ill-quantified and, it would seem from its eventual results, ill-judged.) A more serious threat is that we should drift in what many observers might think is the American direction, where politicization of the relationship is very great. While one can imagine this happening to some extent with Ministers as Parliament's agents, it is patently more likely to occur if Parliament were to develop a more active role after the model of Congress; if one were to imagine the Select Committee on Nationalized Industries administering the Parlia-

---

[1] One of the reasons why the Boards deeply resented Prices and Incomes legislation was because it gave the Prices and Income Board powers to make inquiries as a prerequisite to sanctioning a price or wage increase. The Boards have a reasonable basis for their resentment because of the superficiality in many cases of inquiries undertaken rapidly by people who had no, or next to no, knowledge of the industry. Thus, although in some cases the instincts of the PIB inquirers were sound (though often theoretical), the arbitrariness and conventional wisdom of what they said tended to discredit them in the eyes of the Board. Besides, in practice delay of authority to raise prices or wages has not been used to make Boards *follow* these recommendations. It does not follow from this that it was most efficient to abolish the Board. It might have been more useful to have given it the resources to be better, or, as I shall agree later, to transfer its public sector functions to departments, so as to build up a more specialized knowledge.

mentary function of controlling public money, as congressional appropriations committees tend to administer the same function – it has the same historic and constitutional root – for Congress.[1]

There is no question but that the congressional appropriations committees cut, or even increase, funds against the will of the Government agencies seeking funds. Their cuts can be drastic, and quite frequently they will cut the appropriation for some particular part of a Government department or agency's activity. On the other hand, they can become strongly critical if they feel that an agency is not spending enough money on some activity which a member of the committee feels important, even to the extent of increasing the appropriation to be spent. All the departments and agencies requesting money will have to present papers, and their heads will be examined as witnesses. The relationship is complicated by the existence of the appropriations committees of the two Houses and of the Bureau of the Budget. It is not uncommon for the Senate committee to take a different view from that of the House of Representatives, thus complicating the game an agency must play in presenting its case to each; and in the end, where there is controversy between the two, the matter is settled by a conference between the two committees. The Bureau of the Budget is another force whose duty is to give its own (and the President's) opinion on the appropriations asked for by each department and agency. The convention is that, when the President has overruled a department or agency (usually on the advice of the Bureau), it should not reveal to the appropriations committee what it first asked for. But it is quite clear that the appropriations committees frequently get to know what a department or agency's original requests were, and often make use of this knowledge. The inquiries of the committees are not confined to the formal proceedings of the committees. The committee members are likely to complain strongly if they do not feel they have been visited enough privately by the spokesmen of the agencies, and even on occasion seem to cut appropriations for this reason. On the other hand, they make no secret in the committee that they have been visited beforehand, and some of the more successful department.and agency heads are those who are most assiduous and skilful in talking to the committee members. Thus, a large part of a senior civil servant's time tends to be spent 'on the Hill' with

[1] In what follows I have drawn especially on Aaron Wildavsky's much remarked *The Politics of the Budgetary Process* (1964), which is a clear and remarkably compelling account of the principles on which the appropriations committees actually work. As we shall see in *Chapter 15*, even those who oppose the tendency in general do not question his account of how the committees work.

Senators and Congressmen. Since British civil servants do not talk to MPs in this way,[1] this tends to call for and get very different qualities in the civil service.

While, as one would expect, appropriations committee members develop shrewdness and their questionings are often impressive, it is hard to believe that in the end the process is not bad for financial discipline and for sustained policy. Whereas, in Britain, one can broadly describe the objectives of Boards as commercial and (as we argued in *Chapter 4*) we are beginning to describe the objectives of some other agencies (and parts of departments) as pursuing certain social aims, which are starting to have some more definite content, the policies and the objectives of American agencies and departments are much more at the mercy of the particular interests of the appropriation committee members. (If member A wants X, then he is likely to let member B impose Y on agency P, to get his own way on X.) While it would be quite wrong to think that members always think of their own interest, they make no secret in the questioning that they are interested in what any agency is going to do for their own constituency. There is often no pretence that the interest of the nation ought to come first. As a result, sensible agencies may tend to appease powerful appropriations committee members. Aside from their geographical interests, appropriations committee members are likely to identify with particular interests – it may be in water control, or pollution or the interests of a particular industry. More often than not the identification will be innocent, but it will not always be. Again, this is not unlikely to affect the appropriations that an agency gets. There is a host of professional lobbyists in Washington anxious to put their views to Congressmen, a profession which simply does not exist in the same way in Whitehall or Westminster. (There are lobbying groups, putting their points of view, but neither the scale of their operations or their power compares. The number of really succcessful pressure group operations of this kind which have been successful in British politics, seems to be very few.) While it would be wrong to exaggerate the haphazardness of this process or the narrowness of appropriations committee members – many indeed have a strong view of the national interest on many issues – the results are likely to be less rational and, one may venture, more wasteful, if only because the outcomes are very much

---

[1] Ministers, of course, talk to MPs frequently in the evenings at the House, but because there are no appropriations committees and because Ministers can reasonably plead that they cannot be expected to know detailed expenditures of their departments (let alone of outside agencies like the Boards), this is no parallel with the American situation.

the outcomes of committee compromise. One really has to believe – as some do – that the result of the process is one in which every interest has just the influence on the outcome which is appropriate to the weight of that interest. But this implies a notion of what weight is due to a given interest, which is never made clear and may be circular. Neither is it clear in what sense this can be called a 'democratic' procedure. The difficulty about a world of pressure groups is that one either has to believe in the rational outcome of a largely non-rational process in terms of some social welfare function – and this is a mystical belief – or one finds that the outcome of any particular decision seems largely unpredictable; or a belief grows up that certain groups (the wealthy, private corporations) always win, or at least never lose – which is very damaging to the credibility of Government. In some ways it is anti-democratic, if one tends to mean by democratic a decision-making system in which each man counts for one, that is, has the same weight.[1] The system would also seem to suffer from a certain opaqueness in spite of its openness in many respects. Unless one is an insider, and even then one may not be enough of an insider in certain cases, one may never know why an appropriations committee made a recommendation it did. The basis of a decision can be as secret in Britain; but more recently, where decisions are beginning to be explained in White Papers, one can see the principles on which they are based and obtain some idea of the rationality which dictated the conclusion (even if one may disagree with those principles and the logic of the decision). While with the Boards one has some idea of what would constitute satisfactory performance, even though the wherewithal does not always exist to measure or enforce it, this is far less clear with American agencies – even with those which could quite easily be regarded as purely commercial bodies. While conscious of the shortcomings of our own system, it is not clear to me how it would be any advance to move in the American direction.

This could happen in Britain if the House of Commons Committee were to acquire and use American-style powers of financial control. But it could also happen rather differently if Ministers instead were to become more responsive to pressure groups, or, even without that, were to use their statutory powers more decisively to get their own

---

1 The old Benthamite slogan has not an unambiguous meaning; but it can be given a number of meanings which do reflect various notions of democracy within the context of cost-benefit analysis. One can weight the interests of individuals in coming to a decision to cancel differences in their income, wealth and other characteristics if desired. Nothing similar seems to be the tendency of the interaction of pressure groups.

way without much regard for consistency or the autonomy of Boards. Some of the worst examples of such decision-making seem to occur when decisions are a compromise between different regional interests – certainly this would seem to be true in the United States. The special position of Scotland and Wales in Cabinet in recent years, is an example of this tendency. Perhaps it is a corrective to a situation in which their interests were under-represented; but the result has been that in sharing public expenditure the interests of the two carry more weight, not because of any reasoned conscious decision to redistribute income in their favour by giving an agreed extra weight to a Scottish or Welsh interest than to an English one, but because of their presence in Cabinet and the votes and voices they have there. It is arguable that they have in many sectors got so many more public resources than the criteria used elsewhere would imply, that, at the margin, they are earning substantially lower (social and financial) returns. It is no one's business to calculate how much potential growth in GNP is being sacrificed for a smaller growth in Scottish and Welsh GNP. Some forms of regional government that have been proposed would mean increasing the likelihood of such inefficiencies and inequities. Another possibility of increasing politicization would be to make it not unusual for a Minister to get rid of existing Board appointees and to make his own appointments. Presumably people would have to be paid much more or otherwise honoured, because of the insecurity, but that is not a fundamental point. Again, it would seem to me that security of tenure is taken to rather extreme lengths in Britain; yet for a Minister who may have no special knowledge of the industry and may not have received any carefully thought advice on the subject, to dismiss someone capriciously could be extremely unfair. Better in some respects is the spoils system, where someone dismissed can at least say it happened because he was a democrat or a republican and not because a Minister rightly or wrongly thought him inadequate. Yet in some cases one may imagine that, either from a general policy point of view or to impose a new financial discipline, a clean sweep of a Board and its replacement by newcomers might have a very great effect. But if this were to be common, there are great dangers that it would meet with diminishing returns. There is first the difficulty that Ministers may have in choosing people who are better, either because they are not good at it or because the field of choice is small. There is some tendency to reward political friends and some tendency to appoint people with public rather than managerial qualities. But what is most dangerous is what happens to management just below the level of political appointment. Since life with a succession

I

of frequent changes of head may become intolerable, there is a tendency to capitalize on the fact that someone who stays long has little room to manoeuvre and make a lasting impression, however able. Thus the day-to-day management is likely to fall into the hands of managers who do not mind – perhaps even because they have in some cases a masochistic streak – these particular conditions and are likely to develop an imperviousness to political pressure. While again it would be wrong to think that security of tenure has to be as great as it is now, there are very great dangers in believing that a quick solution to the problems of ministerial influence is to make the top appointments political. While comparisons are difficult, it is not at all obvious that the efficiency of American agencies run on that basis is any greater than that of British public corporations, and may even be less. Although there are cases where one man, or several, put in at the top of an organization, has been able to transform it, they seem rare; and it is far from clear that the politicization of appointments policy would make such success more common.

Politicization, therefore, may be described as taking certain trends towards Ministers' developing a more arbitrary attitude towards their formal powers – trends which have not yet gone far in this direction – and developing them as the main method of Ministers' getting their own way. The powers one has become then a kind of money with which one buys other things that one wants and has no direct powers over. If Ministers come to believe there is too great a divorce between the myth and the reality of their powers towards Boards and any new quasi-Boards developed or hived off to serve purposes which are primarily non-commercial, and unless there is systematic thinking on reinterpreting the existing relationship, this is the most likely way for the relationship to drift because it can come about gradually and, by its nature, in spite of, rather than through, the public discussion of policy in White Papers and legislation. But while any particular Minister indulging in an arbitrary sacking or doing a deal to get his own way with a Board, may feel that he, and even the public interest, has gained, American experience suggests that, in the long run, Boards and bodies gain a new kind of practical independence through a resistance to the virus. They develop skills and opaqueness to combat the skills of the politicians, and because, as Boards, their political lives are longer – however quick the changeover at the top – they have a more than even chance of winning most of the battles.

At best, it may help strong, resourceful Ministers with a gift for diplomacy and intrigue to get their own way on specific, spasmodic issues. It is not likely to increase parliamentary control, as it has been defined traditionally; rather the reverse. Such a development will make sustained financial control and sustained social policy more difficult to effect, because it gets its way by paralysing and side-stepping the formal mechanisms of control. To achieve financial control and sustained social policy, 'the oversight of efficiency and of public policy and the national interest' can be better achieved by the far harder task of improving the imperfect division and specification of powers, and by control mechanisms, latent in what, with liberty, one may call the unwritten constitution that has evolved to give flesh to the statutory bones.

Chapter 12

SUBORDINATION

The fact, as was mentioned at the end of *Chapter 3*, that the departmentalization of nationalized industries is against the trend – the Post Office just having gone in the other direction – is not in itself decisive. Some of the reasons for the trend are powerful without being fundamental.

One is that Boards cannot be run efficiently by people paid at civil service rates. If a Board is part of a department then its equivalents to a Chairman and Board Members will be civil servants. If the departmentalized industry is large, then paying its head the salary of a Deputy, or Second Permanent, Secretary will mean that the salaries down the long hierarchy will have to be squeezed close together, so giving people little incentive to take on the responsibilities of promotion. (This step-pyramid effect is one of the powerful arguments for paying the head of a large company more than the head of a smaller one.) Also, it will be all the harder to attract someone from outside into a managerial position.

This is not a fundamental argument. Why are civil service salaries lower than those in industry? This is partly because Ministers are reluctant to approve increases (but they are also reluctant to approve increases in the salaries of Board Members). However, civil service salary prospects do not cause a large exodus of civil servants; neither do they deter the movement of very capable people in.[1] Some civil servants would argue that they stay either because they are locked in by pension agreements or because the skills they have developed are not marketable. While there is truth in both these, they do not explain why the civil service still recruits so many able

[1] Like everyone else, civil servants often complain that the giants of today do not compare with the giants of a generation ago. Yet one wonders if there are not as many capable people as there ever were. Firstly, the civil service is so much larger than it used to be that even the same number of outstanding people is a smaller proportion. Secondly, much of the time they simply work so much harder than their predecessors did that they cannot keep up the same quality of thought on all issues. Thirdly, what they are asked to do is much more varied than it used to be.

people. The truth surely lies with what Alfred Marshall called the non-pecuniary advantages of employment. Their security of tenure is remarkable, the likelihood of their being asked to move house is small – unless they go, as a few do for a spell, for a rather enjoyable turn of duty in Washington or somewhere else abroad. They will use their minds. Indeed, one can go further and say that a high proportion of their work is intellectual, which appeals to them – otherwise they would not have joined. Also, theirs is still one of the few surviving literary cultures outside the universities. In spite of all the ups and downs there is also the appeal of public service. They will, for example, not wonder why they are spending all their powers for the glorification of soap as some businessmen seem to; and even when they descend, as they often do, to detail, there is usually the compensation that it raises some question of equity or justice. The very peculiarities of the promotion system – which depend on length of service as well as merit – mean there is less jealousy and office politics – at least as far as it affects the permanent officials – and more friendship than is common in many corporations. It is not my present purpose to attack or defend this – though one can in the circumstances defend much of it – but just to suggest that there are compensations in a civil servant's life.[1]

There is a premiss in Britain – which has been abandoned, and rightly, in the United States – that someone higher in the hierarchy should be paid more than someone further down. Thus managers reinforce their conviction that management is the supreme human quality. While one would not expect too many departures from the rule, there does not seem any essential reason why the managers in an industry which was part of a department should not be paid more than some of the civil servants to whom they report – especially if they do not have security of tenure, have less predictable promotion prospects and have a less intellectual life. What one is saying is that there may be a case for an Industrial Civil Service whose salary pension and promotion prospects are much more like those of private and public industry.[2] If there were one, it would probably help if

[1] Nor do I mean to argue whether or not the value of these compensations are declining. As long as the Civil Service Department delays reforming the pension arrangements and so locks senior people in, there is not a fair test of the non-pecuniary attractiveness of the service. But when the Civil Service Department does this – even though it may have to raise senior salaries – one would be surprised if the net non-pecuniary advantages of a civil service life were not thought positive by those who chose it.

[2] One reason why nationalized industry salaries are lower than in private industry is that the chances of staying until retiring age without demotion are almost as great as in the civil service. There this is much harder to defend;

suitable administrative civil servants were able to switch into it.

Another argument is that the Board relationship protects the industry from detailed parliamentary scrutiny as it would not be protected if it were part of a department.[1] It is argued that if Boards were departmentalized, MPs would ask questions about management minutiae: why the coal from a pit was inferior, why a particular train was late, and so on.

Board status also protects the Boards from the Select Committee on Estimates and the Public Accounts Committee. If not, these Committees could take nationalized industry expenditure programmes to task. The Select Committee could require Permanent Secretaries as Accounting Officers to appear before it and explain why certain expenditures were incurred. This would also be a detailed interference in management.

Are these conventions invincible? Nationalized industries are not the only area where Parliament has a self-denying ordinance on the scope of Parliamentary Questions. It would not seem impossible that the Speaker could rule that the same immunity that has been given to Boards could be given to industries organized as distinct divisions of a department. The present rules are not based on a hard and fast principle since, in spite of their (qualified) autonomy, MPs are allowed to ask Ministers certain questions about Boards. It cannot be beyond the wit of Parliament to devise something similar for specified divisions of departments. (Something of the same kind is almost certainly required anyway if there are to be more semi-autonomous, non-commercial Government agencies.)[2]

The argument on the scope of the Committees seems circular. Presumably the reason for which the Boards are exempted from this control is that their own financial discipline is thought sufficient. If not, then some form of financial supervision by the Select Committee is a possible remedy. (See *Chapter 14*.) If it is, Parliament could develop a self-restraint here too. One supposes that this kind of convention, or change in convention, may be harder to establish

---

and there is of course nothing that Ministers can do about this, even were they so inclined. While so-called top-hat pension arrangements in private industry are partly a method of evading tax, while they exist they are probably the most important reason for ambitious people's preferring the private sector.

[1] For discussion of this see A. H. Hanson, *Parliament and Public Ownership*, Cassell, 1961, ch. 4; and D. N. Chester and N. Bowring, *Questions in Parliament*, Clarendon Press, 1962, especially pp. 301–5.

[2] Since this was first written in the summer of 1970, there seem to be murmurings that something of the kind may happen.

than the passing of a statute, but if it were thought worthwhile then surely it could be done.

Those who recommended making the Post Office into a public corporation were probably persuaded that it was easier to secure this way higher salaries and commercial employment policies, as well as less parliamentary intervention, than through trying to establish (i) a new model Industrial Civil Service much more like nationalized or private industry in its pay and conditions; or (ii) a new basis of parliamentary oversight. They were almost certainly right. There is also the disadvantage of subordination itself, that is, that the loss of practical independence, in this form, would deter the heads of the industries and outside candidates for posts. While real, this is in essentials no different from the same situation which occurs after a takeover when the subordinate management of the company taken over finds itself less powerful. The question then becomes whether there are any advantages of subordinating these industries to Ministers, which would outweigh these and other practical disadvantages.

One cannot deny there is a possibility that an able Minister is more likely to get his own way with an industry if it is part of his department. *For* him is that the industry is bound to feel an obligation because he is their chief. He can call more freely on their time and can expect more information and obedience from them. *Against* him is that the more interest he takes in trying to affect decision-making in the industry, the more congestion there is likely to be on his desk. It can hardly be emphasized enough that being a Minister is already a full-time job. This is not just a matter of delegation. Much is now delegated; but if he takes on too much responsibility he will find it hard to take all the decisions he will want to make because he will not have the time to do a thorough job. Therefore he is likely once again to find himself relying on the advice of those below him. There is one reason why Ministers whose departments in effect now have within them large divisions which, but for chance, almost might have been public corporations, can find that they have only little more personal control over what happens in them than they do over the nationalized industries for which they are responsible. A theoretical sovereignty does not entail sovereign power. At the very least, a Minister who had a very different idea of what was important would have to introduce more thoroughgoing reforms in the method of doing business than he usually has the time, inclination and experience for. But these would not be the only costs. A large part of a Minister's time now is spent in dealing with events as they occur, and comparatively little in innovation. Running an industry as well will reduce the time left over for innovation. Herbert Morrison put it that a Minister would not have time to nationalize more industries – presumably as a result of his experiencing the effort needed to nationalize one. But even if a Minister does not want to do that, the chances are that there are things he does want to do. Another cost to him may be the sheer responsibility of so much money, which possibly could weigh many Ministers down into timidity or irresponsibility; and if one were to take another route and multiply the number of Ministers – e.g. one Board one Minister – that number would also have profound consequences for the structure of Government.

What is needed within Government is the improvement of techniques of control to make more effective control possible at the same time as delegating authority. It may not be fundamental, but it is hard to see how the Minister's position would be much improved – or his influence on industrial policy be more powerful in a systematic way – unless and until these kinds of problems of control have been solved enough to increase the Minister's effective span of command.

I will try to argue that there are ways in which Ministers may help impose a more effective financial discipline, and may use Boards more efficiently for non-commercial ends – without subordinating them. The question is then whether there is some other sense in which it would be an advantage to Ministers to have overall command of the Board's policy, subject, presumably, to whatever powers and duties have been laid down in statute. The traditional view is that they would mostly be illegitimate.

First, a Minister would expect to find it easier to interfere in particular issues – stop those closures, locate those new facilities in his constituency – to which we have referred so often. Second, he would expect to find it easier to make up those matters put to him by his constituents and friends – the bad timetable to X, the poor quality of coal on sale at Y. Some Ministers might go so far as to interfere in this kind of detail.

A third, less likely result might be that a Minister might feel better able to mould the ethic of the industry, to define the qualities of public service he expects from it. But this is less likely to be effective. This effect usually takes longer to permeate than he will have. If too many Ministers try to impart rather different ethics, the chances are that the industry will develop the sceptical resignation of the Hindu rolled over by waves of proselytizing religions.

A fourth and more likely result would be that the Minister might try to appoint people further down the organization. Even in Civil

Service terms this would be a departure, since the conventions are that Ministers cannot do this now. But if a Minister were to do this, he had better expect it to consume much of his time if he is to do it well. Of course, if his aim was to place friends and others he feels he owes a favour to, in principle he could be less thoughtful.

A fifth result is that he might feel that he is able to make better top management decisions than the Board. It is possible, but the danger that he thinks he can do better than he can is great; and the greatest danger would be the variability of direction and decision-making which would erode responsibility and about which we have had much to say in the last chapter. One Minister might do exceptionally well, but what really matters is how the industry performs over a long time; and there seems a reasonable chance that if departmentalization did actually increase the opportunities for the Minister to make decisions, the long-run performance could be worse.

At least it seems worth thinking of this solution as one which might solve some problems for a Minister but would create many problems in its turn which would have to be solved; so much so that it is difficult to predict what interest would be served by its adoption.

Chapter 13

COMPETITION

How else can Government effect greater financial discipline with the public corporations? Suppose one accepts for the moment that departments cannot, or should not, exercise more effective financial control than now. What other means can be used to sharpen the financial disciplines of the Boards?

If the dividing line is not to be abolished in practice by greater politicization, or in law by subordination, there is another strategy which might lighten the work of Ministers and Parliament in their 'oversight of efficiency' of Boards – whether or not the Boards in question were important for serving social ends as well. Practical independence would not cause as much concern if competition were strong enough to make and keep the Boards efficient. The principal active relation between Board and Minister could then be political and social. Government would allow its financial powers and interventions to atrophy, and could resume the trustee-client relationship. Parliament would rely on that competition to achieve the ends of public accountability (and even if competition by itself can be shown not to perform that trick, it can certainly help out financial control by Ministers by providing another financial discipline).

While competition and denationalization are often confused in the popular mind, there is no necessary connection. By itself denationalization creates no more competition than was there before. Neither does nationalization *per se* reduce competition. (The relevance of denationalization to this debate is distinct and is to be discussed in the next chapter.)

Once a monopoly has been created it must rely largely on its own internal financial discipline to be efficient. Whether nationalized or not it does not have the stimulus of knowing that it could be undercut by its competitors and driven out of business. A great conglomerate like Unilever or ICI is possibly under less effective competition than the Coal Board or the Gas Council in the sense that, even though they may be undercut by a competitor in one line, they are too big and diversified to fear being driven into the red.

138

They cannot be inefficient in all lines or they would collapse; but they may use their profits earned in some parts of the business to cross-subsidize unprofitable lines which they do not always have the courage to reform or cut out. The big private firm can be inefficient and get away with it, just as the large public firm can; and there are nationalized industries which experience close competition and are unable to make monopoly profits. The nationalized road freight companies in the National Freight Corporation probably get, and give, as much competition as they would if they were denationalized.[1]

Neither can one restore competition simply by breaking up the public enterprises into bits inside or outside public ownership. It is also often argued as if denationalization were a necessary step towards breaking public enterprises up into smaller pieces which would be more competitive. This can be done without denationalization. It can also in some circumstances be done by creating separately accountable subsidiaries, that is, without 'hiving off'. Neither does disaggregation or decentralization necessarily increase competition. It has proved difficult to regionalize the accounts of railways or of other industries interconnected by a grid, like electricity, gas or telecommunications. If one regionalizes them there is not much competition. The old main-line railways competed on only few routes. The old local public gas and electricity utilities did not compete because their clientele was localized. If one were to allow many of these local monopolies to interpenetrate, there might still not be much competition because of the (capital) costs to the consumer or the utilities of changing a supplier. (Just as today if oil prices go up faster than gas prices, the difference has to be considerable and likely to continue before it pays a household or firm to change its method of heating or source of power.) Besides, the industries nationalized – except for some of the *curiosa* – tend to be those where there are substantial economies of scale in monopoly. (Chopping up BOAC into bits and making the parts compete over the same

[1] It is interesting to contrast the experience of freightliners within British Railways and the National Freight Corporation. The latter took over the Railways' small and sundries, known to be a major loss-maker, and also the freightliners, thought to be profitable, when they were sold by the Railways. The NFC found, however, they too were making losses to an extent which was not known because of the inadequacies in those days of the Railways' financial control system. It is not surprising that the NFC predicts that it will take longer now to eliminate the losses. But the rest of the NFC – mostly road haulage – has not got the 'fat' to cross-subsidize the newcomers since they are in strong competition. Their losses were hidden in the Railways for years, even to the Railways; the NFC cannot do this and a policy towards them is now required.

route would create corporations which would find it hard to inter-
nalize the economies of scale necessary to enable them to compete
with foreign airlines while at the same time not adding much to the
strength of the competition they already get from foreigners.)

The sharp distinction between a 'competitive' industry and a
monopoly has long been recognized to have been a false dichotomy
to be found – usually not without qualification – in old economics
textbooks, where a monopoly was often determined as an industry
under single ownership. From this it followed that if coal, steel or
railways were nationalized, they became monopolies. It is now nearly
forty years since Joan Robinson and Edward Chamberlain laid the
theoretical basis of a more profound and realistic analysis.[1] A
casualty was the replacement of the sharp distinction between
monopoly and competition by a continuum. Most firms are in a
position where they would lose some but not all customers if they
raised their price, or if competitors undercut them. There are many
reasons: brand loyalty, advertising, product differentiation, tech-
nichal change, patent rights, superior management and, in a few
cases, possession of scarce factors of production like a mineral or
valuable, because accessible, land. The extent to which a firm would
be hurt by a competitor's undercutting or introducing a new product
is a rough measure of a firm's monopoly power. Because more and
more firms are producing a range of products, often very different,
the damage that a competitor could do in one line is unlikely to kill
the firm. Profits on other lines will help to maintain its dividends
while it licks its wounds. On the other hand, only the largest firms –
and perhaps not even they – can rest on their laurels for too long.
Competition may gradually erode their profitability.

Another casualty was the old idea of an industry as a significant
term in economic analysis. A firm in steel might be more in competition with a substitute plastics product than with other steel firms.
The word 'industry' was only kept on in economic usage, and more
generally, as a convenient word to describe firms that belonged to
the same trade association or otherwise had a family resemblance
because they worked in the same material or used similar processes.
The basis of the resemblance is more likely to be technological
than market-based.

The first relevance of this to the nationalized industries is that
one cannot assume that, because so many of them – but not all – have
monopolized an industry in the old sense, it does not mean they have

[1] J. Robinson, *The Economics of Imperfect Competition*, Macmillan, 1933;
E. H. Chamberlain, *The Theory of Monopolistic Competition*, Harvard UP,
1933.

140

no competition. Electricity, gas and coal compete with each other and with privately owned oil, as well as with products that are not fuels. (A rise in the price of fuel which is likely to last will stimulate firms to find less fuel-intensive methods of production.) The airlines compete with foreign airlines and with independents, as well as with other forms of travel. And so on. All the nationalized industries – except the Post Office – have some competition (which is what one would expect. There are no monopolies without competition. If nothing else, they compete for the same purchasing power).

The second relevance is that one cannot assume that, because in the old-fashioned sense many Boards are monopolies, they experience less competition than private firms do.

A third relevance is that there are no simple statements that one can make about the benefits of more competition. A Board in deficit could be going under because of competition (and despite reasonable efficiency, given its technology) or because it had monopoly power which it had allowed to sap its efficiency. A Board in surplus could be so because competition had made it thrive or because it had enough monopoly power to be inefficient and still make a profit. Unfortunately it is often easier to start at the other end; and decide that because a firm is inefficient it might benefit from more com‧ petition, provided it is not at the expense of economies of scale. And this means finding out first whether a firm is inefficient, some-thing that one cannot tell just from the state of its profit-and-loss account. It also means that deciding whether a Board would benefit from more competition requires calculation of the costs and benefits of introducing competition. There can be no general presumption that it would be good to introduce 'the competitiveness of private industry', whatever that might mean. One must be more pragmatic. Yet having said that, one can illustrate the potential and prerequisites of more competition by example.

(1) There is competition between Boards – sometimes not as a result of conscious policy. The effect of the new, fast trains on the west-coast main line from London to Lancashire has been almost to destroy BEA air services over the same route. The two Boards are sponsored by different Ministers, and at the time the decision was taken to electrify in the late fifties there was little collusion and consultation between them. If there had been co-ordination, one would have feared what is sometimes called an 'administrative' or compromise solution. Even if the return on modernizing this service had promised to be overwhelming, simple pressure from BEA in defence of its profits might have been succcessful in delaying or

substantially modifying the scheme. But, as we know, there was far from an overwhelming financial case. If BEA had objected that the railways had not begun to prove their case that the investment would be profitable, they could have complained reasonably that the railways were proposing to undercut their economic service by one which was unprofitable and would have to be subsidized from other railway profits or from the Exchequer through deficit grants. Even now we do not know if the modernization of the west-coast main line was profitable.[1]

But British Railways could have complained equally that BEA had a number of concealed subsidies and cross-subsidies. While the railways met all the costs of their termini and other stations, both national and local airports have been substantially subsidized. Many of the aircraft flows have also been subsidized for a variety of reasons. Also, for reasons which are not quite clear, there has been a tendency for BEA to cross-subsidize its domestic services from other services. One cannot argue that this is because the competition is between nationalized industries, since there are also private air operators whose use of airports and whose aircraft are also subsidized. One might also want to bring in externalities or social costs. Fast trains on the railways cause limited pollution and noise; they also have a low accident rate. Aircraft cause more pollution and much more noise, as well as tending to a higher accident rate per journey.

The fact that there is competition does not mean there is an efficient allocation of resources between the two. Far from it. Competition (or co-ordination) would only be fair and efficient if (i) there was proper financial control on both sides; (ii) neither side was subsidized or both were subsidized on an equivalent footing (even the definition of what would be meant by comparable subsidy policy towards rail and air is full of difficulty); and (iii) due notice was taken of any difference in social costs and benefits.[2]

The conclusion would seem to be that competition (and co-

---

[1] For a critique of the Modernization Plan see C. D. Foster *The Transport Problem* (Blackie, 1963). The Select Committee were surprised to find that the railways could not produce the information to demonstrate whether this investment was profitable (600); and they imagined that it would have been necessary for internal management purposes. We can be fairly sure that the Modernization Plan as a whole was unprofitable.

[2] All this needs careful watching. It comes to be decided how far inter-city traffic flows are to be met by different transport forms: British Railways' advanced passenger trains, hover trains, conventional aircraft, or vertical take-off aircraft. At present, the rules that govern investment in each are so diverse as to make simple competition between them an absurdity.

ordination for that matter) is only fair if proper financial appraisal has been done on *both* sides (or, if it is a social benefit investment, when it promises a positive social net benefit return. The principle is the same).

(2) The same problem exists more generally where Boards compete with private industry. A common example of the difficulty occurs in debate on any nationalization statute, to which some of the strongest objections pressed will be where it is feared that a Board may compete unfairly with private firms. As we have seen, it often amazes foreigners that our Boards have not been encouraged to diversify and compete more widely. A cynical explanation would be that private industry would rather not have more competition. A defensible interpretation is that it fears unfair competition. When the Chamber of Shipping lobbied in order that the 1967 Transport Bill should have some safeguards against (unfair) competition between coastal shipping and the railways, their case was the chance that the railways, through ineptness and simply not knowing their own interest, would run trains below cost and so undercut coastal shipping unfairly. The same fear explains the hostility to giving Boards powers to manufacture for sale (for example, by using excess capacity in their workshops). While one supposes that private industry does not welcome the powers given to British Railways and London Transport to operate petrol and service stations in their station parking lots, the defensible objection must be that the Boards will not know enough to avoid running these at a loss. (One can sometimes retort fairly – as Boards and socialists do – that private giants can be similarly guilty of unfair, that is unprofitable, competition.)[1]

(3) Again, what is at fault is the absence of enough financial control to make competition efficient, or perhaps the fact that what there is, is not trusted. In some cases, sound investment appraisal may be sufficient to establish whether competition would be fair. If the question is whether the Channel Tunnel will compete unfairly

[1] It is interesting to reflect on another example: the authorizing of Cunard Eagle to compete against BOAC in 1961 on the North American route. Many complained at the time that there was a theft of profitable routes from BOAC, as they have also done as the proposal has come up again in 1971 with the merger of Caledonian Airways and BUA and their establishment as a Third Force airline to compete with BOAC and BEA. This does not seem a good objection, since competition and efficiency imply that if someone else comes along and undercuts an existing product, it is efficient if he got the business. More to the point is the fairness of the competition. Because of the peculiar basis on which Cunard Eagle was then financed there was some doubt about it. Also relevant is the trade-off between economies of scale and the stimulus of competition. Relevant again is that one would have thought there was already enough competition from foreign airlines for extra competition to be unnecessary.

143

with air and shipping services, it should be possible to settle this beyond reasonable doubt by looking at the return on the investment and the analysis on which it is based.

(4) But there are other cases where investment appraisal is not likely to be sufficient (where marginal costs are likely to be a high proportion of total costs). What needs to be known about BR or LT service stations, or BR Hotels, is whether they are profitable enterprises (which may mean knowing the terms on which they acquire land and other assets from their parents). Both public and private interest should be served if such ancillary activities are set up as separate companies or divisions with correctly valued assets and their own (published) accounts.[1] In almost every Board there are many activities which could be given a corporate identity in the interests of public accountability and fair competition.[2]

Ex hypothesi, the suggestions above, and others one could make on the same lines, would only segregate those activities which were easily separable as distinct businesses with meaningfully distinct costs and revenues. But to try to set up separate divisions with accounts may be useless where important costs and revenues cut across divisional boundaries. Even if we go no further, there will still be large areas of most Boards which have been put under no more (fair) competition than before, though one can reasonably argue that the separating out from their accounts of all activities which could sensibly be separated out, must have made the accounts of the residual activities more meaningful than they were.

(5) One can go further by trying to encourage within and between Boards a form of competition which has been growing in the last twenty or so years because the older notion of competition, as existing between a large number of firms selling nearly identical products, has been dying. Kenneth Galbraith has called this *countervailing power:*

> 'In the competitive model, the economy of many sellers each with a small share of the total market – the restraint on the private exercise of economic power was provided by other firms on the same side of the market . . . with the widespread dis-

---

1 Many Boards have divisions organized as companies under the Companies Acts, which file accounts at Bush House; but these are probably less full than they should be and are not treated as relevant information – indeed scarcely, if at all, looked at – by sponsoring departments.

2 I would claim that the 1968 Transport Act and the management inquiries under the direction of Mr John Morris and the late Stephen Swingler, reported in the White Papers, made a move in this direction; but there is further to go. The old THC, and new NFC, company structure is a useful precedent here.

appearance of competition in its classical form and its replacement by the small group of firms if not in overt, at least in conventional tacit collusion, it was easy to suppose that since competition had disappeared, all effective restraint on private power had disappeared . . . In fact, new restraints on private power did appear to replace competition. They were nurtured by the same process of concentration which impaired or destroyed competition. But they appeared not on the same side of the market, but on the opposite side, not with competitors but with customers or suppliers . . . there is an inducement to those firms from whom (a seller) buys or those to whom he sells to develop the power with which they can defend themselves against exploitation.'[1]

The same notion of checks and balances between buyers and sellers can be encouraged within the public sector. Presumably, some idea of this kind was behind the division of the electricity industry into an Electricity Council, which buys and distributes power, and a Central Electricity Generating Board, which makes it; the Gas Council and area gas boards are on a similar basis. One supposes that if the CEGB in a moment of madness was to try to increase its prices substantially, the Electricity Council would try to exercise some countervailing power by protesting on behalf of itself and the consumer. But this is essentially a weak form of countervailing power because there is no competition in it. One has a single seller faced by a single buyer – the area electricity boards have area monopolies. Countervailing power would be far stronger if there were two Electricity Generating Boards, or perhaps three, from which area boards could buy wholesale to retail to the consumer. Then there would be some possibility of a retailing board's switching its purchases from one Board to another – at least at the margin – if the prices of one went up or its service went down. (If there were only one seller and many buyers, or vice versa, the power of the one would be too strong.)

It is important, however, to realize that what we would have, if this developed, would be no simple clash of market forces without oversight. There is unlikely to be enough excess capacity in the industry for even one retailing board to switch all its purchases from a given supplier. (The cost of making that possible would be very great.) In most cases it would be a more theoretical, but not necessarily less effective, competition. The retailer boards would be noting the financial performance of the different supplier Boards,

[1] J. K. Galbraith, *American Capitalism*, Houghton Mifflin, 1952, pp. 117–19.

K   145

especially their prices. But, for there to be no collusion between suppliers, Parliament would have to put this into their statutory objectives and also there would have to be somebody, possibly the Minister, with at least reserve powers to police and monitor. On the other hand, there would have to be sufficient financial discipline to make sure the competition was fair. Something of the kind might be a considerable improvement. In many ways it is more like what a large private firm does when it encourages competition *within* itself, rather than the competition of the market place (because, especially where heavy capital expenditure is involved, the private firm no more wants appreciable excess capacity as the price of 'real' competition than the nation does).

(6) In other cases it is much more difficult to break an industry down into units between which there can be meaningful competition. The railways and telecommunications are examples. Earlier, reasons were given why it was difficult to construct meaningful regional accounts because the region was not a meaningful profit centre. A variable but large proportion of the costs incurred by any one region were for other regions' traffic. Therefore, the attempt by the Conservative Government in the late fifties and early sixties to create some countervailing power and bases for comparison by decentralizing authorities to the regions, failed because it could not be paralleled by meaningful management and financial information for each region. Thus some thought has had to be given to creating competition through countervailing power on a functional basis. The most conscious effort in Government to do anything of this kind was in setting up the National Freight Corporation in the 1968 Transport Act. The Railways' freightliner company was taken away from it and put inside the NFC. The NFC was given a statutory objective 'to secure that in the provision of those services, goods are carried by rail whenever such carriage is efficient and economic'. Mr Burney's committee, already referred to on p. 22, was given the job of hammering out an interpretation of this section which would maximize the joint freightliner profits of the Railways Board and the NFC and would divide them between the two bodies. This was done. The principle in broad terms behind this, as expressed by Sir Reginald Wilson, was that the Railways Board should be the wholesaler selling trains to the NFC which would retail them to the customer. The NFC were given a statutory duty which was interpreted to mean that they should actively try to use the freightliner when it was the more profitable means of transport; and that they should develop a marketing force which would look for opportunities to send by freightliner traffic now going by road. This meant requiring

146

the NFC to develop an objectivity which would mean that they would behave without bias (while providing for the Freight Integration Council as an arbitration council if there should be any disputes on the matter).

Those who argued that this was 'snatching the fairest jewel from the Railways' crown' were missing the point. The freightliner was a new product with considerable potential; but there was some question whether it was not being overdeveloped at the expense of other rail freight to which, it was arguable, not enough attention was being given. There was also some question whether the freightliner system was not being overdeveloped at the expense of its own profitability. Besides, there were complaints from road hauliers and road unions that the prices the freightliners set must be too low to be profitable. Thus there was the cry of unfair competition and the possibility that the railways were embarking on yet another development which would have to be subsidized or abandoned. One could have tried to get the Minister and his officials to do a financial appraisal of the service – though they have no powers to do this[1] – but as it looked as if the problem could run on for many years, there seemed to be something said for giving an outside body a locus. Thus it is for the Railways' Board and the NFC to get together to monitor the freightliner service in the interests of the consumer and the taxpayer. Already there are signs that the policy is being effective (and, to make what may seem a political point, to give the freightliner back to the Railways is likely to reduce efficiency by reducing countervailing power and increasing the chance of unfair competition between freightliners and road haulage).

Of course it is always possible that an NFC in this position could abuse it by biasing its policy against a Board in the position of the Railways (even though there is the safeguard of the Freight Integration Council to arbitrate). But this possibility also exists in private business where a powerful supplier or buyer can very often make a set against a less powerful firm in its power. Such unfairness is not unknown. What one believes is possible – and it is an experiment – is that public corporation can develop sufficient concept of this new aspect of public service to be objective; so that there is a more fair and economic solution than might have been the case if the company had been left to the Railways. (The NFC has a similar responsibility in relation to parcels traffic.) If the experiment fails then overall there is likely to be less effective competition or countervailing power in the public sector because there are many areas

---

[1] Back-checks on investment seem to be rare, perhaps partly because they would appear to require the acquiescence of the Board.

where it is difficult to see how competition can be made to work otherwise.

There have been suggestions in the past for solutions to the transport problem, which involve one Corporation's owning track (rail or road and rail) and others' using it. Often this has been just one more attempt to get a subsidy from the Government. But if something of this kind is to work, then the relations between the track company and the track users will have to be analogous to those between NFC and BRB over the freightliner. Whether these countervailing divisions or companies ought always to be part of another organization is a separate question. But until financial discipline has developed within the existing Boards much further than it has, it will be more effective if it is.

Thus, in conclusion, while competition in many simple and less simple forms could be developed to improve Boards' efficiency and may even, as Hugh Gaitskell hoped, then stimulate efficiency in private firms with which they compete, there must be financial discipline as well. This is because real life can no longer come near to the model of perfect competition when competition itself is enough to keep firms at the peak of efficiency (or kill them off). Thus whatever one does in this way to promote competition, is not a substitute for better financial discipline, since better financial discipline and sometimes organizational ingenuity is needed to make competition work efficiently. Moreover, if competition is to help get an efficient allocation of resources, the rules must bear equally on the competitors. Neither must be handicapped by burdens or advantaged by subsidies which the other has not, and if social costs are important, these should be allowed for. While a careful creation may improve financial discipline, simple forms of competition will hardly ever do so. They often make matters worse.

Chapter 14

THE DISCIPLINE OF THE FINANCE MARKET

There is one form of competition which the argument of the last chapter has not covered and which is also allied to the notion of countervailing power. Boards could compete for funds with private business. If the finance market works well, they will only get funds if it feels the Boards will earn a satisfactory profit. Thus, once again, it is argued that Government and Ministers can avoid exercising financial control. That can be left to the finance market. Again two issues are often confused: creating or copying the discipline of the market, and denationalization.

A Board differs from a private firm, it is argued, firstly because it borrows from the Government while a private firm ordinarily goes to the market. Some of the effects of the difference are more substantial than others.

(1) Boards borrow at fixed interest from the Treasury.[1] The interest payable by it on new stock is governed by the market for Government stock. Because much of its stock will have been issued in the past when interest rates were lower, the average interest payable will be less than the current rate. But this is not of the first importance because the difference is supposed to be taken account of when Government sets the Boards' target rates of return.

(2) Because they borrow on the Government's credit, and not on their own, the Boards usually get money more cheaply than they otherwise would. This may not be true of the Boards which have no difficulty in meeting their interest payments, but it would be of many. Such Boards gain from not having to go to the market. What is responsible is the past failure of financial discipline. If past investment projects had been as profitable as they were held

[1] A few Boards are able to borrow on so-called equity stock from Government, but in present circumstances this is window-dressing, since all it means is that, when times are bad, the Board does not default on its interest payments but stops paying dividends, which apparently is thought to look more respectable.

up to be, the Boards' financial record would have been good and so would their potential credit rating.[1]

(3) Because Boards do not have a stock-market quotation there is not that simple way of noting how the stock market judges their profitability. But while of some value, merchant bankers and often shrewd investors make their own calculations of what a company is worth, hoping to make a profit from their better judgement; and, as we have seen, it is perfectly possible, as well as desirable, for Government to make similar analyses of the profitability of Boards. The quality of the valuation depends on the expertise available in Government, the extent to which the social and commercial interests of a Board have been disentangled, individual evaluation of assets, and on almost nothing else.

What then would one expect if Boards were required to go to the market for their funds? No difference, if they went as they did before 1957 with a Government guarantee. But if they did not go with a guarantee, they would feel, many of them, a severe increase in financial discipline, a financial discipline which could be exercised within Government but which is not, by tradition.

Since the alternative financial discipline within Government would have to be created, sending the Boards to the market might seem an easier alternative (provided of course that the Government continued to find money for social-benefit capital expenditure). But it too would have several serious disadvantages.

(1) The first problem is one of transition. The first charge on a Board's revenue, after it has met its current expenses, is the interest payable on its debt. What happens if the Board begins to go to the market? Does its past indebtedness remain a first charge? For many years, while its fixed-interest indebtedness remained high, the market would require a higher than normal yield on any common shares or debentures. A firm able to finance a high proportion of its capital needs by issuing loan stock is normally one with a blue-chip reputation. Without Government guarantee, Boards would not have this.[2]

---

1 Another possibility is that the assets were over-valued and too much compensation paid on nationalization, a danger that seems likely to recur on the creation of Rolls Royce (1971) Ltd.

2 There are dodges that the Government could resort to but they would all amount to the Government's being prepared to accept a lower expectation of a return than when the stock was issued; that is, some kind of subsidy by Government, or rather by taxpayers, to make the Boards more attractive to investors. For example, the Government might agree to convert existing stock into equity capital or to allow the new loan stock raised from the market to be the first

(2) The second danger is a generalization of the first. As many Boards would face investors not used to and deeply suspicious of them, they would be expected to pay high interest rates. This would probably compel hasty action, either to get funds more cheaply or as an actual condition of obtaining funds. The main difficulty would be with those which had bad financial records or which had not yet disentangled their social and commercial services, as well as with those which had recently done so but which had not digested the implications of the change: in all, a sizeable proportion of the Boards, especially of the larger ones. As things stand the cure would be drastic and could easily kill the patient.

There is a lesson to be learned from the Beeching era. When Beeching and his colleagues joined the Railways Board there was an infusion of stimulating management. All those I have met who worked with him remember him as a lively intellect, a first-class mind, full of ideas, and the best possible man to take one's problems to for a sympathetic hearing. One came away invigorated. Yet, even before Lord Beeching left, the regime had not been wholly a success. I believe that Beeching and his colleagues came into a situation which was far more complicated than is usually found in British industry. As has already been argued, and we will need to return to it again, the fact that the Railways are a network producing a multiplicity of products in such a way as to make it very difficult to attribute costs and revenues, made rational analysis of Railway problems very difficult. Lord Beeching entered an industry which, partly because of this, had nothing much that he and his colleagues would have recognized as a system of financial control, nor management information. The costs on which rates were based were not marginal costs and, indeed, the Railways found it difficult in many cases to know whether what they were carrying was profitable at the rate they were quoting. The new men also found an industry without much by way of marketing or market research, and with a most complicated management structure – which it still has – in which responsibility was more often given to a committee than to an executive.[1] The most able people tended to be railway operators,

---

charge on revenue. It would be even more extreme to allow the Boards to borrow from the market by hire purchase or leaseback agreements.

[1] It is perhaps worth pointing out that the single most important weakness of the Railways, and probably of other nationalized industries, is the size of its administration. It cannot be efficient for them to have so much of it; and it is probably well into the size where there are so many administrators and committees that much of their activity is getting in each other's way. Scrutiny of their accounts often gives this impression.

skilled in the complex skills of actually running trains, engineers, and people knowledgeable in how to deal with Government and parliamentary intervention.

Coming into such a mess, the first instinct of the experienced businessman is usually amputation: to cut out the parts of the business which are losing money, even if some years' work could make them profitable. Thus he is able to concentrate on the parts of the business which are profitable, and on a number of areas where there is a high probability of high pay-off on an investment in better management. It is the most sensible approach for a businessman who is interested in reconstructing a profitable business. The amputation Beeching planned was more sophisticated than the rapid thrusts of the takeover expert. There was analysis – the Beeching Plan – to find out which were the weak parts of the business which should be struck out; and Beeching made it clear that this was generally the passenger business, particularly the part running on local branch lines. Thus he developed his strategy.

One difficulty was that there were some gaps between formulating the policy and executing it. The second difficulty is not wholly unconnected and was that the analysis was, I believe, wrong in many respects. First of all there was the belief that, overall, the future for carrying passengers would not be profitable. Subsequent work suggests that this was mistaken. The market in which railways are most likely to make a killing is in the passenger market, over distances like: London to Birmingham, Manchester and Liverpool, as they already are doing; and London to Sheffield, Leeds, Leicester, Nottingham, Cardiff and Bristol, as they will do when they have faster trains on those routes. Both American and British experience suggests this is the kind of distance over which business travel is building up quickly. In the United States the railways have faded away and are not able to provide as good a service over these distances as the airlines; but in Britain they should, without much additional capital expenditure, be able to provide a better one.[1]

1 Perhaps this is the point at which to mention one of the achievements of British Railways – the research establishment at Derby, many scientists of which came over from Rolls Royce when the prospects for the aviation industry were dimming. The advanced passenger train they have designed is almost certainly one of the few inventions that happen occasionally which are revolutionary in science and have revolutionary practical consequences. Others have built fast trains – some successfully – but they require special track or very heavy track maintenance, both of which tend to price them into unprofitability. The great breakthrough of the advanced passenger train is its promised ability to have stabilizing systems which will enable it to use existing track at high speed. This will be much cheaper and, if successful, should have tremendous effects,

Secondly, by implication, they assumed that the principal future for the railways was in freight; but in fact, while the freight operations of most railways throughout the world are increasing, those of British Railways are decreasing; and this is no serious reflection on British Railways. It is simply that rail traffic tends to be competitive with road only over longer distances than are usually possible in Britain. It is arguable that though Beeching was aware of the relative disadvantage of British Railways, he was over-optimistic. It is also arguable that too much effort went into the new products – the freightliners and the company trains – while very little was done to rationalize the wagonload and sundries traffics, which were the two areas where most of the losses were being made.

Thirdly, it is arguable that while the Beeching Plan made it clear that the branch-line closures it recommended were not the most important steps needed to achieve profitability, yet the Plan almost deserved the uproar it received, because the Railways did not evaluate carefully what cost reduction was possible in these services to make as many of them as profitable as possible. As well, their concentration on closing down routes rather than cutting out surplus track and stock was probably a mistake.

What is important about this is not that the analysis was wrong – after all, one has the advantage of hindsight – but that it was superficial. One can argue that the Beeching Plan was the best that could be done at the time, given the little analysis that had been done, the little good management information there was, and the short time they had to do better analysis and build a decent management information system. But that is simply not good enough, or ought not to be. It would be if we simply did not care what kind of a railway, port or telecommunications system we had, provided the rump was profitable. It is reasonable to suppose that a businessman as able as Lord Beeching coming into, say, telecommunications or electricity generation now – both are said to be inefficient – and being put under pressure to make the business profitable, would either take his hatchet to a large part of the business or raise prices substantially. Unless he was very thoughtful and un-pressed for time he would not sit down and do what is really needed in these key areas: patiently to assemble the data, the data-

---

for example: on the distance over which it is practical to commute from London (at least on some main lines); and on the distance away to the north and west from which it is profitable to produce goods for sale in the markets of the South East and Midlands. The innovation should take some absorbing and could have almost as much relative importance in diminishing journey time within Britain as the railways first did.

processing facilities, the operations researchers, economists, financial analysts, and to establish the interchange between the planners and the managers which would really be necessary to get to the bottom of the problem.

The relevance of this to the point at issue is straightforward. The danger of putting on to the market several of the Boards which have lacked financial discipline, is amputation. The market is likely to be quick in its judgements – quicker than a Beeching – and to require more drastic action from Boards if they are to receive more investment funds. But there are many Boards which simply have not done the planning to be able to move so quickly. This is especially true because of the complexity of their operations. Amputation is likely to lead to a death which more careful planning would avoid. Plannning, to my mind, means, at least for those industries, a period in which Government exerts strong financial discipline while the Boards make every effort to analyse their problems, and plan; or, to put it another way, it is the same argument we have met before. Such drastic action is only likely to lead to an efficient result if a Board has the financial discipline and understanding of its own operations to meet it.

The argument for making Boards go to the market could therefore be circular. If Boards went to the market for part only of their funds, or went with a Government guarantee, it is difficult to see how this would increase the financial discipline on the Boards. If they were made to go for all their funds, without a Government guarantee, there is a danger that if they went to the market in disequilibrium – that is, without their commercial and social duties disentangled and without strong pre-existing financial discipline – they would be in great difficulties, which could easily end in what I have called amputation. If, on the other hand, they have their social and commercial duties clarified beforehand and already have a strong system of financial control, it is not obvious why making them go to the market will exert any additional financial discipline.

However, just deciding whether they should go to the market or not is not the only question. Nationalized industries have one advantage which private firms do not have. Even the laziest, most bureaucratic and protected of these firms must make enough profits to pay dividends to keep its stock-market quotation healthy. If it were to pay dividends out of reserves for any length of time, or not to pay them, retribution would follow. By contrast, some Boards have had a safety net in the deficit grant provision of the statutes which enable Ministers to meet Board deficits. Year after year, Boards have been bailed out at no greater cost than a difficult few hours in Parliament and a wigging from the Minister. The performance is rather like that of the father who always pays his son's gambling debts. The Chairman is likely to reassure the Minister that the end of the downturn is in sight; and he may try to shift the blame a little by claiming that a large part of his troubles has been caused either directly by Government intervention or indirectly by the Government's failing to keep the economy expanding at a rapid enough rate. In the past, and still in relation to many Boards, the Chairmen could argue that some part of their deficit was not a deficit but a vague payment for social services rendered. That the two sides were unlikely to agree how much, did not help the conversation. For one or more of these reasons one suspects there was a tendency to think these deficits less wicked than a private firm or its shareholders would think them.

This is yet another reason for moving to specific subsidies for social services; but by itself this would still leave the deficit grant. One feels that this exists because most of those concerned have felt that it had to exist. But if a private firm goes into the red to an extent it cannot meet from reserves, it does not expect an almost automatic and cumulative overdraft. The Transport Act abolished this power in relation to the Railways (but there is no good reason why it should be abolished only for them. The argument is perfectly general). The reasoning was that it would be a good discipline for a Board to find that if it did go into the red and had exhausted its reserves, it would have to cut into its depreciation provisions.

There is a sensible logic behind this. It reflects a way of thinking about companies which is commonplace in the City, yet strangely uncommon in Government. By and large, a private firm is in equilibrium if its earning power bears such a relation to the market values of its shares that the return on those shares corresponds to what the market thinks right for a company of that type and risk (and if the company's assets would not command a higher value in an alternative use). To some extent, earning power will reflect the market's evaluation of the firm's prospects also. If its earning power or prospects decline, its share values will fall; and there is a prima facie indication that investment by that company is less profitable than it was. Of course, a firm in that dilemma may even increase its capital expenditure to restore its fortunes; but if it has got into a position where it has exhausted its reserves, or for some other reason needs to borrow, its prospectus will have to be more convincing than usual.

It is useful to look at a Board in the same way to see how its capital expenditure relates to its earning power and its reserves.

155

Quite often they are out of line for long periods. One hopes that the abolition of the deficit grant will help financial discipline. It should surely be abolished for other Boards which have it; and not even be contemplated as a last resort for Boards which do not. Also, allowing Boards to borrow to meet a so-called 'temporary' deficit, should be controlled as firmly as similar lending to private industry by banks.

There are, as always, cynics who think that all this is merely window-dressing and that when it comes to a deficit any Government – Conservative or Labour – will find some way of paying it. One possibility is that the Government merely raises the social grant provision. But to do this to meet a deficit on commercial account would be a blatant misappropriation of funds, an illegality which, one assumes, would be resisted by the department's Permanent Secretary as the Accounting Officer responsible to Parliament, and, if not resisted by him, would be picked up by the Public Accounts Committee.[1]

A more likely way in which Government might try to relax the severity of this would be to increase investment appropriations automatically by the amount the Board had had to cut back on its depreciation provisions, so maintaining the Board's cash flow. (If the reserves were zero and the deficit on current account £15 million, and normal depreciation provisions £60 million, depreciation would fall to £45 million, implying that, *ceteris paribus*, investment would have to be cut back by £15 million. But if, in addition, the Board was planning to invest an extra £40 million borrowed from Government on an implicit assumption that earning power would be increased, and the Government was to increase this to £55 million, the Board could continue to invest at the same rate.) While one would be surprised if there was such a shameless manoeuvre, there is just a chance, one supposes, that officials might be under pressure to bend over backwards, as the saying goes, to

---

[1] Mr Morris's Railway Inquiry recommended that grants for unremunerative railway services should be paid on a full, and not marginal, cost basis and that therefore it should cover a contribution to overheads and depreciation provisions. Since most of the capital used on these lines has been written down in the 1968 or some earlier Act, this element was not for the most part a payment towards the capital costs of those services, but a general subsidy, quite small, to the railway system. It would be more rational if the grants were paid on a marginal cost basis, so that any capital expenditure incurred for those lines would be paid for. It would seem that the Public Accounts Committee has picked this point up; and from the point of view of financial discipline there is much to be said for their pursuing it. As they have picked up a point of this sophistication, it seems unlikely they would not pick up a simpler one as described in the text.

be charitable. (Yet on the other hand, if the Board at such a time were to come forward with an increased investment programme which really promised well, after examination, the Government could make the funds available, as indeed could a merchant banker to an ailing firm in similar circumstances.) Even if a nationalized industry was required to go to the market without Government guarantee, it can still be argued that it is in a special position because, it is said, it cannot go bankrupt. There are two aspects to this: the enterprise's and the creditors'. From the standpoint of the enterprise, bankruptcy is the final disgrace and fear of it is a financial discipline. Even if it is thought that actual bankruptcy is impossible for the Railways or Gas Board, a comparable disgrace can be devised. In the past, capital reconstruction has not carried the same stigma as a bankruptcy, though it also implies writing down capital. It has not been a disgrace (i) because the sting has been drawn by the confusion between commercial failure and running into the red to meet social obligations; and (ii) because it was argued in many cases that the private shareholders had been bought out upon nationalization at an excessive valuation. But it would be possible – and, I believe, desirable – after provisions similar to those in the 1968 Transport Act have distinguished between commercial and social business, to attach some of the penalties that go with bankruptcy to a Board whose capital is having to be reconstructed. In particular, the Board should collectively offer its resignation to the Minister who may not, depending on circumstances and the responsibilities of the persons concerned, accept all or any of them. (Indeed, one might go further and make it mandatory that if a Board should find it necessary to use its depreciation provisions to break even for more than two years running, it should also offer its resignation to the Minister.)

From the standpoint of the stockholders and creditors, a Board's not being able to go bankrupt, even though some of the stigmata of bankruptcy were introduced, means they do not have the last resort of forcing liquidation and receiving the proceeds from the sale of assets. It might at first seem to be difficult for this to be done without denationalization, at least when it comes to liquidation. It is useful to look at the experience of the Mersey Dock and Harbours Board here. We have noticed already that this had some claim to be the first nationalized industry; and that it was cited as a precedent for the Central Electricity Board by Baldwin in 1926. By a process which is obscure, it seems as if its stockholders had assumed that the stock carried a Government guarantee. In 1970 the accumulated inefficiency of the Board proved too much for it. The Government decided that it had not guaranteed interest on its stock and did allow the Board to go bankrupt. This did not entail liquidation and the appointment of a receiver in the interests of the stockholders. What has happened, the appointment of a reconstituted Board and quasi-receiver in the interests of the Government, could, but need not, be equivalent. The interests of the stockholders is that the business should be contracted to make the most profitable use of its assets. Any assets of which more profitable use could be made outside the Board, should be sold off (or, at the very least, the business should be contracted or otherwise reorganized until debts are paid and the stockholders earn their interest again). If the Government treats the Mersey Docks and Harbour Board as having no social obligations, this is what its receivers should do. This indeed would be a way in which a public body could go bankrupt in a way which would be in the best interests of its (non-guaranteed) stockholders, and without being denationalized or ceasing to be a public trust. However, there is bound to be a suspicion that the Government will not let the reconstituted Board make the best use of its assets because it will not allow the necesssary contraction on account of the unemployment that would follow or for some other reason. If this is so, the Government is requiring of the Board a social obligation to create unprofitable employment in the Port of Liverpool. To require the stockholders to finance this by getting a lower return through reconstitution on these principles than they would get through an ordinary commercial liquidation, is to require them to shoulder the social obligations, which seems patently unjust. If this is required of them, one would expect in future for stockholders in trusts like these to require a premium interest rate as an insurance against this risk which investors in private industry do not have to bear.

From one point of view it is difficult to see any difference of importance between the constitutions of the Mersey Docks and Harbours Board and other public corporations with loan stock. As we have seen, all public corporations of this kind are their own proprietors. They are trusts. Except that some of them actually have their stock guaranteed by Government while others, it appears, were thought wrongly to have had it guaranteed, there seems to be no reason why other public corporations could not go bankrupt in the sense that the Mersey Docks and Harbours Board has, if the Government were to decide to guarantee no longer the loan stock of public corporations. Thus, if the National Coal Board could not meet the interest on its loan stock, it could be reconstituted. As a financial discipline there would be much to be said for this, provided that the stockholders did not have to bear the cost of any significant obligations – which implies that Government, central or local, bears the full cost of providing any social services – and that the aim of reconstitution was to make the most profitable use of the assets. It also follows from the distinction between commercial duties and social obligations, which, I have argued, should be the guiding principle on what should happen upon reconstitution. The idea that a public corporation has failed in its trust and that therefore it should be reconstituted, does not seem incompatible with the idea of accountability. The contrary notion that it should be protected from bankruptcy, in case it should thereafter be required to make the most profitable use of its assets, does.

The conclusion so far is that any financial disciplines that can be exerted by the finance market can, and indeed should, be exercised by the Government in relation to nationalized industries. Whether or not Government requires Boards to go to the market for funds for its commercial operations, it should *in extremis* be prepared to exert a discipline equivalent to bankruptcy. The major provisos so far are (i) that there will be bad and unfair results unless commercial and social business are disentangled, and (ii) that to throw a Board to the market without previously having established strong financial control, is a crude manoeuvre which invites amputation.

There is an additional financial argument for denationalization, as there is another against it. As long as these enterprises are organized as public corporations with loan stock, they cannot be taken over. Many companies with stock-market quotations face the possibility of takeover if another management believes it could make a more profitable use of the assets. It is arguable that these days this is the single most powerful stimulus to efficiency. On the other hand, many private firms are immune from this threat because they are closely owned, or because they are too large or have too much monopoly power to worry. There are therefore many Boards which would not have much to fear or to gain from denationalization. The chances of another enterprise's taking over electricity, gas or the railways must be small. Moreover, the money market only exerts a minimum discipline. Provided that a Board earns enough to service its capital – which, as in the case of the power industries, it may be able to do so by simply increasing its price – the market will provide it with funds. Either immediately or when the first shock of market discipline has been absorbed, most of the larger Boards will be no more, no less, immune from money-market discipline than similar large private conglomerates are now – and it is generally the larger Boards which require the greater financial discipline now. Therefore, there is one thing that effective strategic control of the Boards by a Ministry alone can do: it can exert over such enterprises a financial discipline which in many cases the money market cannot.

The arguments of the last two chapters would seem to be these:

(1) There are many nationalized industries in effective competition with private enterprise. But some of the most important are too large to become efficient by competition. In this they are in the same position as some of the largest private conglomerates.

(2) Breaking down the larger nationalized industries into smaller pieces creates in some cases more competitive entities. Nationalization is not needed for this. An effective financial discipline is. And there are some cases where the big corporation's operations are so complex that an intensification of financial and corporate planning is needed beforehand to make a rational breakdown possible.

(3) In many cases where public competes with private, or other public, enterprise, the rules of the game – the pattern of subsidy regulation – are such that the competition is 'unfair'. The anxiety of Parliament to restrain nationalized industries from some diversification is one objection to this, but another is the complicated subsidy pattern, for example, in the aviation industry which means that competition between public and private airlines, and between the public and other private and public transport, is not 'fair' and therefore not an efficient allocation of resources. The principle causes of this are (i) lack of financial discipline and (ii) failure to disentangle commercial and social obligations.

(4) In many cases, in order to achieve effective competition, it must be created by means which take care, patience and intelligence to establish 'countervailing power'. This requires financial, managerial and economic acumen and leads to efficient results only within a good system of financial control.

(5) Making the public industries go to the money market for their funds, but having these still backed by Government guarantee, is no sensible increase in financial discipline.

(6) Throwing the public corporations on to the money market without Government guarantee has its dangers. In the short run the money market will not be able to make a good appraisal of long-run potentials of the Boards. In the long run, unless commercial and social obligations with Boards are fully disentangled, unless there is good financial discipline within Boards, and unless the Government's own relation with the Boards can be securely defined in relation to the oversight of efficiency and to the control of social

policy, markets will exact a higher risk premium from public enterprise.

(7) Some of the features characteristic of the discipline of the private money market could, and arguably should, be introduced into nationalized industry even without sending it to the market for funds: (i) Requiring Board Members to offer their resignation for persistent failure as shareholders would require their directors to do so in similar circumstances. (ii) If there is clear separation between commercial and social obligations, then it should be possible to treat a reconstruction as the bankruptcy it is. A capital reconstruction should be an ideal opportunity for deciding on commercial grounds which is the most profitable use of a Board's assets, and for redetermining the extent of its social obligations.

Chapter 15

WHY NATIONALIZATION

The conclusion of the last chapter may seem to have attempted no more than to demonstrate a negative: that public enterprise need not have less financial discipline because it borrows its funds from Government or with Government guarantee. Even the argument that before commercial and social objectives had been clarified and an internal financial discipline constructed, hasty, ill-prepared denationalization, might well cause more butchery than would be efficient in the long run, is not a positive argument for public ownership. Neither is the reflection that there has been as long a history of public corporations as of private. The notion of a public trust is ancient. Legislation enabling the limited liability company antedated by only two years the Mersey Docks and Harbour Board which, as we have seen, many have called the forerunner of the nationalized industries. However, the argument would seem to cut both ways. Unless in a given case there is another reason for denationalizing an enterprise after a long period of public ownership, or of nationalizing one with a history of private ownership, the change might easily seem doctrinaire.

One discipline nationalized industry is necessarily immune from is the possibility of takeover. Companies with stock-market quotations have to be on the watch that another management may attempt a takeover if it believes it can persuade their shareholders that it could make a more profitable use of its assets. Many of the smaller nationalized industries without significant social obligations would have this additional stimulus to efficiency if denationalized. But there are other nationalized industries, generally larger, who would run virtually no risk of takeover. The chances of anyone's taking over the railways, electricity or steel, if private, must be small. Of course, some of these could be fragmented on denationalization to make takeover easier. But we have argued before that in some cases, e.g. the railways, there is such interdependence between the parts that no one has yet succeeded in giving many of the parts meaningful separate accounts. In other cases – electricity or steel – there would be a genuine possibility (i) that substantial economies of scale would be lost through fragmentation, which might outweigh any gains through competition or the facilitating of the possibility of takeover, and (ii) that therefore there would be mergers after denationalization to restore something like the original entity – it would be difficult to argue that this should not be so on efficiency grounds. Thus, following denationalization, many nationalized industries would be joining the group of those private giants which tend themselves to be immune from takeover and, indeed, from the financial disciplines of the market, because of their size. Over such enterprises the market only exerts a minimum discipline. On denationalization they would be exchanging a practical independence, tempered by persuasion within the public sector, for a more uninhibited practical independence in the private sector. In itself it is not easy to see how this would advance financial discipline; and if Government had solved the problem of effecting a strategic financial control efficiently, it is arguable that for such firms then, nationalization of private firms would have more of a chance of improving their efficiency than denationalization of public firms. If the problem of strategic financial control can be solved, the gradual growth of firms to realize economies of scale might mean a continual succession of candidates for some form of public ownership or surveillance on these grounds (though there may be alternative methods of securing the same ends). When such operations are offered to the market, it is not unlikely that there will be few takers. It may be argued that there must be some price low enough to attract bidders for any enterprise; but the risks of such highly specialized or non-standard enterprise are such that they are heavily dependent on national policy for their future. In any case, the risks may seem so great for the private investor or for takeover, that the effective bid, if forthcoming, might be so low that not only would its acceptance be politically difficult in many cases, but it would seem to be based on the break-up value of the business.

One can go further and argue that, over the years to come, more highly-specialized industries, especially those of advanced technology, may fall into the public sector because when their present management collapses there will be no suitable alternative private management. One such example in 1971 is Rolls Royce. The aeronautical firms have a complicated technology which has proved difficult to control. They also operate in a very difficult international context of subsidy and regulation. If they do fail the chances are high that they will either disappear, merge with some overseas competitor or fall into the public sector. Once arrived there, the chance that they will be sold off again is probably small. At least they will have to have been reformed first financially. Thus, ironically, both in the past and probably in the future, it is the enterprises which tend to be hardest to manage and which are in most need of superior and often sophisticated financial control to be made efficient, which fall into the public sector, the sector which, at the moment, has not shown it has anything approaching the superior financial management needed to put them right. But it is also a powerful reason for thinking that no Government is going to rid itself of nationalized industries and so avoid the problems of their financial control.

A second reason for believing that the nationalized sector is possibly more likely to expand than contract, is the growing specialization of management in some industries. Railways are one example of intensely specialized management. Take the example of American railroads. Any enterprise outside the industry is wary of taking an ailing railroad. If there is a railroad with a poor management record, an outside enterprise is unlikely to be willing to take it over, unless it, too, has a tradition of railway management. Because of its lack of specialist knowledge it would find it difficult to reform the existing management and not easy to pick a specialist team from elsewhere. As a generalization, investors as well as specialists in takeover keep away from specialist firms with poor management records and disappointing performance. It is often said that British merchant banks are examples of what, as a nation, we have shown ourselves able to do well. But it is characteristic of most merchant banks, especially British ones, that they flourish without much intervention in management and with no real machinery for investigating the performance of firms. Much the same is true of other institutional investors. If they find the prospects of a company disappointing, their reaction is not to attempt to intervene to ginger up or replace existing management, but to drop those shares from their portfolios and move their funds elsewhere. While takeover specialists do specialize in taking over firms with poor management but high potential, they tend to keep away from firms with specialized management tasks they do not understand and would find difficult to control.

Many of the tasks undertaken by public enterprise are specialized in this sense: whether they are the railways, the power industries, the post office, or because they involve advanced and specialized technology like the Atomic Energy Authority or telecommunications.

So much for the commercial and financial arguments for thinking that nationalized industries are always likely to be with us. But there are also social arguments. If a Government wishes to have a social service performed, it has roughly three possibilities: (i) it can operate the service itself, as it administers driving licences or runs employment exchanges; (ii) it can use the Boards and other public corporations; or (iii) it can use private enterprise, profit-making or not profit-making, on a contractual basis. The argument for devolving such activities outside Government is that it is often not suited for such management activities, and that to make itself more suited it would have to reform its management and devolve responsibility within Government. Thus, whether the activity were put outside the Civil Service or not it would become in form more like a public corporation with its own management, accounts and management objectives. In the United States, private firms have frequently been used to serve public ends and administer public programmes on a contractual basis; but this has in many cases led to such a lack of public control that there is some move towards the use of public corporations. Contracts have to be monitored. The public interest has to be protected against excess profits (as in Britain it was when Ferranti made excess profits out of Blood-hound). American experience suggests that public accountability ends up with Government's interfering more in the detailed management of private firms in the United States than it does in the affairs of nationalized industries in Britain.

Thus, if there is a genuine possibility that there is some social service to be run as a routine operation, whether it is now being run by an existing Board or whether the service is a new one, there is a strong case for its being operated by a public corporation. *A fortiori* the case against denationalization is very strong when, as with London Transport or the National Bus Company, most of its services are social and unprofitable. One imagines that the use of public corporations to serve public ends will grow.

There are various ways in which, because of monopoly power – a tradition of public service ethic or for some other reason – Boards are not expected to behave exactly like private enterprise. Logically the fact that Boards run social services for Government on a quasi-contractual basis should not make it harder for it to borrow from the market for commercial purposes. But it may not be as simple as that. Lenders may fear political intervention to keep prices down and wages, worse management and other forms of intervention. Until events had proved them wrong they might either expect a premium against these risks, or exert pressure in some ways to make public business more like private business.

A socialist can have deeper concerns. All over the world there are signs of a revolt against capitalism and against a socialism which is dominated by the idea that consumption is the aim of existence and in which many people endure the boredom of an unenjoyable day in the hope they will have the energy left to enjoy their leisure and will be satisfied by a life so divided into two parts. The idea that socialism has something to do with conditions of work and enjoyment of work – of production socialism – has been unfashionable for a long time, and is only recently reviving. The Boards would be a natural basis in which to start some experiments.[1] I do not myself believe that financial discipline is the enemy of such experiments, but rather the reverse, since it can provide a fairer test for them than prejudice often has. But all this is so far from the way in which the Boards are run now, that it is properly material for a *Second Essay on Nationalization* than for this one, which is more concerned with what is. The point I want to make here is that if Boards were to be used for anything of this kind, it might be incompatible with their getting their funds from the market, not because the experiments would be unprofitable, but for political reasons and because many people would fear, reasonably or unreasonably, that their money was at risk and would rather invest it elsewhere.

Many of the arguments for denationalization and against it are exactly the same as for and against going to the market. Even setting the social arguments aside, the balance, in my opinion, is against denationalization for those Boards which are thought most inefficient; and, for the same reasons, it would not be a sufficient improvement if they went to the market. There is no magic wand by which changing from public to private enterprise blows away the cobwebs and makes the management superior. It would also seem there there would be no special advantage in denationalization – certainly in terms of efficiency – if there was a demand for a Board's prices to be regulated because of its monopoly of power. In the cases of large Boards and Boards which have not disentangled their objectives, denationalization might have a similar traumatic effect on their being forced on to the money market, or else they would pass from practical independence in the public sector to the same in the private sector because of their size.[2]

---

[1] If I ask why we did not at least experiment in some forms of workers' control in the 1968 Transport Act, the main reason was simply that so much effort went into tackling the immediate problems that not enough impetus was left for this, given all the people who would have had to be persuaded. It was certainly the kind of issue that would have had to be argued out up and down Whitehall, as raising general policy.

[2] But there are a number of Boards and parts of Boards which do not fill any of these categories and where, as they are presently run, there seems a much less convincing case against making them go to the money market, or even against

In conclusion – setting the social arguments aside – it is arguable that either making Boards go to the money market or denationalizing could be too drastic a cure and even then would have limited effects on financial discipline where there was substantial monopoly power. Some of the benefits of market discipline could be achieved more simply – e.g. by abolishing deficit grant provisions and making possible the equivalents of bankruptcy – and in general financial discipline is needed in enterprises for the money market to achieve efficient results. Denationalization adds one additional sanction – the threat of takeover, but this is likely to be effective only for Boards small enough to be taken over.

Reviewing the last three chapters, we see there are many ways in which competition between Boards, between Boards and private industry, and for funds, could be increased and so take the strain off other ways of increasing efficiency. But it seems unlikely that it could ever be a complete answer. Moreover, competition and countervailing power will be much less effective, and in some cases disastrous, without prior financial discipline. Therefore there seems to be an overwhelming case for considering how one might improve the weak financial control that, as we have seen, now exists, unless one is prepared to wait for the Boards to reform themselves, or believes in the ultimate efficiency of persuasion.

---

denationalization. These are the *curiosa* which have fallen into the lap by accident. What is the case for a nationalized travel agents – Thomas Cook's – in a world of travel agents? One argument might simply be that it has high integrity and is an example to others. Another argument made by Hugh Gaitskell was that selective nationalization could be a way of stimulating the efficiency of private firms by competing with them. Without making any comparisons in respect of Thomas Cook's, which may be among the most efficient travel agents and an example to others – I do not know – one doubts if any of the Boards would claim that their efficiency was clearly so superior that their competitors – say in the hotel or shipping industry – would definitely have more to learn from them than they from their competitors. Neither are the things that many of these do such that they are natural candidates for grants to provide social services. It is not impossible that the Government would want to subsidize British Transport Hotels to provide subsidized hostels for homeless families, for example, but there has been no initiative in that direction. Of course, if these Boards were examples of syndicalism that would be another matter. Then one could see their social purpose. But no socialist Government has taken a step in that direction.

Part IV

STRENGTHENING MINISTERIAL CONTROL

Chapter 16

STRATEGIC FINANCIAL CONTROL

The system of financial control that was starting to be developed in the Ministry of Transport, and was described at the end of *Chapter 6*, was far from perfect – though, I believe, a move in the right direction. There were several respects in which it fell short of what a private firm, for example a holding company of that size and scope, might have developed. But the main criticism of it – by Boards and others – is in my opinion right: it was tactical rather than strategic. To make it strategic would imply a further effort but the pay-off might be high: one could relax some of the tactical controls without harming the interests of public accountability.

To see where it had got to as a system of tactical control, let us look at its parents. These were what we have called the administrative or *candle-ends* approach, which was the background from which the administrators tended to develop their ideas of financial relationship, and the *seat-of-the-pants* approach, which is a rough, generic label for the more intuitive methods of investment appraisal from which the Boards, like private firms, were slowly evolving something more systematic.

Most systems of financial control have a strategic and a tactical aspect (as well as third which is book-keeping). Financial control is being strategic when it is thinking about the operation as a whole. It is being tactical when it is looking at particular changes – proposals for investment, for rundown, etc. – to help decide whether they are worthwhile. But there is not a hard and fast line between the two. A system of tactical control can help correct and inform the strategic financial thinking of the operation.

The tactical aspect of the approach we have called 'candle-ends' were described fully enough in *Chapter 6*. The strategic approach is more complex but seems to operate in a number of ways. The first kind of strategic occasion is when Ministers steel themselves to impose a cut in public expenditure (or, more joyfully, to share an increase). What decides the cuts or the increase depends on the occasion; but among the factors, as one would expect, will be some ideas of fairness as between departments, ideas about what it is feasible to cut and what is so far committed that it would be too costly to do so. This is a short-run strategy. Sometimes it is the strategy of crisis. The long-run strategy raises two main questions. The first is how certain programmes increase their share and others decline; and the second is how priorities and principles change within programmes. The way the initiative would often seem to be taken in the second case, and possibly sometimes also in the first, is by way of discussions of principle. The initiative for such a discussion may come from Ministers, Treasury or departmental civil servants. An area will be chosen as one of interest. There will be a committee. Papers will be called describing what is done. Counter papers may be written by some of the outsiders. These may describe how they believe the priorities are chosen to help clarify their minds and elicit more information by way of confirmation or denial; or they may suggest changes. The dialogue may not end with very large or definite changes being accepted in procedure or principle, but the expectation is that something will have been accomplished: those who have been under examination will have got some sense of the direction in which they are being asked to move; those examining them, so to speak, will have got some idea of the difficulties and habits which stand in the way of more rapid change. In a particularly difficult case, the outsiders may come back several times within a few years to help move things along a little more briskly; but in any area there is likely to be come discussion of the kind from time to time. The occasion for it may well be some expression of Government policy. This could be a statement by Ministers that in some general way they want the scrutiny of public expenditure improved, or that they want this done in a given area; or there may be a more political impetus. For example, Ministers may say they would like an expenditure programme to be directed more towards regional ends or perhaps towards helping the balance of payments. It is then the duty of those I have called the outsiders on the committee, to work out the implications. While Ministers may or may not have said something which made it clearer what kind of changes they had in mind, these discussions down the machine are intended to explore how expenditure programmes might be influenced by the change in principle. In a particular case the reaction may be quicker – not that one can expect a whole programme to alter direction for this reason. Some expenditure will have been committed and much else is likely not to be affected by the change; but there are likely to be some changes in the direction Ministers want.

172

While many businessmen may find this approach strange, they must remember the conditions in which control is being exercised. It provides a practicable link between expressions of policy and action, particularly where there are no clear financial or cost-benefit criteria; or, even if there are some, where there are also complex and non-quantifiable factors. (It is also, I believe, the approach that many administrators think natural even when there are more definite financial or cost-benefit criteria that can be used.) Some would think among the virtues of the method, others among its drawbacks, that it tends to be gradual and marginal, requiring patience and giving everyone concerned every chance to make their case. It would be impossible and wrong to argue that this kind of approach is the only one to be found in Whitehall – or that it is exclusively only to be found there and not elsewhere. But it is an approach one might expect where criteria are complex: where it is difficult to provide ex-post checks in any formal way to see if expenditures achieved their objectives; and where also, it has to be said, departments are not to be ordered around. Government is not homogeneous. Departments report to Ministers.

Seat-of-the-pants can be a generic description for the more traditional systems which are still be be found, especially in small or old-established firms. As in the candle-ends approach the tactical element is usually uppermost; and its basis is the manager who has experience and a strongly developed intuition. When considering whether to replace some machinery, and with what, he is most likely to rely on his judgement and knowledge of the business. This may be backed by some figuring he has asked his accountant or someone else to do for him and he may have various rules of thumb which he has found useful; but what persuades him in the end is likely to be a growing conviction in some part of his body that one course of action is right and another wrong. His back-checking may also be largely intuitive. Very often it will be hard to him to disentangle the effects of this decision on the accounts from that of other factors; but he will hope that his knowledge of the business and the feedback from the salesman will confirm his judgement. In a company which has several levels of management the system of tactical financial control will have added to it one man's judgement of the persons below him, and theirs of those below them. Again there will be figures, but they may not be the most important part of the discussions when the managers get together and argue out what is the right thing to do. A lot of what is relevant is likely to be what has not been quantified (whether or not it could have been).

Clearly the success of such a system depends on making judgements which are more often right than wrong. This depends in part on having a high proportion of management who have been around long enough to have developed the intuitions and gained the know-how (just as the candle-ends system depends a little on this but also on having movers, people who move around often enough to be objective and detached). It also depends on having some agreed or intuitively recognized tests of success or failure. The business has to be simple enough, and management's knowledge sufficient, for them to be able to say to each other convincingly that A worked out well and B worked out badly (and that X or not-X was to blame). Learning from experience means reading the lessons of experience correctly.

The system may begin to creak and break down because there is (i) higher management turnover, (ii) more complicated external conditions, (iii) product diversification, (iv) because the company grows much larger, or (v) because profit margins are finer and there-fore judgements have to be more exact. But as these things happen, what one often finds is that managers' assertions that their intuition is their best guide grows in inverse proportion to their ability to manage the business. As their grasp of all that is relevant declines, so what they are doing becomes more of a gamble, until in the extreme they are relying most of all on the pure chance that more of what they are doing will be a success than a failure (and enough of a success to cancel out the costs of the failures as well as make a profit for the firm).[1]

Reinforcing either the candle-ends or seat-of-the-pants methods by more rigorous methods of financial appraisal will first affect the tactical financial control. This improvement often begins as a research activity: a programmes analysis unit is set up to look into methods of appraisal. While this can be a device to keep it out of the way, it is more common at this stage that management wants to control the proposals they look at, or to be able to treat the results of any analysis they may be asked to do as research (which therefore are not necessarily to be taken notice of). The next stage

[1] One of the most dangerous situations is where a business is large and where the operations are so intertwined that no one in charge of one part of the opera-tions is really able to develop an intuition powerful enough to grasp the effect of what he does on the whole concern. Then there is a strong chance that, because investment funds cannot be allocated on the basis of rational analysis or effective intuition between the parts of the enterprise, it will be done on the basis of notions of fair shares or even as a result of internal politics. It is this kind of situation, which is not unknown in either the Boards or some private industry, which perhaps in Britain comes nearest to the situation described in *Chapter 11.*

may be that the unit is given what are agreed to be difficult cases with special features. Very often these may be projects which are politically rather than financially difficult; or they are chosen because they involve many interests, e.g. several parts of a business, more than one Board, or several Government departments. A major breakthrough towards investment appraisal as a method of corporate financial control occurs when projects start to be looked at on a sample basis, the presumption being that in general all projects should now be appraised in this manner, even though only some are looked at. The purpose of looking at the sample is for top management to get 'some idea of how the criteria are applied' with the aid of the investment analysis unit. This, broadly speaking, is where Government normally stands in relation to the Boards, and where the Select Committee thinks it should stand.

However, if the appraisal unit is in a position to deliver opinions on a number of schemes, some of these may be unfavourable; and the possibility has to be admitted that those it advises will, after consultation, want to turn one or two of the projects down. This does not imply a radical change in the more traditional methods of control. The main use of financial appraisal is still to stimulate the judgement of those who initiated the project in the first place. The purpose of a corporate investment appraisal system is not to check figures or force those lower down the line to substantiate with hard fact every argument upon which their conclusion depends. If one does, initiative is damped. Instead, what one is trying to do is to get management to show (i) that they have used their judgement and their experience to analyse the effects of a project in a way which has concentrated their mind on the salient fact: the return the enterprise may expect to get from it, and (ii) in addition, that they have brought the major causes of uncertainty out into the open so that everyone relevant can form their own opinion of them. One is still just as much testing people as facts and figures. Making this into a test implies the possibility of failure.

But if one begins to act with the aid of these appraisals, it is only reasonable for it to affect the way in which the sample projects to be examined is drawn. As departments and Boards explained to the Select Committee, the projects to be delivered to the department were chosen after consultation between Board, department and Treasury. The department and the Treasury said what they wanted to see; and the Boards had their suggestions on what Treasury and departments ought to see. It would be totally wrong to suppose that this meant the department only saw what the Boards wanted it to see. However, there was a tendency for the larger projects to be over-represented, and for the smaller projects and the projects which came rushing up at the last moment to be under-represented or not to be represented at all. This had two consequences. The first was that Boards had plenty of time, if they chose, to apply a different (higher) standard of appraisal to the projects they sent forward. The second was that financial control did not have the element of randomness or system which are the hallmarks of a good system. A private enterprise which is moving from a situation in which investment appraisal is a research activity or reserved for special projects, will realize that it is both fair and effective for it to get some basic system by which all projects, usually above a minimal size, have a more or less equal chance of being picked up for appraisal (and even then the small projects are likely to be picked up in a similar basis somewhere in the organization). One possibility is for all projects (perhaps above a certain minimum amount) to be worked up in an appraisal form and for all of them to be sent to the special appraisal unit for analysis. Some firms certainly do this. Others will require that all projects be worked up in the same form but will only expect a sample of these to be sent forwards for appraisal. It is arguable that a good system of financial control is one in which the controlling agency occasionally calls unexpectedly for a project to be shown to it. It would not be sensible if the controlling body was often changing its mind and asking to see things that it had said it did not want to, or wanting to see things at very little notice. But some element of surprise keeps people on their toes. If everyone knows which projects are to be looked at in advance, without exception, there is a temptation for people to trouble less with other projects. This stimulating effect might especially be true on the small projects, which are usually such a high proportion of the total (and where, in the case of Boards, it is rumoured much of the waste occurs – rumours which could not be proved or disproved).

Again, before investment appraisal becomes a routine, the submissions tend to come up in all shapes and sizes. This tends to be true of submissions from different Boards. Even the submissions that one Board sends in tend to come in variously presented, the presumption being that the Board has the right to present the submission in the form, and at the level, that seems best to it. This is unimportant, and may even be best, when such a submission does not happen very often. But it is arguable that a more efficient system of financial control would be a shade more formal, given the large sums and numbers of projects involved. In the financial systems of large corporations it is not uncommon for submissions

176

to have more or less standard 'front pages' where are collected the most important facts about the project. Behind it will be a number of other pages explaining the arguments in more detail, where the defenders of the project will say what they think is important, anticipate objections and put down the thoughts of other interested parties within the organization. One advantage is that it saves the reader time. He can look at the front pages and get an idea of what it is all about. But there is more to it than that. The controlling body then begins to get an idea of how everything adds up, what the total effect on the accounts of the organization is likely to be. They also realize the proportion of the corporate investment in which investment appraisal seems to be working; and by comparison, what is most important, it reveals the area of the business where people are having difficulty in writing up a satisfactory defence of what they would like to do. These tend to be the areas of very great complexity which I have already mentioned as having been so common in several Boards. There, no meaningful rate of return on a project has been produced, or can be, with existing methods.

It is also common for the financial control systems of corporations to have signatures attached to show who back it and who have dissenting opinions. This is part of the notion that one is looking at people as well as at opinions. Signatures – the fact that someone has laid his name on the line – help apportion praise and blame whether the project is later a success or a failure. It makes clear to people that they are responsible for their judgement and cannot sink their identity in collective responsibility. It is arguable that submissions should come from departments to Boards with signatures and not, as they do, bearing the collective imprint of the Board. (This last also tends to escalate all disagreements into ones where the Board sees itself under an obligation to identify wholly with every detail of any submission it sends.)

While the exact way in which such a system might develop could be individual, what has been outlined gives some conception of what reasonable system of *tactical* financial control might be like for a large organization and for one which would give reasonable assurance that public money was well invested. But there are several objections to it which will be made. Some are not fundamental:

(1) Some may object that departments have not the right kinds of staff to operate such a control; but if this is so, it may be a good reason for acquiring or learning the extra skills needed. (This will be discussed in the next chapter.) Unless there is some great disadvantage in a Ministry acquiring these skills, it cannot be a

M

sufficient reason for abandoning the idea of such a system of control.

(2) What many people will fear is that departments, like the Head Offices of some very big firms, would then demand to see every project (or, at least, all above a certain size) and would exercise a very strict and time-consuming detailed control. The fear is that if Ministries are sent full submissions, there will be more niggling questions and answers *whether or not the submissions are good*, simply because the Ministry officials cannot leave well alone. But this, though an important matter, is something which is endemic in any situation involving delegation. It is very like the traditional view that people in the field have of Head Office, or district officers had of Delhi. This fear of Head Office's meddling and being bureaucratic is common and quite often well founded. It may be a legitimate fear that in giving more information to Head Office, one will get back stupid questions which may only hamper business because they are asked by people who do not really know what is happening. One of the most difficult tasks for a Head Office or a Ministry is to know when to stop, to impose on itself a discipline such that it does not ask questions for the sake of proving it still exists. It could in fact exercise more self-restraint than that. One could lay down a rule – similar rules exist in public service – that even if a department gets a 'front page' about which it has serious misgivings, it has not the right to see the project in detail unless it is one it has already asked to see in detail, as under the present system. What it could then do is to take it up with the Board in some annual discussion, whether or not the proportion of unsatisfactory front pages seems to be rising or falling, and invite comment. Or it could be agreed that the Ministry is allowed to pick up in this way an agreed maximum number of projects. Or there could be an element of randomness, but with it also pre-arranged just how many projects could be picked up in this way. Safeguards of this sort should not be beyond devising; and indeed the Select Committee might interest itself in what they were.[1]

(3) More fundamental is simply the objection made by Board Chairmen to the Select Committee in one form or another that it was not right or was not necessary for Ministries to do this. Often the cry was 'duplication'. Several added to this the question of trust.

---

[1] At present the informal methods mean that projects tend to come over at any time, and are dealt with by their own timetable. Although almost all are approved quickly, some hang around, which is a major and reasonable cause of complaint. A more formal process might help the Boards which reckoned to deal with projects which passed certain minimum standards on the information and signatures they displayed, on a production-line basis, with the project automatically approved by a given date unless the Ministry took certain steps.

Lord Robens argued that 'when one has chosen people to manage the industry and satisfied oneself that they are capable of managing the industry they really ought to be left to manage within the rules that have been laid down' (Q. 489). There were complaints from several Chairmen that there was no need for the departmental officials to do again what their own people had already done. Partly this was combined with a feeling that civil servants were the wrong people, but aside from that separate question, this is again very much like what one tends to hear up and down the line in a large firm. A more penetrating objection is that it presupposes that enterprises as big as the Boards are not large enough to manage themselves. But this of course brings us to the crux of the matter in two senses. We are not talking about management. We are talking about Government's having enough assurance that public money or the nation's resources are being invested with a high enough return; and the question is, not whether the Boards are large enough, but much more simply a question of (public) accountability. Neither is it central that they do not in some cases seem to have developed the financial discipline which would have improved confidence. It is more basic than that. Because the competition of the market is not strong enough to exert a sufficient financial discipline, the basic contention is that no public body should be in such a position that there is no effective external check on the strength of its financial self-discipline. If one does not believe this, one is probably satisfied with the *status quo*, or with what can be achieved by measures outlined in the last few chapters.

(4) But there is a fourth difficulty which, I believe, is fundamental: it is that a highly developed system of tactical financial control will, in many cases, not be sufficient because of its strategic deficiencies. The main reason for wanting to get information on projects is to try to form some impression of how the organization is doing as a whole. The Ministry exercising accountability for Parliament is, or should be, uninterested in the detail of projects. It is, or should be, interested in the net revenue forecast of the organization: what profit does it expect to make; what are the risks; what are the assumptions made about competition, labour costs, strikes, technical progress and so on; what is the chance that public money is at risk. The weakness of systems of financial control that rely mainly on project analysis is that one does not build up a picture of the whole. This is likely to be compounded when there are large areas where, because of complexity, project analysis simply does not work or cannot be relied on in the present state of the art. A situation of this kind may well tempt a Ministry, like any other financial con-

troller in the same position, into great detail on the projects which
can be analysed, in the hope that if one can save pence or even
pounds there, these may offset the pounds being lost in the obscure
areas about which so little is known.

The feeling that it is the strategic rather than the tactical financial
position which matters, has led some Boards and the Select Committee to argue that departments should look at investment programmes as a whole, rather than at individual projects. The trouble
is that there have often been no investment programmes to look at
in the past; or rather, that all there is is a naming of projects with
provisional estimates of cost. Against only some projects is there
an estimated return in either first-year or net present value terms.
This is just another way of saying that Boards are not yet able
to supply all those front pages. Thus if one were to approve investment on the basis of the programmes as they are, it would mean
tending to rely on the impression that the Board has formed about
the effect of its capital expenditure on its profitability. Since the
case for the whole is not stronger than the sum of the cases for the
parts, this, in many cases, would not have a substantial basis. Thus,
to follow this route would have meant, and in many cases would
still mean, going back to little more than the Minister trusting the
Board, and reducing public accountability to the point that Ministers
would have even less effect as a pressure group.

(5) There is another fundamental way in which strategic financial
control based on capital expenditure analysis is incomplete. One
finds that many of the more crucial decisions a Board makes are
not related directly to capital expenditure. One of the useful activities
performed by economists under the control of administrators in the
Ministry of Transport was the appraisal of productivity agreements –
which did not always turn out to be the bargain they were first
thought to be. It is equally as important that the wages policy and
the capital expenditure policy of an organization should be
appraised.[1] The influence of Government policies and actions on

[1] In my opinion one of the reasons why Prices and Incomes policies tend to
fail is because the machinery of analysis has never been developed in a rigorous
way, so that a jaundiced look is taken at the often over-optimistic bargains that
are offered. Another activity of importance undertaken by the economists in
the Ministry of Transport was the economic evaluation of strikes imminent and
continuing, to make an assessment of their effect on the economy. This normally
meant taking one's forces off whatever else they were doing and sending
them out to look into areas which one might expect to be affected. This
was backed by interviews and telephone calls, checking and re-checking
first impressions. I believe this should be a routine activity because of
the very great exaggeration that is often made of the effects of a strike.
Those who complain most loudly are likely to be those worst affected

the labour and wage policies of Boards is quite as great as on its capital expenditure. The discussion in *Chapter 10* of the record on Government intervention to delay price increases, has made it plain that it is also vital for financial discipline that this, too, should be discussed in the context of strategic financial controls. What one is doing in all this is testing the parameters of the environment within which a Board or business works. This is just as important for it and public accountability as the appraisal of capital expenditure projects. There has been a tendency to concentrate too much on the former to the exclusion of the rest.

One can go further than this. In those companies where there is effective financial control of a strategic kind, the appraisal of capital expenditure – which is almost the be-all and end-all of central Government interest in the Boards – plays a subordinate role. One can argue that the difference comes because capital expenditure (the capital-output ratio) is so much higher for many Boards than for much manufacturing industry that the difference in emphasis can be understood. While an excuse, this can hardly be an historical or rational explanation. Historically, Governments have tended to control expenditure as their prime financial duty. They have, if they are wise, tended to concentrate on the larger expenditures – hence the greater attention paid to capital than to current expenditure (not infrequently overdone). This priority Government has tended to transfer to its financial consideration of the Boards.

A very different attitude is often to be found in industry where there is effective financial control. The main topic for discussion is the overall performance of a subsidiary and how this compares with its past performance. In an efficient enterprise there will be monthly and quarterly data. Some of the key magnitudes will be percentage profit on capital employed, rates of sales to inventories, ratio of sales to capital employed, and percentage profit on sales. It is by noticing trends in these that one is able to open a dialogue to oversee the efficiency of a Board – if one has the skill and experience. Such an approach provides a context for approval of capital expenditure. One can deduce what capital expenditure a business can afford if it is to maintain its level of profit. One can relate the rate of profit, the rate of growth in business, and the capital expenditure required to achieve that growth. A business which over-invests in the sense of not maintaining or improving its profitability, will

---

and very often they are even then exaggerating the effect to which they are hurt. It is only natural. Failure to make a reasoned appraisal which requires hard work and rapid quantification, can be a reason why concessions are made too easily to wage demands. Otherwise it may be difficult to resist panic action.

falsify its net revenue predictions. In manufacturing businesses, one would expect the financial effects of investment to work their way through into the profit-and-loss accounts in a year or two. Gestation periods in many, but not all, nationalized industries are longer, which means that more time should be given initially to capital expenditure appraisal. Nevertheless, the public sector tradition of concentrating on the appraisal of capital expenditure almost exclusively may be responsible for ineffective control. While it, too, has its advantages, one might start with a more mechanical approach. Normally an enterprise would be allowed to invest so as to replace its assets so far as justified by its earning power. If it has a momentum of profitable growth the expectation would be that it would be allowed the funds to sustain it. Only an acceleration in growth (or a change in activity or capital-intensity of investment) might require special sanction; and of course there would be argument if the financial programme of the enterprise worsened.

How does one develop circumstances in which strategic financial control is effective, and which will make it possible to achieve meaningful public accountability without looking at so many individual projects? The tendency of all the nationalized industries we have already mentioned to follow the example of the Transport Holding Company and to subdivide their organizations into separate companies and divisions with separate accounts, has helped. It is not always sufficient because, although organizing a business into more homogeneous self-contained units makes net revenue forecasting less complicated, it does not mean that it happens.

Beginning with relatively informal methods is better than nothing; and it would seem to me that the best form of control in relation to the more homogeneous entities and parts of entities would be an annual or semi-annual discussion of each one's financial position. The management would present its investment programme and explain its expectations and its last year's experience as a company might do to a merchant bank which was seriously involved in its affairs, or even as a subsidiary might do to a parent company. One might expect a session attended by the Ministers and his senior officials to be preceded by working meetings at a lower level where explanations were gone over and briefs prepared. This kind of meeting between Board and Minister does not occur now.[1] (The

1 Investment reviews, as conducted in Whitehall and reported to the Select Committee, tend to be inspections of collections of projects – not a look at a corporate plan in which investment is evaluated against net revenue forecasts, and at alternative marketing strategies. That the habit of work has been such

meetings that happen now tend all to be on more specific and partial subjects or to be so much an exchange of generalities that they amount to little more than requests for, and concessions of, trust.)[1]

In many cases, corporate planning, if that is what it is usually called, may not be very advanced by some standards of scientific management, but it may not have to be. But in other cases – the obscure and complex areas we have talked about – a great deal will have to be done to get things to a point where corporate planning and net revenue forecasting are good enough to be meaningful. One of the most hopeful signs for the future is that the Railways have put a great effort into developing corporate planning on this basis. It will only be when they have a good corporate plan that they themselves will feel that they have any control over their own destiny. There are other Boards of which the same must be true.

It is probably worth stopping and asking what a Minister ought to be able to expect to be told at such an annual discussion.

(1) The size of the investment programme. Its expected effect on the net revenue position of the whole organization (and on each homogeneous sub-unit) on a year-by-year basis over the next three to four years. This broken down by the sides of the business so to get some ideas of which are expanding and which contracting and what their financial strengths are. These are not forecasts in the sense that they are expected to come true; but they are detailed best estimates on the basis of explicit forecasts of demand and costs.

(2) An analysis of the sensitivity of these net revenue forecasts to various contigencies and the measures taken to anticipate these contingencies. This might imply, for example, a discussion of the Board's manpower plan and of the effect on finances of strikes, or unexpectedly high wage increases. Also, a discussion of pricing policy to

---

that there are no meetings with overall financial focus was the second discovery that astonished me in Whitehall – the first was, of course, that capital proposals were seldom, if ever, turned down.

[1] In many cases what would seem to be needed is a ministerial power which enables Ministers to talk about the affairs of separate divisions or subsidiaries of Boards and give approval to their financial intentions or corporate plans as such. In order to protect the Board against a Minister who tried to chop a Board into two small pieces to increase his control of detail, or who tried to create divisions or companies which were not homogeneous enough to be meaningful management units, one might require schemes to be approved by Parliament. On the other hand, to protect the Minister against a Board which tended to create management units in relation to which statutes had not given Ministers this power, it would be necessary to have some more flexible machinery, other than another statute, by which Boards could reorganize internally without altering the scope of this kind of control.

make clear what options the Board has here and what room for manouevre. There might also be discussions of what might be reasonably expected from cost reduction and from science and technology. The strategy of the research and development should also be discussed.

(3) There should also be some analysis of out-turn against past forecasts. This must be in financial terms and should be backed by sufficient figures to make a convincing case. What went right? What went wrong? Why?

(4) There would also be on this or another occasion some discussion of the financial implications for the Board of the social services it performs against grant; and there would be some discussion of the effect of future options on profitability.

In some sense, even though strategic discussions are not now normal, they could start without much preparation since one can always begin with inadequate data before it is improved. But one suspects that many Boards, like many private firms, have not got into a position where they discuss these questions in any systematic way themselves. There is a tendency in many to keep going the old kind of representative Board where meetings tend to be a series of reports, detailed questions that have not been settled further down the line and anything else that it occurs to the Chairman to put on the agenda. There is often a tendency for individual Board Members to talk only about subjects for which they themselves are responsible. There may be little feeling of collective responsibility. Again, one believes this may be changing; but the idea that the Board has to present to Ministers and senior officials a systematic account of their stewardship should help to change it a little faster.

Even though some Boards might agree to move in this direction they often tend to suggest that meanwhile the Ministries should give up looking at individual projects. But to abandon the existing imperfect method before getting a better would seem a quite unnecessary act of faith, and there is surely no point in disguising the fact that even the most public-spirited Board will move a little faster if under some pressure. But even when the new deal is possible in a meaningful way, it would seem to me imprudent for a Minister to give up this power, though he would probably want to use it differently. For a Ministry to sample the investment projects of a Board seems as excellent a way then of reassuring itself that all is well, as any that can be devised. One would hope that the sample would be small, but for it not to exist would seem foolhardy. There is always the possibility that something might go wrong in the financial control of a Board, and then an increase in the sample of projects looked at might seem the natural next step.

Thus, one might hope that one might get a strategic financial control developed which is both effective and meaningful, when the present methods which have been so ineffective are replaced by better: when arguments about investment criteria are replaced by discussions about the kinds of economic and operations research tools which are needed in difficult cases for planning; and when, superimposed on these technical discussions, full discussions about the Board's corporate plans and those of their most important divisions or subsidiaries, are conducted between Boards on the one hand and Ministers and their senior advisers on the other. Thus one would have moved away from a system which is fragmented, like the traditional candle-ends and seat-of-the-pants systems from which it would have developed, to one which is strategic and not tactical. The role of detailed investment appraisal of particular projects would then be less important – a way of checking up that all was well below. Just as it is the case that top managers do not submerse themselves in detail, neither do they never get down to detail. Their inquiries, their occasional thunderbolts, fly from top to bottom.

A development of this kind would make the relationship between Board and Minister more meaningful to both Board Members and the Minister. It is an oddity of the present situation that the meaningful contact now takes place several steps below Minister and Chairman. The kind of activity that investment appraisal is, means fair attention to detail and paperwork. Indeed, one of the objections of Board Members to the way that officials operate, is often that it is much more detailed and nitpicking than interests them. While some of them would work off paper, they would not work as financial analysts or economists do, though they might work with material prepared by them. They pay more attention to people and spend much of their time relating one thing to another. They would think themselves mostly occupied with strategic things (while they would see the dialogue on particular investments as mainly tactical) and when they did make tactical forays down the line it would usually be primarily into management and not, except exceptionally, into the quality of an investment submission. One can understand why it is the Board Members often say that when they do get wrapped up in these investment discussions, they are there either because they are blazing with rage that a project they approve of is being delayed or, more simply, because the etiquette of the situation has raised the matter to their level. While the Minister will occasionally receive on

185

his desk a précis of the case for and against an investment sub-mission, he scarcely ever gets the opportunity for discussing with its top management the way the organization is moving as a whole – which, in financial terms, is discussing its net revenue forecasts or corporate plan. In its place he is likely to get generalities, some visits round plants, workshops or goods yards, and the *results* of the enterprise which he may have to defend in Parliament. But there is no point in discussion if there is nothing to discuss. Indeed it is arguable that, quite apart from the merits of net revenue forecasts and material to support them for the enterprise itself, something of the kind is even more necessary if the Minister is to discharge his duties to Parliament. One reason, for better or for worse, why many organizations do not have anything so systematic, is that the business is reasonably compact and that they are experienced. They know each other and the business so well, meeting every day, that they feel there is no need to go through the formality of a corporate plan. But this is simply not true for the Minister. He cannot, and should not, develop the knowledge of the business which would make a corporate plan unnecessary. But he and his officials should be able to exercise financial control more effectively and with less piecemeal intervention with one than now, which means that he would have a more rational basis for saying No, when No should be said, and a running basis from which to appraise performance and influence so far as his powers permit him.

What I have described is how one might make the present system of financial control effective and more meaningful. Since the general practice is a system which now is persuasive and educational rather than firm, this would mean an attempt to make the reality approximate more to the myth of how financial powers are operated. Ministers' financial powers tend to be latent insofar as they do not establish financial control.

It is not how Boards, or apparently the Select Committee, would like the system to be operated. Or rather, the Select Committee might be interpreted as liking it but imagining that it would come by consent and would require no policing. The drawback to the Select Committee's notions as sketched in *Chapter 8*, was that, in distinguishing between normal and critical times, they seemed to imagine it feasible for Ministers to go along most of the time listening to whatever the Board chooses to tell them, asking a few questions, and finally approving – what I have called the trustee relation. This seems to deny the most elementary truth about a successful power relationship which is that, while one delegates, one also manages. There must be a certain (friendly) tension so that while the Board feels they are trusted, they never have enough rope to hang themselves. What the Select Committee seem to be requiring is a much more detached attitude from the Minister than this; and there is much in the tradition to support them. My contention is that the tradition is too lax for an effective basis of trust and a degree of public accountability that makes sure that the return on the large proportion of Britain's economic resources is protected.

Therefore there would seem two ways in which a better financial discipline could be secured. The first is to improve the system of tactical control as it was developed in the Ministry of Transport, to a pitch where it is more efficient and better placed in the context of the financial framework of the exercise. But even if one went all the way with this, there would still be large amounts of capital expenditure in many Boards where there would not be enough information to yield meaningful investment appraisals on a piecemeal basis. The second route is to move towards a more strategic system of control; but this will mean several Boards' developing a much deeper and, in some ways, sophisticated analysis of their predicament, so that they can produce net revenue forecasts sensitive to assumptions about investment, pricing and other policies (a corporate plan), that are worth the paper they are written on. Then, and only then, should it be possible to pass into an era of less (financial) intervention in detail without a serious sacrifice of financial discipline and public accountability. One must not duck the risk that in practice such a system could be developed where the Ministry is interfering in detail as much or even more than it does now. This is the challenge: to design a system which achieves the overall end but protects the Boards from the tentacles of *candle-ends*, except where a strategic discussion has shown clear evidence of major Board failure; and even then, the descent to detail should be in context of an inquiry into the Board's overall financial management.

Thus, one is suggesting that the Minister's financial powers should be exercised seriously to achieve public accountability, which many people believe is now the purpose of a Minister's financial powers but which the traditions of the system do not permit. Whether the financial powers need to be redefined (in relation to the need to approve a corporate financial plan) or whether the power to approve the lines of capital expenditure or borrowing would seem secondary, I would have imagined no change in formal powers was needed,[1]

[1] The only additional power he would probably need would be one to be able to call for, see and discuss the corporate plans of the major subsidiaries or divisions of the Boards. Many of these are named in the statutes so that there would be no problem in defining the scope of this power; but there are others

since the purpose of the practical innovation would be what it has
always been assumed that this aspect of ministerial control has been
for: to ensure that the nation's resources are being used efficiently
and productively.

which are the creatures of the Boards themselves. A statute could be drafted so
that the Minister had the same rights in relation to all of these. The Boards might
then argue that this would be a disincentive to them to organize their business
so that the Minister could exercise this power on small parts of their business.
Alternatively, it might seem as if the Minister could designate any small part he
is interested in as a 'division' – though not a company. If the power were confined
to 'companies' this would ignore that large parts of Boards may not be organized
as under the Companies' Acts. It is probably sensible that Parliament should
be required to approve a Minister's claiming this power in relation to any division
or company, while the Board would be required to submit any major reorganiza-
tional plans to the Minister. As the preceding argument of the book will have
made clear, to think that one can define a power in a statute so closely that
there will be no disputable cases, is hopeless.

Chapter 17

MEN AND MACHINERY

In this sort of book, at this stage in its course it is not uncommon for the author to come down from the mountain and catch the reader, before he is quite tired, with some weighty proposals about organization. It is the best time. The end is in sight. The reader will stumble through a few rocks rather than give up at this late stage, and as he totters through the end of the book there is just a chance that some of these weighty proposals may have lodged in his pockets.

Many people's reactions to what I have said will be to say that there must be the wrong sort of people in Government if things have worked out quite like that. They will be burnt up with impatience. Jam a few businessmen in and the whips will soon begin to crack. But it can hardly be said often enough that the system we have is in part the system we have wished on ourselves; and the people who are operating it do so in part because that is the way in which a developing tradition has required them to. This is not to say that they can just turn round and operate it quite differently. People take time to do things differently and efficiently. Neither is it obvious that businessmen can work their way into this kind of activity without having to learn something in their turn.

This last point is quite often made, so that it is perhaps necessary to say why. Some of the Boards have talked for some time of how much they would like to exchange staff with Ministries; and one of the ideas they have had was that more of their own kind of people would be listening to them on the other side of the table. They have assumed that businessmen like themselves would have more understanding of their difficulties – by which they sometimes mean an understanding of why they cannot do what they are being asked to do. Occasionally one feels that they are not talking of the genus 'businessman' but are rather seeing themselves on the other side of that table listening sympathetically to themselves. When I have been near businessmen who have involved themselves deeply in an interest in a Board, it seems to me that I have seen them torn between conflicting reactions. Firstly, those who have been with one business most of their working lives – and this is true still of the majority of British businessmen – have a deep, only partially analysed knowledge of their own organization and a tendency, of which most of them are aware, to see the problems of a Board in terms of their own organization. Therefore they first have a problem of deciding what in their experience is relevant and what should be discarded. Secondly, not only have they their deep knowledge of their own firm but they have many sources of information about new people and new developments in it, many familiar ways of approaching a problem before they make up their own mind. Here they are in a situation where they have to size up the people before they can form their opinion on the problem. Quite often they are likely to go through various stages of trusting and distrusting the accounts of the people they are listening to before they feel they know where they are; and this process may take them a longer time than they have. But if they then do make up their mind and decide what is wrong, they are likely to come fairly quickly to an opinion on what should be done: who fired, who moved, what changes in policy. If they have a management consultant background at this stage they are likely to look round to see who has the power; and they may quickly decide that it is not the Ministry, so look in the Board itself for whoever it may be that is most likely to feel the way they do and to have the power or the diplomacy to get things through. If there is no such man they may be tempted to compromise drastically on their recommendations and to cut them to fit the men they have to deal with. Such is a large part of the life of a management consultant. But if that is not their background, they may still expect the Minister to put through the conclusions they have come to, quickly and decisively, but they then find and perhaps do not even believe, that the powers of the Minister are as limited as we have shown them to be. The best they can hope for is that the civil servants will take their ideas on board and, one way or another, will gradually implant them in the process and bring all the pressures and influences to bear which will begin to move the enterprise in that direction. If they try to do these things themselves they may acquire the knack of influence, but experience seems to show that they find what has to be done distasteful and too long drawn out. If they have to put their thoughts down on paper, it is usually the proverbial sheet or two, and it is likely to be a much more assertive piece of paper than a civil servant would produce. Very often one feels that they expect what they say to be taken notice of because they, with all their experience, say it, rather than for any reasons they give. But there are a number of reasons why this does not quite work in the Civil Service, which it would take me too far astray to go into now. One reason is simply that the notion of good administration – with the shadow of the Ombudsman darkening the land – is that things should be well reasoned and argued and should not be accepted on the basis of anyone's authority, however eminent. A second is that many people are likely to have to be persuaded. A third is that if it is worth doing it will be a long process: a memory of it must be deposited in the files and men's minds so that the thing can keep moving. If the businessman were to try to act like many do in this area of Government (I am not speaking of what may happen elsewhere), he and the Boards would find that for him to act in any sense like a manager, would be a serious breach in the practical independence of the Boards which would probably be frustrated by the resentment it would cause. Businessmen who have had more experience of an arm's-length relationship would probably do much better than those who have come up as managers. Those who have worked mostly in merchant banks or in Head Offices where the subsidiaries have not been easily ordered about, would have a better notion of what has to be done.

But there is another aspect to this: what is the businessmen for? I have said how it seemed to me that administrators and economists together made a more useful bunch of people than either group separately; and that the fact that some of the economists had worked in business was a great advantage also. I am sure that businessmen who are used to working in an analytic, appraisal sort of way would be welcome additions to the team, but they would not, I think, be revolutionary. Where I do believe a Minister is likely to want most advice, as control moves from the tactical to the strategic, is when he listens with his senior officials to the accounts given by the Boards of their affairs – the discussions of the corporate plan which do not take place at present. It would be useful if he could have sitting with him a number of experienced industrialists with whom he could discuss afterwards what he had heard on a strategic level, and who, in asking the questions, might make some of the running at the meetings themselves.

Thus it would seem to me that as long as Ministries exercise a tactical financial control they will need a group of analysts to help them, and that, while to rely on administrators only to do this may be narrowing too much the basis of skill, no revolution is needed. Add a few economists and financial analysts who have had commercial or industrial experience and one has the kind of group which many enterprises have for the purpose. As a Ministry moves over to being able to interact with a Board strategically, the same kind of group will be needed to service the working groups and perform the necessary analyses. The more 'hiving off' there is, the more this kind of activity will be required of a department and the larger the group will have to be. To be without such would be a return to the days which, one fears, still exist in many departments where highly intelligent administrators and even Ministers have to take decisions on the basis of too little analysis.

But where there may be a need for a kind of person who is found rarely around Whitehall is when it comes to advising the Minister on these strategic matters; and what matters here is wisdom, experience, insight into people, adaptability and perseverance, as well as an ability to interpret and use figures and analysis, since so much of the relation between Board and Minister is financial. This is the kind of area where one cannot expect even the ablest administrators to have developed a relevant wisdom since they have spent their own time acquiring other experience, equally valuable for its own purposes. Therefore I would like to make a modest suggestion that Ministers be encouraged to acquire a small group of such advisers. In order that they should not detract from the Minister's responsibility to Parliament, they should be appointees and not have any formal status. He should be able to appoint whom he likes (perhaps with the provision that they should be drawn from people with an industrial, financial or other relevant background) and give them up when he likes. They should have no responsibility except that of giving advice. The justification would seem to be this: while there will be a sufficient need for the analysts and the economists for them to make a career within the Civil Service (but including some years spent in industry, as we shall see), it is much less likely now, or for many years to come, that one can provide a career structure within Government which will produce the prized commercial top managers whose advice Ministers will need on many aspects of the financial strategy of the Boards and other 'hived-off' public corporations.

This seems to me a preferable solution to some which may seem a little like it. The Canadian National Railroad, which is a nationalized industry, has, for example, a Chairman and Board of Directors appointed by the Minister who are a Board above the executive Board. The members of this upper Board are in some sense more political, more the Minister's men, than the lower Board. Then there are all manners of suggestions for interposing Boards and Councils between Ministers and the nationalized industries. While in the first place devices of this kind may get something accomplished which was not being done before – while the new Board or Council is fresh and united (if it is fresh and united) – in the end it becomes the Board running the business or some insulation between Minister and Board, a way of reducing external pressures for efficiency.

All proposals for interposing Boards into councils in departments and nationalized industries and public corporations as they are now – whether they appear to be socialist like the old clamour for a British Transport Commission to be revived, or for some Board to stand between the Department for Trade and Industry and the aviation corporations – are, in my opinion, based upon a false analysis, though also, on a profound instinct. In talking to Board Chairmen, and others within the Boards, one finds over and over again the belief that civil servants simply do not have the right experience and training to operate either a practical or a strategic system of financial control. At the extreme, Lord Robens would insist that such people employed by Government must be business-men and must be separated from the ruck of the Civil Service, so that they, too, can have some independence as well as having business conditions of pay and service. But many others say the same thing to a lesser degree, especially in relation to the power industries. This is not a criticism of civil servants as such, but the critics will recognize that, while civil servants are good at the things which civil servants are trained to do, simply the irrelevance of the civil servant's experience and indeed his particular kind of intelligence, limit his ability to do what is required. I have argued, and strongly believe, that a mixed team of traditional administrators and financial analysts and economists with different backgrounds, is stronger than either group apart. It is also arguable that in the old Ministry of Transport we were going some way towards providing a team to interact with the Boards who had the right mixture of public service and financial experience. I believe that the principle we were intro-ducing needs to be developed further. Demand for financial expertise within the Civil Service is growing and will grow. Therefore I would like to make a second proposal, which is really a distillation of the essence of something which was said by the Fulton Committee on the Civil Service and of another thing said by the Select Committee. The Fulton Committee argued that there was a case for separating administrative civil servants into two types: financial and economic administrators on the one hand and social administrators on the other. Perhaps the Committee did not make it clear enough what they may have had in mind, because few people have found it persuasive. But while the distinction is a little vague, because they

N   193 never got down to understanding what kind of specialized skills an administrator needs and, indeed, never defined his function in a satisfactory manner to my mind, there is an important point here. One of the most important tensions in most organizations and throughout Government is between the financial mind and the executive mind, between the No-men and the Yes-men. It is the job of the Yes-men, the executives, to have ideas, to do things. It is the job of the financial men to put them through the hoop, to force them to say why what they propose will be value for money. A healthy organization has both a highly developed imaginative or executive faculty and a highly developed critical or financial faculty. I am not asking for the traditional kind of accountant, but for the type of the modern financial man whose face lights up with a smile when he has been finally persuaded that the company's money would be better spent doing this one thing rather than something else, and whose impulse is not to save money but to get the most for it. In general, the kind of personality required for the one thing is different from that required for the other. It is not so much a question of training as of temperament. Though there are people who are equally good at either, there is no reason to suppose they are less rare in the Civil Service than elsewhere; and if there are such people, by all means let them move around. The basis of such a distinction is well planted in the forms of Government. There is the House of Commons with its traditional special financial role; however, it does not, as we have seen, act as a financial controller as Congress does, partly one imagines because the political and the dour financial mind of integrity do not go easily together. There is the idea of the Treasury as the centre of the administration; but we have seen that in relation to public expenditure the Treasury has not traditionally acted as a financial controller, and it would make a very big and almost unthinkable dent in the basic constitutional principle that a Minister is responsible for his department, if the Treasury (or a Bureau of the Budget) were to try to take on a more decisive role. Within a department the basis of the distinction is to be found again in the traditional distinction between the Minister, who has overall responsibility but a special responsibility for initiating policies and otherwise taking initiatives, and the Permanent Secretary, who has his special role as Accounting Officer in which he is responsible not to the Minister but directly to Parliament. There is here a notion that financial responsibility can be kept slightly distinct from ministerial responsibility; and there is some advantage, in terms of influence and propriety, in emphasizing this by giving the Permanent Secretary this special position. But while

194

the basis of the distinction is valuable and does have a moral effect, the Permanent Secretary, like the general manager of a company, is much too busy with wider responsibilities to act the role of Financial Controller to the Minister's Chairman. The distinction is, however, preserved within the department itself where the pure doctrine of the generalist – if it ever existed – has been breached by the existence of a Finance Division; the special responsibility of the Permanent Secretary in financial matters has been observed by making the Finance Officer directly responsible to him, even though he may be two steps below him in rank.

The genesis of this special Financial division, as in most organizations, is a book-keeping one, and this is still a large part of its function. But just as the accountancy sections of business organizations have developed an interest in financial policy, so there are more and more questions in which the Finance divisions would expect to be involved to present the 'finance view'. When one has something of this sort it seems to me sensible to build on it rather than create new machinery or introduce people with new responsibilities. Because of the great importance of getting value for money and of public accountability, this section of departments is too small a proportion of the whole. It is not easy to make comparisons, but when one remembers that Government has few production or marketing functions, financial control one way or another is a large part of its business. In many departments it would seem that there are really a rather large number of issues involving the expenditure of money where the finance divisions will not be asked to present a case; by contrast, it would seem to me that a very definite finance case should be presented in relation to all non-negligible expenditures of money. What this would imply would be something like, but broader than, the role of a vigorous Financial Controller's division in a company. It would be the duty of this section to take a view on the return of all expenditures, and this would be so whether it was expressed in financial terms, cost-benefit terms, or what is loosely called output budgeting. One might expect the Ministry's Finance Officer to have a higher status in the organization than he does now and, perhaps taking advantage of the Permanent Secretary's special relation to Parliament as Accounting Officer, to have the duty to perform expenditure appraisal and see that the results of these appraisals are before the Minister when he makes his decisions. To do this effectively would mean taking over some of the more financial functions now done by the civil servants who are responsible for the other divisions, and making a clearer distinction between financial and other policies (and also incorporating

195

some of the work done by economists, as at the Ministry of Transport).[1]

[1] To be more specific, an Under-Secretary now responsible for the business of a nationalized industry will be responsible for forming a view on the financial position and social obligations of that Board. He will also advise his superiors and Ministers on a wide range of day-to-day questions involving the Board – some trivial, some not. He will get advice from the Finance Division where there is a financial question, and from other divisions in his own and other departments where their interests are affected. My proposal is:

(1) There should be a financially oriented division which would be primarily part of the Finance hierarchy and whose responsibility it would be to oversee the financial position of the Board and to relate all policy proposals to that position. It would be their responsibility to see that the effect on the financial position of Boards was considered in decisions at all levels. They would be more or less single-minded in the view they represented, which would be a purely financial view – the view that a merchant banker or Head Office might take – whichever is thought the appropriate analogy. The social obligations and other policy questions would be the responsibility of a policy division, that is – to observe the old dichotomy – a Generalist Division.

If there were not some moves in this direction already, the proposal would not be so useful. But acceleration is needed if we are not to have, as is not unknown, a gradualism where steps are so shallow that one cannot prove that the Civil Service is not continuing along the flat. As a minimum, besides the last proposal, I would suggest these also:

(2) Every civil servant of Principal grade should be designated primarily – either Generalist (in the new sense of the last paragraph), Establishment, Financial, or some class of professional – and their career programme thereafter should be in such posts only, unless there is an excellent reason for a change. The Financial cadre should have some responsibility outside departments in a Board or the private sector – virtually without exception and if possible on exchange, since there are many financial posts where outsiders could usefully be used for a stretch. The Civil Service Department moves in that direction, but in my opinion, less thoroughly than it could. In the past there would seem to have been two main reasons why exchange has been infrequent. One, the difference in salaries, reinforced by the fear that civil servants seconded to the private sector would not return—an attitude which possibly exaggerated the lure of high salaries over the non-pecuniary advantages of security of work in Government. Secondly, there are comparatively few posts in industry which demand exclusively the qualities that generalist administrators have tended to acquire. This may be changing as British corporations follow American ones in the practice of appointing high level and responsible personal assistants to the most senior executives and co-ordinators. But the qualities required of the financial cadre I have in mind would be much more similar to those required by large companies in industry.

(3) Within each department, an officer should be appointed at a level below the Permanent Secretary to co-ordinate the financial view and take steps to see that there is strategic financial control as outlined in this chapter, not only of Boards and other autonomous or semi-autonomous bodies, but also of departmental expenditure. He needs more authority than the present Finance heads tend to have – because they are too junior – as well as a greater concentration of relevant expertise. In short, departments require, in my view, a Financial Controller.

Where temperament comes in, I think, is where one might expect most administrators to specialize more on the one side or the other. There are indeed many administrators whom one thinks of first as financial men, and often very good ones by any standard; but the way in which the service operates means that from time to time they are likely to find themselves in non-financial jobs. On the other hand, I do believe there are some admirable administrators who find themselves in financial posts but who do not have the granite perseverance and unrelenting financial perfectionism needed to make the weight of this job distinctly financial and different enough from the approach of other administrative functions. They have the skills of presentation and diplomacy and knowledge of the machine which the good administrator has, but these at times may make him not push through the analysis to the point where the financial consequences of policy are transparently clear. It would also have the advantage that those who became financial specialists could have more training and relevant experience than it is easy for them to have now. The Centre for Administrative Studies has made a difference for the younger administrator, and there are several who have been to business schools. It is also surprising to find quite a number who have accountancy or other financial experience. But something systematic would imply, I believe, that the financial specialist would have had more finance training them most of them have had the chance to have, and would have had the opportunity to pick up the skills which many of them now do not have. Quite as important, it should be easier to arrange for them regularly to spend a period in a merchant bank or the financial controller's office of a firm. On the other hand, it might also be easier to arrange for people from outside to come into this kind of job from time to time than into the rather mixed jobs which so high a proportion of administrators now occupy. It is rash to make international comparisons, but one might be making strides towards developing a corps of people like the French Inspectors of Finances, which would have a good effect on the efficiency of Government at the place where it matters most – that is, in departments – and in a manner which would only be a development of a distinction already existing – so that there would be no violent disruption. It would then seem to me that such a group within a department would be able to exercise over nationalized industries the financial discipline that is needed, without getting engaged in management or feeling that their experience does not equip them for this role. They would also be there to undertake all sorts of financial functions for departments which equally require a greater financial professionalism.

197

POLITICS, FINANCE AND THE ROLE OF ECONOMICS

All suggestions which involve hiving off such people into a special department or offshoot of Government, seem to me ridiculously inferior. For example, the Select Committee argued that there should be a special department to deal with the nationalized industries, leaving policy in some sense with the departments. This has so many disadvantages that it is difficult to know where to begin. The Cabinet is one of the weakest links in the British system because it is always threatened with congestion. What cannot be agreed at lower levels has to be decided by it; and it is a democratic body which, even under a strong Prime Minister, is not likely to let him decide controversial issues without discussion. The idea that one could have one Ministry primarily responsible for the financial affairs of Boards and a number of others for their social and general policies, would be bound to increase considerably the congestion at Cabinet. If this went so far as to diminish the number of financial posts within a department, one would find also that its own sense of financial responsibility would be weakened. The chances that issues would be decided at Cabinet level might in the end weaken the financial control that the measure set out to improve. Besides, improving financial discipline is not a matter of setting up one or more great entities called 'Financial' and other great entities called 'Non-financial' or 'Political'. It is a question of increasing the interaction of financial and non-financial ways of thinking at all levels throughout Government. One can hardly think of a measure less calculated to do this than a separate Ministry. Another basis for believing this desirable would be if one thought that in future one was going to be able to operate nationalized industries more purely as commercial enterprises, performing even fewer social functions. But this seems so much the reverse of what is probable that it is hard to believe that the net effect would not be to lessen financial control and increase waste – probably, too, to increase the risks of politicizing government in the American style. Indeed, I would argue that a strengthening of the status and influence of a corps of financially minded administrators is a necessary prerequisite of the topic I want to discuss in the next chapter.

I would argue that any notion that one should invent new supervisory agencies, whether another department or quasi-autonomous, will be a retrograde step. It will complicate further the already overloaded channels of administration, but not even then in a way which is likely to lead to good financial control or good policy-making. It is likely to reflect too many decisions to the political level in a manner where they are likely to get a political, rather than a dispassionate, attention. All ideas that are based on the belief that

198

one should interpose a body between politics and the Boards, are, in the end, only likely to perpetuate the practical independence of the Boards in another form. Indeed, they are often based on the false diagnosis that Boards need less control. While one can agree that there may be too much ineffective intervention, this does not seem to me to be of financially effective intervention. Besides, if Parliament and Ministers are to use quasi-autonomous agencies to perform public services, the problem of their relation has to be solved, not distanced. Moreover, if the financial arm of Government in general needs strengthening, which I would argue that it does, the place to begin is within Government, there to develop the already existing financial disciplines in a way which will be beneficial to all Government. The financial and the policy-making are so intertwined, and rightly so, that any forced separation into distinct bodies must in the end weaken financial control, not enhance it.

Chapter 18

A DIGRESSION ON THE CONTROL OF SOCIAL POLICY

I call this a digression because it has been pointed out to me that, while it is essential to the argument of this book, it could as well be the first chapter of another. This is as it should be. There has been relatively little thought on how one controls social policy and the social obligations of Boards. But of course the relevance becomes much wider. There are many public corporations – from London Transport and the BBC to the British Museum – which are scarcely commercial entities at all. Their financial control by Whitehall can be in no sense related to what we have so far called a corporate plan. There are countless non-commercial activities within Government which require financial control if the money is to be spent efficiently to achieve financial ends. Many of these may be hived off to become public corporations. There is a danger that their practical independence in determining their social policy will become very great – even greater than the practical independence of the nationalized industries from financial control. Therefore it is right to make clear what issues are involved in the financial control of the social policies and obligations of public corporations, while admitting that there is much more to be written in detail.

It has been a leading theme of this book that a prerequisite, or price, of greater financial discipline for the Boards, is that there must be a sharper line between their commercial and social activities. There are some aspects of their social responsibilities which are mixed up inextricably with the style of their management. These are the old Morrisonian beliefs that public Boards have a special necessity to be honest to customers and employees beyond the ordinary honesty and restraint from deception of the private firm, and any developments of these beliefs which are likely. But apart from this, the framework that seems to be developing is the notion that Ministers should give grants to specific services to be performed by Boards when these are unprofitable.

200

But what of the control of this money? As was suggested in *Chapter 4* the mere fact of specific grants, brings into being an apparatus which has a symbolic significance. As these grants will be voted by the House of Commons because they will be part of public expenditure, they will be subject to scrutiny by the Public Accounts Committee. The Minister not only will be able, but will be expected, to have a policy on how this money is to be spent. While the scrutiny given by the Public Accounts Committee does not begin to compare with thoroughness of the appropriations committees of Congress, they do pick up points of detail and castigate what they regard as wrong procedures more forcefully than the Select Committee on Nationalized industries is expected to. There is something more to this different intensity of scrutiny than just a symbolic distinction. Its rational basis is that by now we know so much about financial control and discipline of commercial activities, as a result of the development of accountancy over many years and of scientific management more recently. This knowledge has not always been effective in securing financial discipline in private or public corporations, but where there is a will it can be established. (Among the chief exceptions, as we have seen, have been those whose technology has been so complex and interlocking that a major planning, economic and operations research effort is needed before financial control can be put on a firm foundation. What is lacking here is knowledge not of financial control techniques as such, but of how they may be applied in these complex cases.)

By comparison, the control of non-commercial operations is in its infancy. Where operations are not commercial there has been less development of investment criteria, let alone of what is more important: the apparatus of financial control which would make possible net social benefit forecasting (by analogy with corporate planning to achieve new revenue forecasts), of which the definition of investment criteria is a necessary, but tiny, part. Because it is in its infancy, there is a case for the greater scrutiny in principle that is implied by being under the watch of Ministers and the Select Committee on Estimates. The natural way for Ministers to control such activities is the historic way. Financial and other control is not easily disentangled. Tactical control is exercised, roughly speaking, by the candle-ends method described in *Chapter 6*. Strategic control is largely the periodic discussion of principles described at the beginning of *Chapter 15*. One imagines that Ministers and their officials will be able to have considerable and legitimate influence on the way the money is spent.

Therefore the natural way ahead would seem to be for the commercial activities to be subjected to more meaningful financial discipline – if it is agreed that that tendency should be strengthened – and for the social services to be subjected to the same kind of control that is exercised now over social services performed within Government. The way in which a department looks at the money spent by the Railways on unprofitable rail services would be essentially the same as the way in which money is now looked at which is spent, say, on prisons or school-building.

It is quite common to believe that social and financial control can be improved by the manipulation of organization. Some recent thinking seems to have assumed that to set up separate agencies somewhat like the Boards, and devolve Government activities to them, would be an improvement in management. What we have discussed should make us question a little more carefully why this should be so.

(1) There are a number of activities within Government which are, to a large extent, commercial in that they provide services for which the public pays. One thinks not only of the Stationery Office, but also of much smaller operations: testing services, information services, the Public Trustee, the Royal Mint, and so forth. Many of these will also provide services for Government, who may buy the same services from them as the public does, or some special services. In many cases it could be sensible to turn them into Boards, so to speak. But if they had quite the practical independence of Boards, competition, in many cases, would not be strong enough to establish a sufficient financial discipline. Thus, if nothing were done about financial discipline (which could even be reduced in the process), it is not easy to see how management would improve (unless one really believes that simply giving the running of such things to persons other than civil servants will do the trick, even without outside pressure to be efficient). If there were to be a better financial discipline, there might be some advantage in setting up such entities as Boards. A major benefit would be that it would help free officials and the Select Committee from the more gruelling and time-consuming traditional methods of control. In many cases, such entities disgorged from Government would be considerable monopolies – in some cases legal monopolies: for example, the operation of drivers' tests could be such an entity. It would be as necessary in discussing their target-setting to make sure that they did not abuse their monopoly power as it is for electricity.

(2) There are several organizations which are given an independence because they perform judicial or quasi-judicial functions.

On high there are the Courts themselves. On a much smaller scale there are the Licensing Authorities, for example, who perform quasi-judicial functions in regulating road freight transport. They too have a considerable autonomy because of the importance that their decisions should be seen to be independent of ministerial influence, and, in some cases, to ensure that a right of appeal to a Minister or the Transport Tribunal should be a genuine opportunity to appeal. There are many agencies of the same kind, many of them integral parts of departments.

(3) There are other organizations which raise questions of equity and justice in their operations in rather a different way. In at least one case this has been a reason for giving them independence. Because of the possibility that if Ministers had greater control over the BBC they might misuse it for electoral ends, it has been given a very great independence from Ministers and Parliament. But in many cases, where the direct interests of Ministers and MPs are not as closely involved, this becomes an argument against independence. The Boards of Inland Revenue and of Customs and Excise are departments which no one would ever think of pushing outside the Civil Service, principally because of the very great need to believe them trustworthy, fair and above suspicion. A more interesting case is the question of a Roads Board, because it is nearer being a marginal one. Many interests have urged that the Highways side of the Ministry of Transport should be given a separate existence and perhaps turned into a public corporation like a nationalized industry. One important reason why this is difficult – there are other arguments on both sides – is that highway construction is very much bound up with questions of the rights of the individual. A large part of the time of the administrative civil servants engaged in the roads programme is taken up with public inquiries, problems of land acquisition and compensation where the Ministry is dealing with many small people. Now, while it is perfectly possible to argue that the basis of compensation is sometimes unfair, and even that small men are sometimes trampled on – inadvertently but painfully – this system has advantages. The administrators will have served in other sides of Government. They will have had some experience in equitable administration. In this respect they will not be completely identified – as it is often accused American highway officials are – with the construction of the highway programme. It is difficult to see how the creation of a separate Roads Board would be an advantage from this point of view. It would take the everyday activities away from Parliamentary Questions and the Ombudsman; and the sheer volume of questions

suggests this is just the kind of administrative casework where these kinds of procedure are most effective. It is also likely that if the Roads Board were given a separate existence, one would find a growth in litigation between it and those with whom it dealt, just because it had lost its quasi-judicial character. Again, while not maintaining that the present system always acts in the best interest of the individual, it is difficult to see how litigation would secure better justice, especially for poor people.

(4) There is a sense also in which the mere setting up of an agency with the independence of a Board can achieve an apparent increase in financial discipline which is quite spurious. Supposing one was to lay down as a general policy that the right way to perform a large number of social functions would be to pay bodies with the independence of Boards and autonomous agencies to do them, through an extension of the social grant procedure. Then there would be a very limited sense in which one could say that one had solved the problem of *financial* control. If the preponderance of their activities was paid for by user charges and only a small part consisted of services performed for Government, then the case would be as strong for doing this as it was said to be in *Chapter 4*. But, formally, one could go much further than this. There are virtually no subordinate, semi-autonomous agencies or divisions of departments which could not be given the same financial framework. At present, we can suppose, they receive money by parliamentary vote with which they perform the services required of them. It would be quite possible to regard this as revenue and to require them to earn a predetermined return on their assets (whatever these may be), with the revenue coming either from charges imposed directly on users or from Parliament. Formally, Government or Parliament would be a customer paying for services rendered, on a contractual basis. As far as the enterprise is concerned it can judge itself, and be judged, by what are near enough ordinary financial criteria. We could, at an extreme, extend the same principle to cover all manner of activities, from embassies to the Economic Section of the Treasury, or the parliamentary draftsmen.[1]

Unless the commercial, profit-making, non-Government activities of the organization are not negligible, it is questionable to what

---

[1] The same point may apply when administration of such activities is devolved outside Government altogether. The financial control of the National Health Service is far from perfect. But the administration of health service finances through non-Governmental insurance schemes in the United States appears to have been unable to control cost increases, themselves at least in part the result of monopoly power.

extent this would imply an increase in financial discipline. The point can be put quite simply: it makes sense to distinguish between the commercial and social activities of an organization *when it has both commercial and social activities*; but if it has no commercial activities then to give it commercial accounts and a commercial financial discipline is mere window-dressing.

There are, indeed, Boards of public corporations where financial discipline in the ordinary commercial sense is an irrelevant discipline because the Boards do not, or should not, be seen as ordinary commercial profit-making bodies. One such is London Transport (and the new Passenger Transport Executives are, or ought to be, in the same position). Until a few years ago it was possible for it to be profitable, but the growth of car ownership has cut into its profits to a point where most of its capital has had to be written off in order to get some correspondence with its earning power. This cannot be a stable financial position because it implies a much smaller capital structure than is needed to maintain the business. Thus, even though London Transport has assets (tunnels) which will never need replacement, it has many other assets which do (rolling stock, buses, escalators, power stations, etc.). Therefore, as these come to be replaced, they will have to be written off continuously (which is the same as their being a free gift from the GLC and Government) or London Transport will automatically find itself in deficit. Given its earning power, it cannot retain its present level of operation as a *profitable* enterprise. But there are very strong social, political and economic reasons for not allowing London Transport's services to contract. The reason is one which we have already encountered in *Chapter 13*. There would not be fair competition between public and private transport (especially for the underground lines) because there is not the required financial discipline on the road side. As has often been argued, and demonstrated, most urban roads are underpriced, especially in the peak, and this is nowhere truer than in London.[1] If one were to impose a

---

[1] One reference which is particularly relevant because it is in the context of a justification for building its newest tube line, is C. D. Foster and M. E. Beesley 'Estimating the Social Benefit of Constructing an Underground Railway in London' (*Journal of the Royal Statistical Society*, Series A, 1963); but see also M. E. Beesley and C. D. Foster 'The Victoria Line: Social Benefit and Finances' (*Journal of the Royal Statistical Society*, Series A, 1965) in which there is an estimate of the inefficiency of pricing to cover costs.

The recent announcements by the Greater London Council that they mean to run London Transport as a profitable enterprise just shows that they do not understand the issues involved. That kind of financial discipline is not

rational pricing on urban roads then it would make sense to impose a normal financial discipline and normal investment and pricing criteria.

What then remains is the heart of the problem: how does Government go about getting value for money when the objects of an activity are not commercial. We are able to broaden the scope of the discussion. The same problem arises for: (i) the Boards of nationalized industries who perform such services; (ii) other autonomous agencies, existing or to be created, which are in the same position or whose main *raison d'être* is to perform social services (e.g. Arts Councils, Government laboratories, and many more); as well as for (iii) the activities of the same kind conducted within Government of the same kind. The question is whether better methods of control can be devised than the traditional ones.

This is the point in the argument at which to introduce what is commonly, but very loosely, called *output budgeting*. Its introduction does not depend on any particular organization, as one of those most responsible for introducing it has pointed out. 'The effectiveness of Planning and Programme Budgeting does not depend on reorganizing operating units to conform to programme categories, as is often claimed. In fact, this would be harmful in some cases and impossible in others.[1] It is primarily a mixture of methods for achieving better financial control and discipline in just the cases in which we are interested.

By now PPB, or PPBS, as it is usually called, was introduced into American Government has become widely known: how Charles Hitch and some associates worked for some five years at the Rand Corporation on problems of optimization in defence; how when Robert Macnamara became Secretary of Defence under Kennedy, Hitch became an Assistant Secretary and PPB was introduced on a grand scale into the management of the Defence Department and the evaluation of military strategies; how, on August 25, 1965, President Johnson announced 'a new and revolutionary system of planning and programming and budgeting throughout the Federal Government – so that through the tools of modern management the full promise of a finer life can be brought to every American at the

---

relevant in this case and, if persisted in, can only damage London by leading to a rundown in its public transport which will not only be inefficient but, one imagines, also political suicide. More recent announcements still (1971) suggest they may be coming round.

[1] C. L. Schultze, *The Politics and Economics of Public Spending*, The Brookings Institution, Washington DC, 1968. Schultze was Director of the Bureau of the Budget under President Johnson.

lowest possible cost'.[1] A year later the Committee for Economic Development in the full cry of enthusiasm wrote that it should result in 'improved operational management of programmes, more effective budgetary execution, and a more intensive review of budgetary performance . . . if carried through in all its implications – including congressional consideration, budgetary execution and performance review – initiation of this planning-programming-budgetary system may come to rank among the main events in federal budgetary history'.[2] Three years later it was reported that:

'Since 1965 the new system has spread rapidly. It is now being introduced, used or misused by: hundreds of bureaus and divisions throughout the Federal Government; the Comptroller General as a tool in trying to modernize the General Accounting Office; congressional committees in appraising executive programme proposals and writing legislative prescriptions for future programme review; many governors, mayors, and state and local agencies (a tendency accelerated by a growing belief that applications for federal aid may be more successful if justified in PPB terminology).'[3]

It is ironical that enthusiasm for it in Britain has blossomed just at the time, or even a year or two later than the time, when enthusiasm in the United States dropped very sharply. Even the protagonists have to concede that:

'PPB has had a rough time these past few years. Confusion is widespread; results are meagre. The publicity has outdistanced the performance by a wide margin. In the name of analysis, bureaus have produced reams of unsupported irrelevant justification and description. As Schumpeter said of Marxism: it is preaching in the guise of analysis.'[4]

[1] 'Introduction of New-Government-Wide Planning and Budgeting System', Statement to a Cabinet meeting, August 1965.

[2] *Ibid.*

[3] B. M. Gross, 'The New Systems Budgeting', *Public Administration Review*, vol. 29, no. 2, 1969.

[4] A. Schick, 'Systems Politics and Systems Budgeting', *Public Administration Review*, op. cit. The difference in optimism between this and the December 1966 issue of the same journal is remarkable. Both were given over to discussions of PPB. The first was generally enthusiastic and self-confident. But by 1969, even those most identified with the system were apologetic and hesitant. For example, Schick's basis for belief that in the end PPB must win – echoed by Dror – was simply that the entrenched system with its gradual incremental procedures simply was not adequate to deal with the major non-marginal problems of American society. Therefore, in the end, a procedure like PPB, which could evaluate non-marginal changes, must prevail.

Even Schultze, the ex-Director of the Bureau of the Budget and among the most important of those who tried to spread PPB in Government, finds himself asking in a series of lectures which is generally a defence and exposition of PPB, 'whether . . . PPB as a system, and cost-effectiveness as an analytic technique, can fit into the political decision-making process', and recognizes that the answer is far from an unequivocal Yes.[1] Aaron Wildavsky, who in 1964 to his mind had demolished the possibility of PPB before it started, was able by 1969 to argue that the experience of PPB, if anything, had made decision-making less rational: '. . . its difficulties have been so overwhelming that there is grave danger that policy analysis will be rejected along with its particular manifestation in PPBS'.[2]

Gone almost completely are the ringing tones of confidence. But some of the reasons for disappointment should be avoidable. It is said that when President Johnson announced in his August message that PPB would be developed in all agencies, it was only after the Bureau of the Budget had begged him to start in a few areas. As Schultze has said, 'I must admit that in first establishing PPB procedures in civilian agencies, too little consideration was given to the problem of selectivity'.[3] (In British Government the idea that something could start on all fronts at once is, for better and for worse, unthinkable.) It was also a fundamental error to introduce special people into departments and agencies whose responsibility it was to develop and produce *programme budgets*. While one can understand the belief that this would get PPB moving more quickly, it is hardly surprising that in the end that it moved more slowly. The established financial administrators did not take kindly to being overridden; and because, in practice, one cannot develop a financial programme without the co-operation of the established financial people, there was inertia and hard-fought resistance. (This was not only culpable, but human, irritation at being by-passed. It was also an incentive to the established financial people to point out PPB's shortcomings more persistently than they otherwise might have. One would hope that one could avoid this mistake, and work with and through departmental financial officers, even though it looked as if it would take more time, though in fact it would take less.)

Other errors seem to have been partly, but not wholly, a consequence of the last two. Because every department was to be tackled at once and because largely new men were used for the job,

1 Schultze, op. cit., pp. 1, 2; also p. 101.
2 *Public Administration Review*, op. cit., p. 190
3 Schultze, op. cit., p. 80.

not far short of a thousand people were assigned to PPB duty, about half of them analysts of one kind or another from outside. Everyone was looking around for some of the few who had made a difference to the Defence Department, but in general such a rate of expansion had the expected effect: many of the PPB practitioners and prophets were of low quality. There were many complaints of arrogance, stupidity, even quackery and charlatanism. It was mostly because there were so many people – of various levels of ability – that such fantastic quantities of paper were created. Schultze says again 'although agencies were asked to focus on "central questions" the original Budget Bureau instructions could have been interpreted as requiring a comprehensive analysis of all programme elements. As a consequence, initial submission of programme memoranda from many agencies took up six-foot bookshelves, described (not analysed) programme objectives and content in excruciating detail, and burdened harassed budget examiners with a flood of irrelevant material'.[1]

One would hope that a more sensible approach would avoid some of these extraordinary results; but there is a more fundamental reason for believing that PPB has a better chance of succeeding in Britain. Some of the defenders of PPB in the United States have said that, in the last resort, what it has done is to increase the power of the Bureau of the Budget (or of the parallel institutions in state and city). The mere fact that there is a new process to be gone through, for which they have the most responsibility in the end, has given them more leverage in the budgeting process. But even so there is a profound difficulty which comes from the nature of the American political process. PPB is a reformist movement. This goes further than a mere desire to get the work of Government done less wastefully. It also goes further than an attempt to help Government develop new policies and programmes. It is, or was, a concerted effort to make politics more rational and, in order to achieve that end, to defeat the porkbarrel politics and politicization we described in *Chapter 11*. Some who are, and always have been, most opposed to PPB, like Wildavsky, are those who have found most virtue in the traditional system.[2] Some who have been keenest

---

[1] Schultze, loc. cit.

[2] See also Robert C. Wood's oft quoted statement: 'Despite our predictions, disaster has not struck: urban government has continued to function, not well perhaps, but at least well enough to forestall catastrophe. Traffic continues to circulate; streets and sewers are built; water is provided; schools keep their doors open; and law and order generally prevail.' (*American Political Science Review*, March 1958, p. 112.) It was also one of the main messages of his *1400 Governments*, his study of the political structure of New York.

on PPB have been most dissatisfied with the old process and have seen what they are doing as necessary preludes to the substantial changes American society needs because of all the current dissatisfactions with its way of life.

But what is relevant for us in this, is that it imposes an additional strain upon the use of PPB. Not only is it trying to introduce a new style into decision-making, but also new values. A more impartial approach might take the kinds of values and decisions made by congressional committees, with all their log-rolling and side-payments, and try to find more efficient solutions in the light of those values. To do this it might point out to the Senator from X that the expenditure which he thinks will help his constituents will not do this half as well as he thinks, nor half as well as another project might. Or it might show Congressman A who has a particular interest at heart – it may well be a disinterested one – that the best way for him to get his way is through collusion with Congressman B. But of course this is not what the advocates of PPB mean by improving the efficiency of public expenditure control. Thus they try to present to congressional committees alternatives based on very different value-systems which, for the most part, they regard as reflecting more the national interest. It is this which gives so much force to Aaron Wildavsky's observation that:

'. . . there is little or no realization among the reformers that any changes in budgetary relationships must necessarily alter the outcomes of the budgetary process . . . proposed reforms inevitably contain important implications for the political system; that is, for the "who gets what" of government decisions.'[1]

Therefore, quite apart from all the confusions and ineptitudes that PPB is reported to have got itself into in the United States, even if we imagine these absent, the fact that it is trying to achieve both greater efficiency and a change in value-systems may have meant that it was attempting too much. Not that better analysis cannot make fundamental changes: if it is possible to analyse a problem in such a way as to help people to see more clearly the implications several steps ahead, there is a chance that their decisions will be less 'incremental, fragmented, non-programmatic and sequential'.[2] Similarly, one reason why it is more difficult upon a change of government to get a change in political values reflected in a change in policy, is that if this is held to imply a large change, the sheer uncertainty of doing something more than marginally different from the *status quo* is likely to be so alarming as to damp

[1] Wildavsky, op. cit., p. 127.   [2] Wildavsky, op. cit., p. 136.

down enthusiasm for change. While not claiming too much, analysis can make the future a little more predictable and less frightening. It would also seem to be the case that in certain areas the congressional appropriations committees have seized on PPB and turned it to their own advantage. Thus they have made it mirror their values, rather than remake their decisions to fit it, or ignore it altogether. But, in general, one should not be surprised if one cannot use PPB to promote a revolution in values as well as in procedures.

Why it seems to me that there may be more hope for PPB in Britain than in the United States is this: not only may one expect that it could be introduced more carefully, but also it is more likely to succeed because British Government is relatively less politicized. I am not thinking here just of porkbarrel politics, but also of what Schultze is saying when he states that:

'It is impossible to make a policy proposal in Washington without stirring up an incredible array of interest groups, each joining in the debate and uncovering real or alleged relationships between the proposed policy and its own interests – relationships that the policy proponents may never have dreamed existed. There are thousands of individuals whose full-time occupation is the careful examination of proposed legislation or executive actions, seeking to discover implications for the interests of the groups they represent.'[1]

In legislation this describes a situation I can recognize. There are many interests; they are reasonably representing their own interests. They perform a necessary function. It is against their

[1] Schultze, op. cit., p. 51. Schultze also talks on a more technical level of the difficulty of defining a determinate social welfare, or decision, function: 'In practice, however, there are so many "dimensions" to most public programmes that there is no possibility of determining, in the abstract, multidimensional trade-off functions among different, usually noncommensurable, values' (p. 39). While the concept of a social welfare function is the kind of jargon one would really wish to introduce into a policy discussion, I have found that what is involved is perfectly comprehensible to administrators. If $U = U(u_1, u_2 \ldots u_n)$ is a social welfare function where $(u_1, u_2 \ldots u_n)$ are the interests of particular groups, in my experience it is not usually difficult to agree on which are the groups to be taken into consideration. The point of departure is usually the classical Pigovian social welfare function where utilities are additive. If there is a wish to use the function distributionally, there is usually no disagreement on what groups are to be given special weighting (though there may be a problem of precise definition of such groups). What is likely to cause more problems – because it is an activity to which politicians and administrators are less used – is assigning the actual weights; but this has proved tractable in several situations. Much more important than these are the empirical difficulties of estimation. These are much more likely to sink an analysis.

211

criticism, their opposition that a notion of the value of proposed legislation is developed. If they are not listened to, legislation will be worse; and there is always a chance that they may be able to bring enough influence to bear to kill it. The queen of the political arts lies in recognizing these interests, treating them, yet having a clear idea of what is important in what one wants. Successful legislation should please most of the people most of the time, and yet be a power for good. If it does some group a disservice it should be possible to show why this was done, in a way which will persuade most people that it was deliberate, reasoned and not unjust. All this is commonplace, and has often been discussed.

But in relation to executive action, what Schultze describes is not a situation I can recognize. This does not mean that people within the administration do not think of the effects of their actions on interest groups outside. They do. It is arguable that perhaps they do not give enough weight to some groups, or even recognize the interests that some groups may have in a decision. But in the end, Ministers and officials have a certain freedom to make up their own minds. They are not under such duress from pressure groups. (If a decision is made as a result of the exertions of pressure groups, this will often be because no one can think of a better way to make it.) If decisions involve more than one department then there is perhaps more chance that a decision will be taken because of the relative weights of the immediate bodies concerned, rather than on the basis of a rational calculation of how it will affect the people who will ultimately be affected by the decision. It is far from my contention to suppose that all decisions in British government are taken on the basis of carefully calculated analyses in which immediate political pressures or pressure groups have no part. That would be ridiculous. It is clear to anyone watching that, of course, bad decisions, as well as good ones have been taken for all sorts of reasons and in all sorts of ways. What I would maintain is that most administrators when faced by analysis which is rational and relevant, have a predisposition to make use of it and even to welcome it.[1]

---

[1] This is subject to several not unreasonable provisos: (i) the analysis arrives in time so as not to disrupt the decision-making process; (ii) it is not presented to Ministers in such a way as to seem to make a fool of administrators; (iii) the opinions of the administrators have been sought and taken notice of at several stages; (iv) the values are relevant values reflecting ministerial policy; and (v) the jump in policy is not too big. This last is the most difficult. The important tensions are between the administrator's possibly having a more limited, and experienced, idea of what is possible than has the analyst, and wishing to go more slowly. Occasionally, too, though the administrator is unlikely to resent

Those who revel in decision-making in the dark on the basis of less adequate information, are a minority.

Therefore it seems possible that for these reasons Whitehall is a more fertile ground for PPB than Washington. While there has been far less display and no general directives to introduce PPB in Whitehall, reading the literature makes one wonder if it is not possible that more actual decisions – including some extremely complex ones – may have been taken with its aid in Whitehall than in Washington.[1] But so far we have managed to talk about PPB without discussing what it is or the nature of its relevance to the topics of this book. This is not so strange as it may seem, because it is difficult to find a clear description of what is meant and impossible to find a rigorous one. The key word which is used can have the most various meanings in different contexts; the picture is one of an orphan, claiming as its parents whoever it thinks will impress those it is talking to, and using words to describe its activities that are impressive rather than meaningful.[2]

If there is no consensus, no account of what is meant by PPBS can be definitive, but to try to clarify its leading ideas: there would seem

---

rational modes of analysis, he may on occasions be more likely to think that he may even get more enjoyment that way.

[1] In early 1969 we did an analysis of some hundred or so projects undertaken at the Ministry of Transport in the preceding three years, some quite small, some very large, but all of which would come under the general heading of PPB. The success ratio was 90 per cent. By success, one does not mean an analysis which disagreed with a decision reached by other means. Happily the need for an analysis was usually agreed early on and success meant that its results were agreed to be relevant and useful. Some of the failures were where the analysis was not finished in time, or the data was not good enough.

[2] 'All these confusions have been magnified by fantastic terminological tangles. Into the older jargons of budgeting, accounting and efficiency engineering have been mixed new terms from microeconomics, systems engineering and business management. Bumbling attempts at popularization have been successful in little except slowing down the essential processes of improved conceptualization. "System", "output", "planning" and "programming" have become fad words, used with a false sophistication that often masks a narrow-minded naivety. In fact there seems to be an unspoken "gentleman's agreement" that the basic terms need never be defined' (Gross, op. cit., p. 115). This seems like fair comment. Gross goes on to show that the Bureau of the Budget itself had its doubts. 'By the summer of 1967, Budget Bureau officials reluctantly but officially found that "the longer-term objectives of PPBS are now unclear to many". By identifying many alternative future relations between PPBS and *the* budgetary system, they highlighted the fact that the new system was merely an increment on top of the old and that integration between the two in the near future is unlikely. Indeed, they even came to the conclusion within the Bureau itself: "The definition of PPBS is a source of disagreement and confusion." '

to be a *tactical* and a *strategic* strain, a distinction as useful here as in previous methods of control we have considered.

The three major tactical forms of analysis would seem to be:

(1) *Cost effectiveness.* Although one finds variation in the definition,[1] a convenient definition is that it takes an *output* and compares the costs of doing it in various ways, and also the costs of its being done by various organizations. To think of it as a simple ratio, a cost effectiveness index will be of the form: $C_i = X/c_i$, where X is a given output and c_i is the cost of producing it in a particular (the ith) way. It is usual to define the output in clear *physical* terms. Therefore a cost effectiveness index of road construction might be one which compared the costs of building a mile of (four-lane, dual-carriageway) road.

(2) *Output budgeting.* The index is still a ratio – the numerator and denominator are incommensurate – but the measure of output will be more abstract. It will not be the mile of road itself but a service the road provides. To quote Schultze, '. . . it is not sufficient to ask how many miles of concrete are laid, but what the programme produces in terms of safer, less-congested travel – how many hours of travel time are eliminated and how many accidents are prevented.'[2] Thus it becomes possible to compare roads of different widths and with different traffic intensities, to decide how many vehicle- or person-hours a day will be saved by different improvements, and how many accidents. One can go further since hours saved is a general output of transport improvements – road, rail, sea, air. If there are two or more outputs which are incommensurate – here we have two: person-hours saved and accidents – then it is up to the decision-maker to whom the facts are presented to decide the weight to be given to each output.

(The kind of abstraction used to define the outputs is the defining characteristic of many variants of output budgeting with many different labels.)

---

[1] Cost effectiveness is often used to mean what I have called output budgeting; but the difference between the two definitions is not sharp, as will be appreciated, and the words perhaps suggest the meaning of cost effectiveness that I have given. It is not easy to think of a better nomenclature. If one was starting from scratch it might be: (i) cost minimization where the output is defined in physical terms; (ii) cost minimization where the output is defined more abstractly; and (iii) cost-benefit analysis.

[2] Schultze, op. cit., pp. 20–1. For a fuller analysis on the same lines see D. Novick's (ed), *Program Budgeting: Program Analysis and the Federal Budget* (Harvard UP, 1965, ch. 6). There are many state publications which set out objectives in similar terms: e.g. 'California, Division of Highways', *Planning Programming Budgeting System for Highway Program* (Sacramento, 1969).

(3) *Cost-benefit analysis.* In this the ratio is replaced by a single number. Outputs and inputs become commensurate, both being expressed in money terms. If a number of alternative highway improvements are considered, the benefits might still be the number of hours and accident savings. But on the basis of experiments to determine how people value their time,[1] and on some calculations of the money costs of savings as well as imputed value of the loss of a human life,[2] one can produce a money figure of the benefit to be derived from alternative investments. One can substract the costs (having discounted to allow for time) and produce a single figure value showing the worth of the programme; this is formally identical to a net present value calculation of financial return such as we have seen the Treasury urging and the Boards slowly adopting. It is an extremely flexible instrument since, if it is desired to give any group of persons a special weight in the calculation, this can be done. If one wants to benefit a group of people whom one defines as poor, one can weight the benefits and costs they incur by some factor to reflect the weight one wants to give. Or, if one has no *a priori* idea of what weight one wants to give, then one can test the sensitivity of the results to a number of different weights. So ends and means may interpenetrate and help the decision-maker to reach a conclusion.

What determines one's choice of method? Principally it should be the nature of the data one has. The more comprehensive and flexible method is cost-benefit analysis; the others are conceptually and empirically inferior, to be chosen only because one has not the data to do better. Output budgeting, as it has been defined here, is better than cost effectiveness. Cost effectiveness tells one only the cheapest or most efficient means to a narrowly defined end. Output budgeting extends the range of rational choice – but at some cost. The time saved on one road will not be equally valued by those who gain it as will the time saved on another road. Small time savings are not normally valued as much as large. Richer people tend to

---

[1] There is an excellent discussion of the many experiments done and the considerable consensus there is on values in A. J. Harrison and D. A. Quarmby's 'The Value of Time in Transport Planning: A Review' (paper presented to the Sixth Round Table of the Economic Research Centre of the European Conference of Ministers of Transport, Paris, November 1969).

[2] The giving of a money value to a human life is often misunderstood. There are minimum calculations of the loss experienced on average by society and by his family when someone is killed. But by raising the value above this in stages one can test the sensitivity of an investment programme to successively higher values. An infinitive value on a human life would of course imply that one would never spend resources on anything else except saving human life (unless of course it was held there were other things which also had an infinite value).

value time savings more than poor people (if only because they can afford to pay more, a fact that can be nullified in the calculations if desired). People tend to value the time they save on one mode or one kind of journey more than they do on others. Output budgeting calculations which talk, for example, of the output of a school as the number of graduating students or of a hospital as the number of days off work, reduced can seem to very be crude measures, but they may well be much better than nothing. Simple measures of this sort can often show up peculiarities in a system which suggests that something should be done about it.[1]

All these techniques are used to illuminate decisions by the British Government, as they are used by many Governments. If one makes a comparison with the history of the stages of the growth of financial discipline given in *Chapter 15*, the stage most British departments are at is an early one where such techniques are either in the research stage or are used to throw light on particularly difficult or otherwise special cases; this is precisely the stage at which many American departments and city governments are. This is far from suggesting that even at the tactical level, this is the best of all possible worlds. There are departments where nothing of the kind is heard; and there may be others in which research in techniques is used as euphemism for a situation where boys in a backroom work away, but not so as to affect a decision. As well, there are complex decisions where British Government has been slow to recognize that they were not susceptible to the traditional decision-making methods – at least, the output was not sound enough to satisfy public opinion.[2]

[1] Suppose one found that in two prisons the cost of keeping prisoners differed: if one was Broadmoor, one might see a good reason for it and pass on; but if they housed the same kind of criminals and one could see no good reason, this might be a useful pointer to action, the starting point for discussion.

[2] A classic case has been the third London airport. A committee sat on this and one has no reason to suppose it did not go through all the issues conscientiously and thoroughly in the traditional manner. But when it produced a report the quality of its arguments was not enough to allay the strong interests affected. They were not prepared to accept that a committee of good men and true had sifted the evidence and had come to a balanced decision. Because of this debacle a commission was set up with a staff which, as part of its activities, has quantified many of the factors for and against placing the airport at a number of sites. Thus they produced a cost-benefit analysis of the problem. As it turned out, few who had their say seemed to like the conclusion. Partly this was because of the values assigned to particular factors by the commission. If people do not like those values, it is the essence of cost-benefit analysis that they should be able to work out the implications of giving different weights to these factors. Unfortunately, much of the opposition was inconsistent and overrode many of the facts with dubious argument, but the silence of the commission and its staff meant

Neither could it follow from my earlier arguments in this book that a solution which implied only a tactical use of PPB methods to give them the generic name, was ideal. Even the use of PPB methods as a strategic weapon has gone some distance.[1] One can use them in some cases as a routine method of appraisal, as in some cases one can use financial present value calculations as routine – that is, when the techniques have been developed enough to make sense of the relevant facts, and these are known. But this is still tactical control in the sense developed in *Chapter 15*. It is the piecemeal examination of cases. Thus, one could imagine a department (i) administering a social grant paid to a Board or a nationalized industry, requiring a cost-benefit study in each case, and (ii) assessing a project on the basis of it. It will be interesting to see whether Boards accept this in relation to social expenditures where they would regard it as excessive interventionism in relation to commercial projects. Probably for a time they would not, because it will take both sides in each case a certain time to explore the facts and each other's minds before coming up with a rational set of options that can be put to Ministers and Parliament. Again one might expect that once this stage was through, Ministers might relax their vigilance a little and attempt a more strategic control. Financial control of social expenditure would then be beginning to pass through the stage of innovation, when close detailed control is reasonable, into a stage where it is unnecessary and where Ministers and departments can pass on to spend their close attention on other problems.

---

that its critics' arguments were not exposed. Whether otherwise the interests of the people of Cublington would have received quite so much weight, is hard to say. One of the great dangers of the traditional methods in contentious cases is that a decision keeps on being postponed, because there is always a strong enough minority against a solution but never the factual basis to convince the majority in favour of any solution. In this particular case, when the clouds have blown away in a few years' time, it should be possible to make a dispassionate analysis of the politics of the final decision-making, and to learn from this how to improve the decision-making process in the future and make it more useful.

[1] To cite again the department I know best, the Ministry of Transport has been using output budgeting methods of highway appraisal for many years. More recently it has developed cost-benefit methods for inter-urban roads which are being adopted as a routine method of appraisal. Some progress has been made on the research level in the much more difficult problems of developing cost-benefit appraisal for use in towns and also to reflect environmental considerations. For some years it has been routine to require cost-benefit analysis to justify new underground lines and extensions, and for surface rapid-transit facilities. Cost-benefit studies have begun to be made of unremunerative rail-lines in such a way as will help develop a rational policy towards these. Cf. Ministry of Transport, *The Cambrian Coast Line: a Cost Benefit Study*, May 1970.

But again it would seem to be wrong, and for reasons I will not repeat, to let things relapse into practical independence. To make the public trust, so to speak, the prime engine for social policy, seems an extraordinary devolution of parliamentary and ministerial control of that policy. Financial control of Boards of nationalized industries and other agencies within and outside departments, would seem to be as sensible as for commercial programmes and could be conducted, one would hope, on the same kind of basis. An investment programme would be presented as part of a corporate plan. Instead of forecasting the effect on net revenue of different strategies, it would forecast the effect on net benefits (as defined in relation to that programme).

But even to sketch the problem in those terms points out how far we have to go. At the moment, practical independence of the Boards means in many cases no effective financial discipline of commercial projects at the tactical level. To move through that and on to effective financial discipline at the strategic level, will take a major effort of will which, as a nation, we may not be up to. To move likewise in relation to the financial control of social expenditure will take not only another great act of will, but also much more work and analsyis, a task which, if the omens are favourable, might be beginning to supersede the more traditional methods at the strategic level within the next ten years.

Meanwhile, what has happened to PPB in the United States as a strategic method of control, may be a dire warning against letting apparatus strangle achievement. The six-foot-long shelves of indigestible tomes on departmental programmes are one manifestation. The fact that no one can point to a success on this level is another. In a way it has been a situation analogous to the Beeching influx into the railways, though much more mischievous in its results. The similarity was in trying to impose a financial discipline in that case, a PPB discipline in this, before there was the capability to analyse the organization to find out the causes of changes in revenues (benefits) and costs. One can appreciate in the United States why it was likely to happen the way it did. The impetus came from a strong President, and, as many have pointed out, the intention was to increase the power of the Chief Executive. Profoundly irritated by his lack of control over a machine which had grown too large and unpredictable, he would seem to have seized at an iron claw which would gather all together in his power. If this were the impetus, then an attempt at strategic control, at the very highest level, was inevitable. After all, it can hardly have mattered much to President

218

Johnson whether a particular decision in an agency was taken on the basis of cost effectiveness or by grace and God. Except in the most striking cases, particular decisions do not especially interest high-ranking politicians. But the belief that Macnamara had a method which gave him a much publicized control of his department, was too tempting.[1] The idea of a departmental head's, let alone a President's, increasing his power is bound to be seductive. Moreover, there is a sense in which the effective power, as opposed to the nominal power, of Presidents has declined to an even greater extent than that of Ministers as Government business has become more complicated; there is much to be said for techniques which will increase it in a rational manner.

Why then did PPB fail at the strategic level? It was not just the style of confusion and impulsiveness with which it was introduced. To a large extent it was based on output budgeting. Programmes were grouped together out of projects which were thought definable in terms of common outputs. Now, it is true that, in a sense, a departmental head can increase his power if he has displayed in front of him a large number of, let us say, transport options, where he is told that A improvement in an airport, B in a port, C in development of a new aircraft, and D expenditure on more highways will save different amounts of travellers' time. He can be Draconian and try shuffling round the funds to where these crude indices are highest. But as well as the unreasonable resistance of inertia and self-interest, he will also meet a reasonable resistance from administrators who will argue, rightly, that the objectives they are in administration for are not as simple as that and cannot be reduced to one or two output measures. Quite apart from the intellectual and economic crudity of such a supposition, they will also argue that the political backlash against such crudity could be considerable. They should have the sympathy of businessmen who have themselves

---

[1] Scorn has been poured on this too: 'Those willing to give Macnamara credit for a "managerial revolution" in the strengthening of military capability must ponder his role – and that of cost effectiveness analysis – in an Asiatic military operation of high costs, low effectiveness, and questionable wisdom' (Gross, op. cit., p. 115). People tend to be remembered, naturally enough, for the most striking things they do. So the noble Duke of York is remembered for his up-and-down hill-climbing rather than for his efficiency in producing an effective army for someone else to use. To say that Vietnam inevitably has been the supreme test of Macnamara's methods, is not to say that it is a fair one. Someone else may reap the benefits. But what is more interesting is why PPB was so much more quick in application in defence than elsewhere. Among reasons given are: (i) that Hitch and his associates had put in five years' work first; (ii) that defence was much freer from congressional interference; and (iii) that it came first.

got beyond cost effectiveness and productivity indices towards the sophistication of profit centres and management by objectives related to profitability. One trouble about such crudity is that it may encourage administrators to take up an attitude which is less defensible in the face of a more sophisticated approach: namely, that their activity is so complex in its objectives that no rational analysis is possible. If the resistance was not too great and a departmental head was to play games of strategy using such crude indices, that too, though maybe increasing his power to throw his weight around, would not increase the power of rational Government nor, except in the most unlikely circumstances, help him get what he really wants. Thus, whatever happens is not for the best unless it is carefully done.

The most interesting moral to be drawn from this would seem to be rather like that drawn for the Boards if they should abuse their practical independence to the extent of not being responsive to the changing demands of Parliament. Similarly, a system of Government which does not develop within it, or develop fast enough, the means of control and discipline to provide the wherewithal of a sufficient political control, finds that politicians rend the firmament from the heavens to the foundations in an agony of impotence, in the hope that by a great gesture they can find power—a process which does nobody any good.

To conclude, in relation to the social policies of Boards and of other autonomous and semi-autonomous bodies I am saying:

(1) These policies, in significant cases and where what is at issue is a product or service provided by such a body, rather than the style in which it is run, should be regarded as the Minister's policies.

(2) This means the net cost shall be paid for from departmental funds and should be generally negotiated by the Minister and his officials to get value for money.

(3) This implies under the present system, parliamentary control of a different and closer kind than that exercised over Boards as commercial entities; instead, the expenditure will be under the scrutiny of the House of Commons Public Accounts and Expenditure Committee.

(4) There are traditional administrative methods of scrutiny, but they have similar defects to the analogous methods used tactically and strategically to oversee the financial operation of Boards.

(5) The sensible method of improving control of social policy, which is logically similar to financial control of profitable operations, is through cost-benefit analysis. Whitehall has pioneered this but

usually as a tactical piecemeal administrative technique, not in order to achieve the strategic control which is as necessary here as it was said to be in *Chapter 15*. We have much to learn from the American PPBS experiment – much of it, unfortunately, being how *not* to go about the task.

Chapter 19

CONCLUSION

And so one ends this discussion of our public corporations and the triangular relationship between Parliament, Ministers and Boards. The aims of my argument have been to show that the relation is something of a muddle, that the public perception of it is dangerously inexact and that there is probably a better way we should go than the way we appear to be drifting.

The relation is obscure because our public perception of it is built on the sandy foundation of not one, but several, competing fictions:

(1) There is first the fiction that the relation between Minister and Board is to be described by a distinction between the laying-down of policy and its execution. This might be a useful description if Parliament had ordained ministerial sovereignty over the public corporation, so that the Boards exercised their powers by delegation from Ministers. It is a fiction because it represents neither the statutory nor the real power relationship. It is a dangerous fiction because it is used at times to puff Ministers up as if they had more power than as is the case; they are tempted to talk as if the nationalized industries were 'their' industries and the acts of those industries were their acts. Puffing them up, it can also let them down when they are blamed for acts by those industries or failures of execution for which neither in statute nor in fact are they responsible. It is in terms of this fiction that public opinion, and Parliament in debate, imagine the relation between Ministers and Boards. The rationale of what Parliamentary Questions MPs may ask about nationalized industry affairs, and also many arguments used by the Select Committee to define the relationship, seem to presuppose that this is a good description of the facts.

(2) The second fiction is that of the division of powers and responsibilities as it appears to be laid down in the statutes. These give certain powers to Ministers and other powers and duties to

Boards. The Boards also have the residual autonomy over matters where powers are not expressly given to Ministers. The description one therefore has is of a Board with corporate personality and with freedom to interpret the duties laid on it by Parliament, subject to certain powers laid on Ministers by Parliament. In particular, the statutes are often interpreted publicly as if Ministers have a responsibility to use their statutory financial powers to secure the financial viability of the industries and a satisfactory return on the public funds invested in them. This is a fiction because it understates the interest of Ministers, which tends not to be confined to the matters where they have explicit statutory powers; for example, until recently, Ministers have had few powers relating to the social (non-commercial) activities of Boards. It is a fiction also because Ministers do not operate their powers, especially their financial powers, as this description would seem to suggest they should. They have not exercised financial control, but, as we have argued, have given the Boards a very great practical independence, almost that of a public trust.

(3) The third fiction is that of the Boards as public trusts. While it is close to the truth in many respects, it is not widely held to be a good description, just because the statutes appear to give Ministers more powers than this. The public trust was in many areas the original concept. The 1857 Mersey Docks and Harbour Board was a public trust, meaning that it had almost perfect freedom to interpret the duties laid on it by Parliament. Many of the early nationalized industries and non-commercial public corporations had a not dissimilar status. The original Morrisonian or Baldwin-Morrisonian Board was not far removed from the public trust, since Morrison seems to have seen the influence of Ministers as persuasive rather than mandatory. Over the years the statutory powers of Ministers have increased and much less has been heard of the nationalized industries as public trusts. Yet their practical independence to interpret their statutory duties has kept them more like public trusts than one might have expected. But while expressing some of the truth, it is still a fiction. If it were true, one might expect Governments to allow the nationalized industries to go bankrupt when they failed in their trust, as they have the Mersey Docks and Harbour Board (though even there Government felt that it, rather than someone else, should interfere to secure a succession). As it is, Governments have responsibilities without power (or rather powers which they are ready to use decisively). It is, of course, the responsibilities which Governments have felt for various aspects of nationalized industry activity, which have led them down the

223

primrose path of persuasive, but indecisive, intervention. All this would seem to make the concept of nationalized industries as public trusts a fiction (as well as being incompatible with the statutory description of the relationship between Minister and Board, which is a separate argument, since this, too, appears to be a fiction).

(4) There are a number of other descriptions or metaphors around, such as those which would find a commercial analogue for the function of the Minister as a holding company or merchant bank. They are also in contradiction to the facts. Firstly, they presuppose an effective interest in the profitable use of capital. But Ministers do not exercise their powers to secure this, as either a holding company or a merchant bank would. (Indeed, the idea of the Treasury as, in part, a piece of machinery to allocate public funds between competing uses in order to secure the highest [financial or social] return, is itself a fiction. The Treasury has hardly begun to operate in this way.) Secondly, this kind of description would seem to deny, or ignore, the interest of Parliament and Ministers in the social policy of the Boards.

(5) There is also a fiction of *realpolitik*: that Ministers have all the informal power they want if they are skilful enough. They can wheel and deal to get their way, subject of course to the pressures imposed on them by others. While there is a sense in which it is a truism to say that a Minister's success depends on his skill in negotiation and the way he reacts to external pressures, it is a far from adequate description of the relation between Ministers and Boards because it overstates the freedom Ministers have to engage in *realpolitik* here. Law, constitutional habits, departments' habits of work and the sheer volume of pressures on their time, limit the scope Ministers have to translate this fiction into fact.

No description can capture all the facts, but much nearer the truth would seem to be one of the Boards as public trusts. Ministers show much more interest in many of the policies and performances of the Boards than they might be expected to show in 'ordinary' public trusts. Ministers also act as if they had certain responsibilities for these policies and performances; but they do not exercise these responsibilities as an ordinary trustee would, that is, by being on the Board of the trust or being represented on it.[1] They exercise their responsibilities by a flow of persuasive argument to which the convention is that the Boards have to listen without in the end having

---

[1] It is a subordinate fiction that a Minister should appoint his Board. The majority will have been appointed by a sequence of predecessors.

to obey, unless they are inclined to be persuaded. The truth hardly corresponds to any of the current fictions.

One attitude would be to sit back and let what I have here called politicization of the relation develop. This would mean that the constraints imposed by the statutory framework and constitutional practice would gradually relax as Ministers gradually attempted to make a reality of the fiction of *real politik*. I have argued that this is not compatible with consistent government, and that it is likely to lead to less effective financial control and control of Board social policy than at present. The influence of Parliament will diminish. Because more than one can play at this game, and Ministers are temporary phenomena, the chances are that the influence of Ministers on Board policy could also diminish. Therefore I would argue that this, the most likely outcome, because it represents an already existing tendency, would be to no one's, unless it be the Board's, lasting good. Only naive pluralists who believe that the outcome of conflicting pressure groups is in some sense a democratic outcome, can welcome this development. I gave also argued that reversing momentum and departmentalizing the nationalized industries, and so subordinating them to Ministers, is not a solution. If introduced, it would be another fiction. When the Postmaster General was the head of the Post Office, when it was a Government department, the apparent position, but not the reality, was that his word was law.

I have also argued that to accept the mess of fictions and to improve the efficiency of nationalized industries by increasing competition and introducing more of the discipline of the money market, is a useful, but not a sufficient, solution. If not prepared for properly, it may be catastrophic. Preparation means: (i) separating out in advance the commercial from the social obligations of the Boards (otherwise, more competition may merely mean that the Boards fare badly because they carry social obligations, not because they are truly uncompetitive); and (ii) building up an apparatus of financial control and planning in advance, since throwing an unprepared enterprise into competition can mean its collapse, a result which more careful preparation could have avoided. In any case, most of the large and more important nationalized industries, like many large private corporations, are unlikely to be vulnerable to increased competition or to the discipline of the money market.

I conclude that it seems important to improve the quality and effect of ministerial control over the financial performance and social policy of the Boards. This is right for several reasons: because there has been so much waste in the past; because the proportion of the

P

national resources employed by the Boards is very high; because it is unlikely that there will be any overall reduction in the size of the nationalized sector; and because the general policy of forming new semi- or non-commercial enterprises from within Government and giving them a certain independence apart from Government as public corporations, will not lead to more efficiency or consistent social policy unless the machinery of control is improved for them also. The size of the public sector is not likely to diminish. While some of the smaller enterprises may be denationalized, there are many reasons why the larger will not be; and there is the strong possibility of specialized enterprises like Rolls Royce, heavily dependent on public funds and with non-standard managements and advanced technology, falling into the public sector and not escaping, as their non-standard nature makes them unattractive, because exceptionally risky, to private and institutional investors. Moreover, even if there were to be denationalization of commercial state enterprises on a large scale, there is bound to be a growth in the number of enterprises performing functions which are not wholly commercial. Our concern as a society with the environment, with health, education and poverty and many other things, must mean this. We will have hybrid bodies to give effect to these public concerns. Unless we develop a machinery of control there will be wasteful use of funds, and muddled and conflicting social policies.

Quite apart from this there seems a clear enough indication that Parliament wants more effective financial and social policy control over the nationalized industries. Much of the muddle we are in results from unsuccessful attempts to express these parliamentary concerns.

I have argued that the fiction which could be developed and turned most usefully into a reality is the second: the statutory. The Board should have the residual independence (except insofar as this may be altered by legislation). This is the only practical way of reducing the very great burden of Ministers (while telling the truth) which would result from Ministers' attempting to subordinate all these Boards to themselves and their departments. The Minister would then exercise his financial powers decisively in order to get an adequate return on capital. To make his existing powers a reality, he would move at least as far from the normal situation as the tactical financial control we were beginning to operate at the Ministry of Transport. But it would be better if it went further than this towards a more strategic financial control. This would mean working through the approval of a Board corporate plan to which capital expenditure approval should be subordinate. It would mean departments' developing the capacity to interpret corporate plans and the competence to advise the Minister so that he may act decisively. At present we have the wrong system, used wrongly and, despite their great qualities, with, in part, the wrong people operating the financial aspects of it. Yet an efficient system is neither in terms of its statutory description nor its operation, so far from the present situation that it could not be achieved by a small number of definite steps.

I believe we should avoid any machinery which would turn the triangle into a polygon by introducing other intermediate or associated bodies to ensure financial control. These would make the power relationships more complex and the outcome less determinate. The argument for them is basically a belief, widely held, that civil servants cannot exercise this financial responsibility. I believe such negativism absurd and, moreover, if we are to have a chance of retaining democratic parliamentary control and avoiding waste, they must do so. The level of their financial probity is extraordinarily high and the importance of this is not to be underrated; but discipline and control with the aim of getting value for money has not been developed. (PESC and PAR are attempts at a framework, but they hardly represent the first steps towards exercising financial power within Government or towards the Boards.)

Parliament, through Ministers, needs to exercise some control over the social policy executed by Boards, especially if the number of these is to grow. The notion which has been developing, that the Boards should be paid to do these services, is a powerful one. It ought then to be the responsibility of the Minister to decide what he will spend money on and to negotiate with the Board how it is to be spent and what services he is to receive for it. The Board's main interest will be to undertake services which are useful and profitable to it. It will be the Minister's responsibility to determine the public interest and the desirability of spending money on this rather than on other social ends. Therefore the Minister can avoid for the most part an interest in the other activities and management of Boards, except so far as these affect the Boards' financial viability. Present procedures imply some machinery for the parliamentary control of public expenditure for these purposes. But there are possibilities of building up a more sophisticated and useful approach described in *Chapter 18*. Unless some determination is shown there are also possibilities of this sliding back into a position where the Boards have a practical independence in relation to providing these services, tempered only by sporadic persuasive interventions by Ministers.

What seems clear is that nothing can be done without a certain determination and trouble, but also that one ought to be able to construct a good system to secure parliamentary concerns without having to invent something new. The dividing line may never be sharply defined at all points, but it could be less blurred than it is now, with advantage.

Index

229

231